MIRACLE
AT MILE MARKER 313

THE TRUE STORY OF TRAUMA, TRIALS
AND SOME TIMELESS TRUTHS...

To My Great Friend Ed! + Joyce + Anna! You so very much!

Ps. 102-18

CRAIG STEPHEN SMITH AND
LADONNA J. SMITH

Xulon
PRESS

Miracle at Mile Marker 313
The true story of trauma, trials and some timeless truths...

by Craig Stephen Smith and LaDonna J. Smith
Editors: Dave Fessenden and LaDonna J. Smith

Printed in the United States of America

ISBN 9781629521299

www.xulonpress.com

DEDICATION

This book is dedicated to our children and grandchildren.

Nizhoni;
Dallas, Elizabeth, and grandson Colin;
Shandiin and Stefan Lucas and granddaughters
Lydia and Violet;
...and to the generations to come that are not yet born. As it says in Psalms 102:18: "Let this be written for a future generation, that a people not yet created may praise the Lord."

Our family has gone through great trials and tribulation, but it has been used by God to draw us closer to Himself and to each other. As painful as this journey has been, we are grateful for a deeper understanding gained from our sufferings.

Have mercy on me, O God, have mercy on me
for in you my soul takes refuge.
I will take refuge in the shadow of your
wings until the disaster has passed.
I cry out to God most high, to God,
who fulfills His purpose for me.
Psalms 57:1–2 (NIV)

A NOTE FROM THE AUTHOR

In one sense, this story is about LaDonna and me. In a larger sense, it's the story of our *family.* We experienced intense pain in this journey—psychological, emotional, and definitely physical. It's not possible to write when one is in a comatose state. That's why you'll be hearing not only my perspective, but from those it impacted most, LaDonna and our children.

We love our family deeply, and as parents we want to keep and protect them from harm. That's just not possible in the horrific world we live in. At some point in all our lives pain visits us. It did for us in the aftermath of mile marker 313. This book chronicles both the physical and spiritual realms in our lives as we experienced deep trauma. I'm sure you'll agonize with our kids as they describe the horror and pain they felt.

The good news is, LaDonna and I survived. The best news is, so did our children and their families. We have been drawn closer to the Lord and to each other.

Through many dangers, toils and snares, we have already come.

'Tis grace hath brought us safe thus far, and grace will lead us home.

As many times as we've sung those words, they have a deeper meaning to us now. Thank you Lord!

Craig Stephen Smith

TABLE OF CONTENTS

Chapter 1   Journey's Mercies 13
Chapter 2   Miracle at Mile Marker 313. 20
Chapter 3   Trauma Value Client. 31
Chapter 4   Where's My Husband? 33
Chapter 5   Those Early Days. 40
Chapter 6   My Darkest Days 52
Chapter 7   Three Weeks and Counting. 68
Chapter 8   My Crazy Comatose World 94
Chapter 9   Here in the Real World 126
Chapter 10   Our Biggest Save 137
Chapter 11   Movin' On Up 143
Chapter 12   Kindred's Care 150
Chapter 13   Advancing My Care at Advanced Healthcare . . 165
Chapter 14   Finally Home. 181
Chapter 15   Settling In on That Long Highway 50 188
Chapter 16   The Long Hot Phoenix Summer 202
Chapter 17   Our "Tour de Thanks" 208
Chapter 18   Back Under the Knife. 222
Chapter 19   Hip Hip Horray. 247
Chapter 20   Let These Horses Run! 256
Chapter 21   Anybody Seen My Six-Pack Abs?. 273
Chapter 22   Lord, I'm Coming Home 283
Chapter 23   More Scars A Coming.... 291
Chapter 24   Me and Her in the Men's Rooms 310
Chapter 25   It Happened Again and Again. 318
Chapter 26   Reaching the Home Stretch. 328
Chapter 27   Lessons Learned 338

PROLOGUE

From our youngest daughter, Shandiin Lucas' personal journal:

Daddy,   June 9, 2009

Today was the day the rollover happened. It's crazy how fast life changes.

Here's what Mom and Uncle Zane said happened: The three of you had just finished having lunch with Uncle Joel. You traveled past Santa Fe, NM and were almost to Las Vegas, NM when the rollover took place. Uncle Zane was driving and Mom was resting in the passenger's seat. You were laying in the back.

The wind patterns were extremely strong, causing the SUV and trailer to swerve all over the road. As the wind continued to move the rig, it sent the vehicle towards the median. Uncle Zane felt the shoulder's rumble strips and thought he had the vehicle under control. As he looked in the side mirror, he saw the white trailer lift up in the air and start to flip (eyewitnesses said they thought a tire popped). You and Mom were still sleeping and woke up when he yelled, "Hang on, we're going over!" Mom said that everything happened so fast. She couldn't quite remember the actual rollover, but was aware of all that happened right after it. Uncle Zane was aware the whole time and said he could see the glass cracking as the car rolled.

Daddy, you took the brunt of the impact and when the accident was over, Mom began singing the old hymn, *'Tis So Sweet to Trust in Jesus.*

There were off-duty firefighters as well as a Christian woman (who happened to be a gospel singer with her husband) as the first Samaritans to the scene. I can only imagine what it was like to witness the crash, to come upon it and hear songs of praise to Jesus!

The firefighters went to work, keeping you and Zane alert and stable until the medics arrived, and Mom's new singing partner stayed with her. I also need to add that along with singing, Mom also kept talking to you and Zane, to make sure you stayed alert.

You and Zane were the first to be placed in the ambulance. Zane wanted to stay with Mom (who had to be taken out by the Jaws of Life). The medic told Zane he had no say in the matter and needed to go with you, Daddy. You were able to talk and communicate some. Zane was concerned about getting the cell phones so he could contact the families, but you said, "That is the least of my worries." You kept asking how Mom was doing, and Zane kept reassuring you that she was OK.

While you were en route to the Santa Fe hospital, one of the medics asked Zane if you were Christians, because he heard Mom singing songs about Jesus. Uncle Zane said, "Yes, we are Christians."

It's just so amazing that even in this crazy situation, all three of your lives are testimonies of Christ Jesus!

After you arrived at the Santa Fe hospital, the staff realized that you would receive better care at UNM Hospital in Albuquerque. Daddy, by this time you weren't in very good shape. We still don't know exactly when it all happened, but you went into cardiac arrest. Thankfully, and all praise to God, the doctors and nurses were able to stabilize you. You responded really well to the medications.

Your body took a beating, Daddy. You broke your right and left femur, shattered your pelvis and broke your hips and ribs. You also had some damage to your vertebrae.

Uncle Joel was the main point of contact during this time, driving back and forth between his home in Albuquerque and Santa Fe to check on Zane, Mom, and you. Meanwhile, the rest of the family prepared to make their way from Phoenix and Wisconsin to be by your side.

Chapter 1

JOURNEY'S MERCIES

In March of 2009 I celebrated my fifty-second birthday. If my calculations are correct I had seen well over 1.6 billion seconds tick by in my lifetime. On June 9, it took about four of those seconds to change our lives.

I'm an Ojibwe, aka Chippewa Indian, born and raised on the Leech Lake Reservation in northern Minnesota. More importantly, I am a committed follower of Jesus Christ. I have had the wonderful privilege of serving Him for over forty years in public ministry, most of it with my wife, LaDonna, by my side. We've done everything together all these years, including almost dying and going to heaven together. It was close—oh, so close!

It was about 3:45 in the afternoon and a beautiful day to be out on the road. We were heading northbound on Interstate 25 about thirty miles north of Santa Fe, New Mexico, at mile marker 313 when "fate" and the Sovereignty of God collided, and we just happened to be along for the ride.

Our SUV and trailer full of equipment and supplies fishtailed as my brother-in-law, Zane, lost control going 75 miles per hour—rolling us and our belongings at least three frightening times. We landed back on our wheels in the median between the north and southbound lanes after gut-wrenching panic and pain.

That's where the miracles began.

In the days leading up to the trip, we had just finished a wonderful but busy week in Louisville, Kentucky at the biennial gathering of our ministry organization, The Christian and Missionary Alliance (C&MA). I had just finished speaking to the military and institutional chaplains as the final event of that year's General Council. A few short days at home were all we had to get ready for another one of our extended trips that would take us through the summer and early fall.

While in Louisville we received news that one of the young Native American men we had the privilege of working with and mentoring for several years in a ministry called On Eagles' Wings (OEW) had passed away from a brain tumor. He was twenty-five years old. We had hired Ricky Bird to help with this rapidly growing Native ministry, founded by our dear friends, Ron and Karen Hutchcraft, committed to bringing the hope of the gospel to Native America's hurting youth. LaDonna and I grieved deeply for this young man. He showed great promise as an up-and-coming leader for his generation, and we would miss him dearly.

Instead of flying directly to Arizona from Louisville, we re-routed to eastern Oklahoma, Cherokee country, to attend Ricky's funeral. When we finally arrived home in Phoenix we had even fewer days to get everything ready for our departure.

Ministry events were confirmed in a number of diverse communities that summer. Speaking, teaching, and concerts were scheduled in Minnesota. Outreaches to Hispanic youth in the inner city of Chicago awaited us, then it would be off to the far north fly-in communities along the Hudson Bay to the Cree Indians of Quebec. We looked forward to visiting a multicultural church in the New York City area. Literally thousands of miles of travel were awaiting us, but that really wasn't anything new to LaDonna and me.

Not only were we heading north for ministry events but Zane, who had recently accepted a new ministry assignment in northern Minnesota, had meetings to attend at the Center for Indian Ministries at Oak Hills Christian College.

"Why not travel together?" we decided.

Zane could fly back one way to Arizona once his meetings were over. It seemed a great way to save him some money. When you're in ministry work, that's often the challenge. When you're in Native ministry work, that's always your challenge.

Our first stop was to be Colorado Springs, home of the national office of The C&MA. Time was budgeted to meet with several divisional leaders and IT guys to help answer website questions. Being a low-tech Indian looking at all my high-tech gear is like two old mules standing and staring at each other across a new gate. Neither the gadgets nor I really know what to do next. It was good to know that much-needed help was only a long day's drive away!

Getting ready for any trip is a huge hassle. When you've been on the road as long as we've been, you get used to the packing pressures as part of living on the road.

Along with the normal stresses of packing, we had recently put our house up for sale. Our dear friend, Lynda, had been busy helping us stage it to make it look as appealing as possible to potential buyers—you know, doing the HGTV thing!

While LaDonna was busy cleaning and packing, a ministry colleague, Miles Fagerlie, and I were purchasing a new cargo trailer to pull behind our SUV. The trailer would carry our sound equipment, media gadgetry and other supplies to be used in our upcoming events.

The wait at the motor vehicle office seemed to take an eternity, but finally our brand-new trailer was licensed, insured, and ready to serve us for what we thought would be years to come. I was so happy to know that the trailer's license had no expiration date. Never again would I have to darken the doors of that MVD office. It was licensed for life! I didn't know it then, but its lifespan would be a grand total of one unbelievable day!

I brought the trailer home only to find out that I couldn't do any packing, because a couple was coming by to see the house. In all honesty, that was the last thing I wanted to hear. Couldn't they wait until we packed and were out of there?

Our realtors told us when we listed the house that, on average, it was taking four to five months to sell homes in the depressed Phoenix market. We decided that now would be the right time to list the house, since we'd be gone for at least four of those five months. We'd do the trip, and then get home in time to get that perfect offer.

We'd be ready to move in the cooler fall months once the desert furnace known as Phoenix summers was in our rear-view mirror. Little did I know our rear-view mirror would only last one more day as well!

The staging of the house was simple and beautiful. The couple lingered, and then lingered some more. They just wouldn't leave! After about six drive-bys with the SUV and new trailer, LaDonna, the family pooch, and I decided on fast-food Chinese. By then the sun was setting and we needed to be packed and ready to go by 5 a.m.!

Even though we were tired, I was excited as I loaded the equipment and supplies. I thought and prayed about the upcoming ministry opportunities that were awaiting us.

We always looked forward to climbing out of the Valley of the Sun, heading north through Black Canyon City and up that long switchback on I-17 to Sunset Point. The car windows would be rolled down and the joy of feeling the cool high desert air blowing in our faces would once again welcome us.

It was around midnight when I was finally able to plop into bed and get some much-needed rest for the big drive the next morning. Unfortunately, LaDonna's laundry list was a bit longer than mine. Around 1:30 a.m. she finally climbed into bed. It seemed only moments later that the alarm went off and the coffee was on. With everything finally packed we drove the few blocks to Zane's home to pick him up. Once he was on board, we stopped, as we always did, to commit the day's travel in prayer to the Lord.

I must have said this prayer a thousand times before heading out on a trip: "Lord, we ask You for Your *journey's mercies* as we go." These kinds of phrases can become repetitious; much like, "Have a good day," "Take care," or "See ya." Maybe there was some triteness to that simple prayer that morning in our tiredness, but unbeknownst to us, that would be the morning when we needed the Lord to hear and answer that prayer and give us His *journey's mercies.*

LaDonna dragged herself into the back of the SUV, stretched out, and remained virtually motionless during the seven-hour drive to Albuquerque. She was physically and emotionally drained from the long process of getting our home ready to sell, taking trips to Kentucky and Oklahoma, and also grieving the loss of our dear young friend. The middle bench became her resting place for the long trip ahead.

The first leg of the journey was quite uneventful, except for the ceremonial rolling down of the windows at Sunset Point. While she finally got some sleep, Zane and I drained the thermos, talked sports, discussed ministry, and kept company with the pundits on XM talk radio. It was an awesome start to the trip, and time and miles seemed to fly by quickly. It wasn't long until we had Albuquerque in sight. Plans were made to meet my brother, Joel, for lunch at one of my all-time favorite New Mexican-style restaurants, Guarduno's.

Joel had moved to Albuquerque a number of years ago after serving as the Superintendent of the Bureau of Indian Affairs in Minnesota. He now worked for the Office of Special Trustee in the Department of the Interior.

No trip to Albuquerque would be complete, in my book, without stopping to see Joel and having him buy me lunch. As would often be the case, I'd get him into the restaurant, but he'd have to get me out of it.

What I didn't realize as we walked out of the restaurant to our vehicle that afternoon was that walking normal would soon become past tense. The last thing I did standing on my own two feet was to give my little brother a big hug, knowing I wouldn't be seeing him for several months. Within a few short hours, he'd be searching for me in emergency departments from Albuquerque to Santa Fe, wondering if I was dead or alive.

Zane offered to drive the next leg of the trip, so LaDonna and I negotiated as to who would ride shotgun and who would get to spread out in the back and get some much-needed rest. It would be my turn to sleep and LaDonna would take the front passenger seat. We didn't realize the importance of that one seemingly insignificant decision. Had we decided the other way, according to the doctors, LaDonna would not be alive today.

After my *small* trip through the buffet line, I was ready for a nice siesta. As I settled in for a long summer nap, Zane got us back on track to our first night's stop in Colorado Springs.

One of the last things I remember was peeking out between the two front seats as we merged onto the on-ramp of Interstate 25. I asked LaDonna if she wouldn't mind keeping her window rolled down so the cool high desert breeze could find its way to the back and help serenade me to sleep. That was another one of those simple requests that would take on incredible significance for both of us in the hours to come.

It wasn't long and I was out, sleeping deeply enough to know I was in la-la land, yet awake enough at times to occasionally and happily feel the cool mountain air swirling around me. Little did I realize that ninety minutes away, things would dramatically change and life as I knew it would be gone, all because of four unbelievable seconds and the Lord's *journey's mercies.*

Chapter 2

MIRACLE AT MILE MARKER 313

The sleep was deep, and the cool mountain air made for a picture-perfect afternoon. I've always thought the drive on I-25 in northern New Mexico was actually quite boring, so I was looking forward to sleeping through most of it. All that changed as we approached mile marker 313.

There's a bit of a ridge near that mile marker and as we crested the top, something went horribly wrong, and it all happened so quickly.

"Hang on! We're going over!" Zane shouted from the driver's seat.

I remember shooting out of my sleep like a bullet, and in that first awkward waking moment when one does not have any sense of his bearings, Zane uttered those frightening words. Sensing great danger I instinctively reached under my seat to try and hold onto whatever I could. The vehicle was shaking violently from side to side and I could tell my brand-new trailer was fishtailing like an out-of-balance washing machine. The over-correcting caused the vehicle to go into a violent rollover—rolling, rolling, and rolling until we finally came to an abrupt stop.

In that frightful moment all I remember was hearing the trio's screams overshadowing the horrific sounds of glass breaking and metal crunching. Incredible pain took over, as I was knocked unconscious. I remember coming to as the vehicle finally settled back on its wheels as we landed in the median between the north and southbound lanes.

The trailer totally blew apart, coming to rest against the driver's side of the vehicle and blocking the doors. Its contents—sound equipment, supplies, clothing, and food items—were strewn over the freeway and median like a huge picked-over yard sale.

As I came to, I vividly remember those first images as huge amounts of dust and dirt landed on us. All I could do was lay there and moan for what seemed like a very long time, grateful to know I could see and sense things around me. I was still alive, and at least my head seemed to be OK. I knew we were in a rollover accident and I was definitely injured, but I didn't know just how badly. The questions that immediately came to mind were, "How is LaDonna? Is she OK? How is Zane? Did they survive?"

The vehicle rolled towards the passenger side. The force impacted LaDonna's head in such a way that her neck snapped as it was thrown outside that recently opened window, breaking her C-1 neck vertebrae. This is the top vertebra that helps support and turns the head, and is the worst kind of neck fracture a person can have. We later learned that her fracture was *through and through*, breaking both the front and back part of the vertebrae.

Zane said he was sure that this was the end for him as the car rolled. His position in the driver's seat caused him to be suspended by the seat belt as if in a carnival ride, keeping him from more serious injury.

Then there was me. Unrestrained, I ended up being thrown around like a rag doll. My body slammed several times against the ceiling and floor as the vehicle rolled. Grabbing onto the bottom of the seat frame with my right arm kept me from being ejected out of the open rear window. Had that happened, perhaps I would have flown over the median and landed on one of the southbound lanes, filled with summertime travelers in vehicles large and small. I don't think about that a lot, just enough to thank God at least a thousand times over.

As we settled down in that dusty median, one of the first reassuring signs for me was to hear LaDonna's voice from the front seat. In between her moans she asked if I was OK. I responded to her as best I could. It was reassuring to both of us to hear each other's voices. We both were grateful to be alive.

She asked Zane how he was doing, and in between his moaning he responded as well.

At that point I remember thinking, "OK, we've all survived, so everything is going to be all right."

For the next few minutes, I faded in and out of consciousness several times. I forgot that even though one may survive initially, death could still be lurking just around the corner.

When LaDonna first asked me if I was OK, I remember telling her, "I'm alive, but I can't move my legs!"

I was facing the back of the vehicle, lying on the floor behind the front seats. I sensed that my torso was caught between the two front bucket seats and my legs were somehow over LaDonna's body in the front seat. The feeling I had from my waist down was nothing I had ever experienced before. The only comparison is that of a huge blood pressure cuff being wrapped around my waist and legs, and inflating it to near bursting. Painful? Yes, but it seemed at the time to be more like intense pressure than intense pain. Regardless, I was helpless and couldn't move. My survival depended on someone showing up to rescue me. The next few hours would be crucial as my life hung in the balance.

I knew I was hurt badly, but my thoughts and concerns were for LaDonna. Experience volunteering with my tribe's ambulance service and in a level-one trauma center in Phoenix had taught me to detect signs and symptoms of injuries.

Hearing LaDonna talking was both reassuring and scary for me. Reassuring because I knew she survived and was conscious, but scary because she was rapidly repeating herself, which was indicative of a potentially serious head injury. Little did I realize that her EMS training also kicked in; she was repeatedly asking Zane and me the same question to keep us from losing consciousness.

The damage to our SUV   *Our totaled "day old" trailer*

It isn't the first time this husband and wife of thirty-plus years of marriage looked at the very same thing from two distinctly different but totally understandable angles!

That's when she began to sing out the old hymn, "Tis So Sweet to Trust in Jesus." She later told me that when she knew we were going over, she relaxed her body and the words of this song came to her.

Help started to arrive; complete strangers came to our aid. I remember hearing one man on his cell phone frantically calling 911 as the dust continued to settle on us. Rays of sunlight were cutting through the dust. In a small way it brought reassurance to me, though nothing seemed to make sense at the moment. Light continued to shine on, a wave of peace engulfed me, and then I was out.

Right behind us in another vehicle was an off-duty nurse who stopped and helped organize the initial response. Just behind her another group of men stopped to help. We found out later that they were four off-duty military men trained in firefighting and responding to crisis scenarios. They immediately went to work to move the trailer out of the way so they could gain access to Zane and me.

I came to again as I heard the grunts and groans of these men trying to move what was left of our trailer from the driver's side of the vehicle.

LaDonna was still singing when I heard the voice of another woman.

"Hey, I know that song," she said.

"Will you sing it with me?" LaDonna asked.

And that she did.

"Are you OK? People are stopping and helping pick up your things! It looks like a yard sale!"

LaDonna looked down at her left hand. It looked more like a balloon.

"I think I may have broken my hand and injured my left knee," she said.

LaDonna asked her if she was a Christian and she responded, "Oh, yes, I am!"

Along with singing and praying, these two "sisters" asked God to help us, and those who were coming to our aid.

I can't tell you how comforting it was to have these complete strangers there with us until the "official" help came. It wasn't long before we could hear the sirens in the distance as the fire and EMS personnel arrived on scene.

As they began to assess the damage, several things became very evident to them. There were not a lot of outward signs of injury, such as profuse bleeding. Instinctively, though, they knew something serious lurked beneath. EMS folks are trained to consider the mechanism of injury when assessing potential injuries.

The fact that a totally crumpled SUV and demolished trailer were lying between the north and southbound lanes after cruising the interstate at freeway speed causes one to think the worst. We're grateful that they employed the life-saving assessment training.

While I don't remember being conscious for all of the rescue process, I do remember quite a bit of it. An older man (probably my age) wearing the paramedic patch on his uniform got into the back of the vehicle with me. His co-worker was a female paramedic. I kept thinking, wow, between Zane, LaDonna, and me, did they have their hands full!

As they began to assess Zane and me, I remember hearing the fire personnel discussing LaDonna's situation up front. They yelled back to the guys at the rescue vehicle to bring the Jaws of Life. The roof and doors of the SUV were crumpled in and around her. The only way to get to her would be to cut her out of the vehicle.

She was hoping that we could all be taken to the hospital together, but the fireman told her they were going to have to take Zane and me first. Once they got her out, another ambulance, which was being dispatched, would be there to take her in separately. LaDonna found comfort in knowing that Zane and I were in good hands. She then lost consciousness.

Once the trailer was moved out of the way, the driver's side doors opened without a problem. Zane was extricated first. My head and neck were stabilized, and then they attempted to roll me enough to slide a backboard underneath me. That's when I lost consciousness—and thankfully so!

I found out later from the paramedic, Mr. Dana Gingrich, of Pecos Valley EMS (yes, he is a relative of Newt), that when they rolled me onto the backboard my whole pelvic region flopped open. The image that came to my mind was what I normally do to one of those rotisserie chickens once I bring it home from the supermarket.

Once they got me on the backboard, my blood pressure plummeted, and a crude yet crucial technique was employed that helped save my life.

My flopping pelvis indicated severe internal injury and bleeding which was made worse as I was rolled over. The paramedics quickly put a folded bed sheet underneath my pelvic region, pulled the two ends up over my torso, and tied it in a big knot. That procedure squeezed my pelvis back together, much like a giant tourniquet helping to suppress the massive bleeding.

I regained consciousness long enough to know I was being pulled out of the vehicle. The brilliance of the sun was blinding.

Zane was already in the ambulance on a backboard strapped to the bench, and I was placed on the gurney and lifted into place beside Zane. It was then and there that the scariest part of the experience happened to me. I thought, "Will I ever see LaDonna alive again?"

My fear wasn't because I was so close to death. I was worried that she might be dying!

It went against everything within me to leave her there, trapped inside the vehicle. My husbandly instincts and Zane's brotherly love kicked in big time, and we both protested leaving without her.

We were strapped down, immobile, so the paramedics won that battle; soon the sirens sounded and away we went. From what I remember, both paramedics were with us in the back and the ambulance was driven by one of the firemen commandeered for the moment.

Both Zane and I were moaning in pain as they established IV lines in our arms. Zane was experiencing a lot of back pain and the paramedics did their best to manage that with some IV medications. Medics don't want to give a lot of pain medication in the early onset of trauma, since it can mask symptoms that need to be uncovered in the examination process.

I guess I'm the exception to the rule. They sensed the necessity of giving me the largest dosage of pain medications they could and started multiple IV lines, because my blood pressure was dropping.

My last glimpse of consciousness was the ambulance arrival at St. Vincent Hospital in Sante Fe. We made the last turn and the vehicle rocked from side to side. That's when the lights went out for me—for how long, only the Lord knew; I sure didn't.

My stay at St. Vincent Hospital was short-lived as the extent of my injuries became clear. My unstable blood pressure confirmed internal bleeding, and the initial portable X-ray was telling.

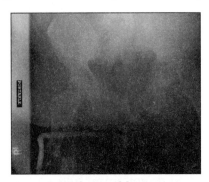

Initial portable x-ray

It showed the following fractures:
- L2–L5 lumbar spinal fractures
- Multiple rib fractures
- open-book pelvic fracture
- Right femur fracture
- Crushed and dislocated left femur head
- Fractured coccyx (tail bone)

A CT scan was ordered to get the best read of what was going on inside my body, but the question was, would I live long enough to get one done?

The fractures and violent dislocation of bones meant important veins, arteries, and nerves were compromised in the accident. The difficulty they had in maintaining blood pressure meant I was bleeding out on the inside, and trauma surgery was needed if I was to live.

Only a level-one trauma center is equipped for that kind of specialized surgery, and the nearest one was fifty miles away—in Albuquerque at the University of New Mexico Hospital.

I survived the CT scan, thanks to fluids being pumped back into me through the IV lines. Once it was determined that I needed to be transported, a life flight helicopter was dispatched and on its way to get me.

Somewhere in the blur of those critical minutes, the worst-case scenario happened. The trauma I had suffered caused my body to finally succumb to it all. My heart stopped beating. My fifty-two year life came to a stop on that emergency room gurney as I passed through death's door. Massive amounts of blood were infused into me, and they were able to eventually restart my heart. The race was on to get me out of there to the awaiting trauma surgeons in Albuquerque.

As I coded, without a doubt, I had the most significant experience I have ever had in my life, but more about that later.

The helicopter crew was stationed locally, at the Santa Fe airport, so it was a short flight to pick me up. I had always wanted to fly in a helicopter, but this wasn't the kind of flight I would have wanted.

While I don't remember much of the flight at all, I'm so thankful they were there for me that day! I do have a fleeting memory of a crew in red jump suits (and one in particular wearing a flight helmet) standing by my gurney, and then of being wheeled out of the hospital to a big red-and-white chopper. I have a brief recollection of rolling under the whir of those massive blades overhead and then, once airborne, of sagebrush-laden ground flying by underneath me as we covered the fifty miles to the trauma center at top speed.

Erin, the flight nurse on duty that day, told us later that normally she doesn't remember the details of many of the flights they make, but "I sure do remember you, Craig," she said.

Erin didn't think I would survive the flight. She knew I had just coded and was clinging to life when they came to retrieve me. I was as white as a sheet due to blood loss and would flail my arms about as I fought for life. My breathing was labored, but at least I was breathing. The short flight ended on the landing pad at the University of New Mexico Hospital and Trauma Center. That's when Dr. Stephen Lu and UNM's trauma team took over.

It was early evening by now. My brother Joel was in Albuquerque running some errands. On his way home he received a call from our Dad. He asked Joel if he was sitting down. Sensing an ominous tone in Dad's voice, he knew something was wrong.

"Craig, LaDonna, and Zane have been in an accident," Dad said. He didn't have much more information, other than the name of the hospital we had been taken to: St. Vincent's Hospital in Santa Fe.

On hearing the news, Joel jumped into high gear and started the fifty-mile drive to see us and find out how we were doing. Halfway there, he got another call from Dad saying I had been transferred to UNM, but Zane and LaDonna were doing OK in Santa Fe. It seemed the best thing for him to do was to turn around and head back to Albuquerque to try and find his big brother.

30

Chapter 3

TRAUMA VALUE CLIENT

By the time Joel arrived at UNM Hospital, it was already late in the evening. Making his way to the emergency room, he asked if there was a Craig Smith that had been admitted.

"There's nobody here by that name. Maybe he was sent to another facility," the registrar reasoned.

He didn't want to think the worst, but it still crossed his mind that I might be dead.

Uncertain of what to do next, Joel spent time at UNM seeking more information about where his brother might be.

"Maybe he didn't have his identification on him. Maybe they got his name wrong. Did communication through the grapevine get mixed up?"

It made for a few hours of frustration as he continued the search. All he knew was that I had to be injured severely enough to warrant a transfer to UNM Hospital.

Meanwhile, his phone began ringing off the hook. As the news began to spread, many friends and family who knew Joel lived in Albuquerque thought he might have the scoop on what had happened.

In between phone calls he went back again to see if the staff had any more information.

"Are you sure there is not a Craig Smith who checked in tonight?"

"No, we've checked again and again, and we don't have a Craig Smith here!" the registrar repeated. Then an idea occurred to her. "Wait a minute! My records show a helicopter transfer from Santa Fe. It's a male and he has the generic name "Trauma Value Client." That's what we call the patients until we confirm their identity. Maybe this is your brother."

After a couple of calls, she was able to confirm that "Trauma Value Client" was being treated in the trauma intensive care unit. Joel made his way there and got clearance to go to the room.

As I lay unconscious, Joel came to my bedside and confirmed my identity to the staff. "Yes, this is my brother Craig! I'm going to stay here with him, if that's OK."

For hours on end, Joel was there with me when I was severely injured and out of it. I've always loved my little brother, but words fail to express how grateful I am to him for being there with me and being that connection to the family when I was alone and in such bad condition.

LaDonna had her brother Zane, who wouldn't leave her side. I had Joel, who hung with me through the night as I hovered near death's door.

Chapter 4

WHERE'S MY HUSBAND?

One of the first things a first responder is trained to do after assessing the "ABC's" of trauma (airway, breathing and circulation) is to stabilize the head and neck in case of fractures to this critical part of the body. The paramedics and fire rescuers did just that for LaDonna.

The backup ambulance arrived on scene, and she was transported to St. Vincent Hospital. She doesn't remember the extrication from the vehicle or loading her onto the gurney. The only recollection she had is of a second or two of her surroundings, with our possessions strewn across the roadway and median. It really did look like a yard sale! My wife loves yard sales, but this one certainly held no attraction for her.

Zane underwent a barrage of evaluations, X-rays, and other tests, and was cleared of any serious, life-threatening injuries. As the driver, he also had to endure questions from the highway patrol officer who responded to the scene. Later we learned that Zane was made to "walk the line" to verify that he was not intoxicated. This made LaDonna furious!

Zane's injuries were primarily to his lower back, aggravating an existing back problem that had plagued him for several years. Thankfully his seat belt prevented any further injury. He was kept overnight for observation and released the following day but refused to leave his sister's side.

LaDonna's initial hours in the ER were similar to mine in that she was in and out of consciousness. Somewhere in a moment of lucidity she asked one of the nurses where her husband was and learned that I had to be airlifted out.

That's when she asked for her phone. "I've got to call our kids and let them know what happened!" she said.

Eventually her phone was found and while lying immobilized in St. Vincent emergency room, she attempted to reach our kids in Arizona. No one was answering.

"We've been in a terrible accident. ... Zane and I are okay, but I don't know if Dad made it," were the words she shared on the voice mails to each of our kids.

Zane also tried to reach his wife, Roberta, and had better success than LaDonna did.

LaDonna called our former pastor and his wife, Jay and Lynda Letey, and her best friend, Bertha Medina, to make sure our kids were aware of what happened. Aunt Bert, as she is lovingly called, gathered the kids at our home and waited to get more news.

We have three kids: Nizhoni is our firstborn daughter; our son, Dallas, is married to Elizabeth; our youngest daughter, Shandiin, is married to Stefan. Their firstborn daughter, Lydia, was eighteen months old at the time. LaDonna did not receive much information about me during those early hours, so nothing concrete could be passed on to the kids.

By late evening, as I was being kept alive by the trauma team, the kids decided the best thing they could do would be to try and get a good night's sleep and make the seven-hour drive in the morning. They slept while their Daddy, "Trauma Value Client," began a long and arduous journey of recovery that started at death's door and inched toward the land of the living.

Employers graciously gave them time to come and be with us. Dallas and Elizabeth were about to take a much-needed vacation in Hawaii, but changed their plans, and they all made their way over together. The hardest part was not knowing what they would see when they arrived.

My father (we call him "Jeep") was next on the call list. He and my step-mom, Barb, got word at their summer home in northern Wisconsin. LaDonna's parents, Herman and Fern Williams, got the news as well. From there the cell phone world of voice and texting went into high gear as news began to spread to extended family, friends, and coworkers.

LaDonna is an amazing woman who loves and trusts in God. Though suffering from her injuries and not knowing if I was dead or alive, she was thinking about others and how they would take the news. That is a characteristic of my wife that I have long appreciated, especially on that fateful day.

Routine tests on LaDonna were ordered, including a barrage of X-rays. One of the first ordered is always a cervical spine X-ray, along with films of other obvious damaged body parts. Initial radiology reports indicated LaDonna had suffered a fracture of her C-1 vertebrae. The doctors and staff were stunned that she had survived this injury.

We were later to find out how severe that neck fracture was, and how few survive it. We were told that 90 to 95 percent of people with a C-1 fracture suffer instantaneous death. Most who survive this *hangman's break* end up paralyzed and on a ventilator for the rest of their life.

The late actor, Christopher Reeves, suffered the same C-1 neck fracture as LaDonna did, but with a much different outcome.

It is hard to sleep on a waiting room couch, but Joel managed to shut his eyes for a few hours while the trauma team began their initial work of assessing my injuries and putting together a game plan for addressing all that needed to be done.

I was facing massive internal blood loss and a dislocated left hip with a crushed femur head. It was dislodged from the hip joint and pushed up my back. My right femur (thigh bone) had been broken clear through with razor-sharp bone chips compromising important blood vessels that could be easily cut with the slightest movement. Four of my vertebrae were broken in multiple places as were my ribs, and that was just the start of my challenges. Other life-threatening issues would surface in the days to come. My chances of survival were slim if at all.

By morning's light I had survived my first night. The medical staff's attempts at stabilizing my vital signs worked as they kept infusing me with new blood and fluids. Frequent blood tests indicated what medications needed to be tweaked on an ongoing basis. Surgical procedures were prioritized and I began what would become way too many visits to the operating room.

Humpty Dumpty was beginning to be put back together again!

Joel was at my bedside the next morning when a visitor came into the room.

"Hi, my name is Julie. I'm a nurse at St. Vincent Hospital in Santa Fe."

"Hi, I'm Joel. I'm Craig's brother. I've been here with him through the night and just hanging out with him. He's in pretty bad shape, and they still don't know for sure if he will survive these early days. Hey, thanks for coming by."

She took a look down at me lying there on life support and turned to Joel as she continued sharing with him.

"I was there last night treating your brother. Normally I don't do this, but for some unknown reason, I was drawn here today. I needed to see how Craig was doing. There's just something about him."

Joel thought to himself, *Wow, even in this condition, God seems to be working through Craig.*

Before she left, she asked if she could talk to Joel outside the room. She had something to share with him that she didn't want me to hear that could have thrown me into further complications.

"Joel, I don't know if you know this or not, but last night your brother coded in our emergency room. I was so thankful we were able to resuscitate him and get him stable enough to transfer him here. Maybe that's why I needed to come and tell you this. I pray that he will get better."

It was such an encouragement to Joel; at a time he really needed it. The agony of family trauma, combined with lack of sleep, can easily wear on a person. Julie's visit, and in particular the fact that she had *been drawn* to look for me, was one of many God moments in our journey.

Many trusted God on our behalf to do His work in our broken bodies. We were already seeing the mighty hand of God ministering to those closest to us who would be facing many days of uncertainty. It was good to know our faithful Lord was continuing to pour out His *journey's mercies.*

From Shandiin's personal journal:

Dad,   June 10, 2009

You continue to remain stable. The doctors and nurses are pleased with your progress.

Nizhoni, Elizabeth, Dallas and Shandiin left Arizona around 12 p.m. Grammy Barb and Jeep had their plane tickets ready and were scheduled to arrive in New Mexico around 11 p.m.

As all this was going on Uncle Joel continued to be at your bedside at the hospital in Albuquerque. As he was by your side one of the first responder nurses who took care of you in Santa Fe drove all the way down to UNM to see you. It's not usual for nurses to go out of their way, let alone, drive almost an hour to check up on a patient. They only met you briefly, Dad. Those who know you are not surprised, though.

There's something different about you, Daddy, something that comes only from above. Your heart and love for Christ is evident and radiates from your life. The nurse introduced herself to Joel and they stood at your bedside for a while. At first Uncle Joel was confused as to why the nurse from Santa Fe would come all the way down to see you. He thought it might be procedural or something needed to tie up the ends for their records.

She simply said that she was "compelled" to come see you, Dad. She said that she couldn't get you off her heart and mind.

Dad, that just goes to show, and all praise to God, that even in a state in which you cannot talk or move, your life shines Jesus and it radiates His glory. You are a wonderful, special man, Daddy, and your life touches everyone you meet because of Jesus Christ in you, the hope of glory.

Chapter 5

THOSE EARLY DAYS

The social media world lit up as our kids began posting what they knew about the accident. It wasn't long before word spread. Within twenty-four hours, our kids, my dad and my stepmom, Barb, had arrived safely in Albuquerque. They were escorted by Joel to see their very sick dad and son.

Zane's wife Roberta and daughter Jineane went to the impound lot and located all our 'yard sale' belongings piled high in the wreckage of our totaled SUV. What was left of our four months of stuff was recovered and secured in the back of Zane's truck just in time before an evening thunderstorm hit.

LaDonna's mom and dad were unable to come due to her dad's deteriorating health, but they joined an ever-growing network of family and friends who became our much-needed prayer warriors.

Continued from Shandiin's personal journal:

June 10, 2009

Nizhoni, Dallas, Elizabeth, and I arrived early evening around 7:30 p.m.

Uncle Joel met us and Dallas and Elizabeth went in first to see you. You were responsive and eager to shake your head so as to communicate. Nizhoni, Uncle Joel and I all joined you in your room. It was so difficult to see you like that. You had tubes in your mouth and all over your body. The Lord really rained down His peace and love in that room. Our hearts hurt and our pain was and still is covered with assurance of God's abounding and measureless love for you, Dad. He loves you more than we ever could!

We spent some time talking to you and you responded by shaking your head and opening your eyes. It was obvious you were a little uncomfortable and hot. You moved your hands around a lot and you were obviously restless. You tried signing to us what you needed and Elizabeth was the one to figure out you were feverish. We spent the majority of the evening wetting towels with cold water and placing them on your forehead, belly and arms. They would get hot quickly so we all took turns rewetting and applying them on you.

Chuck Harper and his wife, Cindy (missionaries working with Native youth) stopped in to bring dinner to the family. They stayed and talked to us, and you, for a while. They also prayed for you. You were responsive to them. Jeep and Grammy Barb came around midnight—and Dad, you were *so excited* to hear Jeep's voice! Your cute little heart rate went up when you heard his voice. You opened your eyes and nodded a lot. We also mentioned how much Lydia loves you and is praying for you with Stefan, and how she is waiting for her teddy bear Papa to come home. Your heart rate really went up when you heard Lydia's name! Brother,

Liz, Jeep and Barb all went back to Uncle Joel's to get some sleep. Nizhoni and I stayed the night with you.

I do not remember anything of that visit, nor of all that went on in that trauma facility for the next two months.

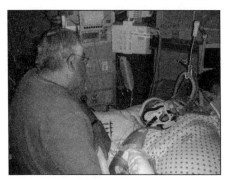

Jeep at his son's bedside

The trauma surgeons made a choice to put me in a drug-induced coma. The family was told it was necessary because my body could not handle the huge amount of trauma I was going through. The best thing for me would be to live in this comatose state for now. It would help my body begin the long journey of healing. That surreal underworld was where I stayed in the weeks that followed, except for a few of quick visits back to the land of the living.

The family divided their time between the Trauma ICU unit in Albuquerque and St. Vincent Hospital in Santa Fe. The wear and tear on them was obvious in body, soul, and spirit.

No doubt the thought crossed their minds in those early days about whether we would live, due to the severity of our injures. It was without question one of the greatest challenges our family would face in our lifetime.

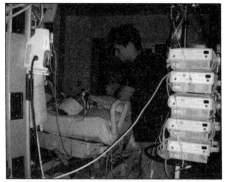

My son, Dallas, standing watch and praying for his dad

It would be important for the family to be together as much as possible in Albuquerque as my condition continued to be extremely critical.

From Shandiin's personal journal:

June 11, 2009

Today is Nizhoni's birthday. What a wonderful present to have our parents and uncle alive and stable!

Today was more of a waiting game. Doctors would come in and out. You had a weight attached to your right leg to take the pressure off the fractured femur and some kind of brace around your hips.

We were actually told a bunch of different things about what happened during the accident. We were told you were ejected from the vehicle, so word spread like wildfire about that. We were also told you had a compound fracture where your bone had protruded out of your skin. Turns out you were *not* ejected and you did *not* have a compound fracture. We had to do a little clarifying with everyone just so they had the accurate news.

As the day progressed, the doctors were concerned about possible blood clots forming. We waited to hear what surgical procedures they were planning before we made our way to Santa Fe to see Mom and Uncle Zane.

The doctors decided they wanted to insert a net into your main vena cava that leads to your lungs. The filter will catch any potential clots which could be life threatening.

We decided to make our way up to visit Mom and Zane. Mom was resting peacefully when we arrived. She looked tired but brightened up extremely fast. I think she was happy to see her family.

Zane and Mom cleared up a lot of misinformation about what happened before, during and after the accident.

Dallas and Elizabeth graciously brought food for the family and we had, to the best we could, a celebration of Nizhoni's birthday. While there in Santa Fe, we got news that Dad's IVC filter operation was successful. They also did a procedure to look for potential bleeding in his pelvis. They didn't find what they expected, and we gave great praise to God!

After our time in Santa Fe we drove back to Albuquerque to see how you were doing. Jeep and Grammy Barb stayed the entire time with you, and we met up with them in the waiting room.

Before we arrived they saw the surgeons and nurses wheel you out of the operating room and back to the ICU. Shortly after, we went in to see you. However, this time they only allowed two visitors at a time because of the surgery. Daddy, you looked great and we are so grateful for God's mercies.

We found out they also repaired your fractured right femur. They inserted a rod from your hip down to your knee area. After spending some time with you we all thought it would be best for you to rest and heal up from the surgery. We returned to Joel's house for a good night's rest.

The doctor determined that LaDonna's spinal cord was not damaged. She would need only to wear a rigid "Miami J" neck collar for six weeks until her cervical bone healed.

Her other injuries were treated. What she needed now would be time for achy bones, muscles and emotions to heal.

Three days later, LaDonna was discharged from St. Vincent Hospital with strict neck precautions and follow-up orders for evaluation and therapy. She, Zane, and the family made their way down I-25 to Albuquerque.

Most the family camped out at Joel's home, but space was at a premium. As word spread of our situation, friends and ministry colleagues in the area rallied around us in a remarkable way.

The Galegors, another ministry family, were away for a while and offered their home to the family. It became one of several that would be a "home away from home" for the next five months.

Four days after the accident LaDonna was able to see me for the first time since mile marker 313.

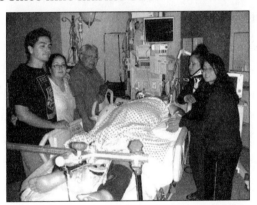

*LaDonna joins the family for the first time
at my bedside in the Trauma ICU unit.*

She recalls an amazing level of strength and stamina God gave that allowed her to spend hours on end with me. She was at my side during early visiting hours and until visitors needed to leave. No matter what level of pain she was in, she was there with me and for me!

One of my first visitors would be a dear friend, Dr. Julian Gunn, a well-respected indigenous leader with the Church of the Nazarene. Albuquerque has been home for them for many years. LaDonna and I love Julian and his wife, Bernita, deeply.

LaDonna recalls Dr. Gunn walking into my room and heading directly to my bed as if on a mission. Without hesitation, he anointed me with oil and stormed the throne room of heaven in prayer on my behalf. He cried out to God to spare my life, imploring our Savior to pour out His healing power on his old friend from Phoenix.

Updates to family and friends became a regular part of our family's daily activity. Facebook friends received ongoing updates as those early hours wore on. As inquiries grew, the family spent more and more time answering many postings and e-mails sent from a growing list of concerned folk.

Our oldest daughter, Nizhoni, remembered a website called CaringBridge.org, where people going through health challenges could post updates on a single site. Interested people could sign up to receive e-mail notifications when a new journal update was posted. There is an overview page that explains the illness or injury, a place to post photos, write journal updates, and a guestbook page where people can respond with comments and words of encouragement. It continues to this day to be the place we update our extended support group.

The site is www.caringbridge.org/visit/craigladonnasmith.

LaDonna was able to write her first post on the CaringBridge site shortly after seeing me for the first time since the accident:

Sunday, June 14, 2009 3:28 p.m., MST

With my family by my side, encouragement and help continues to overflow. I know Dad can hear us, so I'm taking time to just read through the Psalms. Psalms 1 reminds me of Craig: "Blessed is the man that does not walk in the counsel of the wicked or stand in the way of sinners or sit in the seat of mockers. But his delight is in the law of the Lord. And in His law he meditates day and night. He is like a tree planted by streams of water which yields its fruit in season and whose leaf does not wither. Whatever he does prospers."

Craig is that tree. His roots go deep. I know the Lord is ministering to him even as he lies on his back facing each new day of challenges. When he came to Christ at 13 years old, he began that walk of a blessed man. He lives that to this day. His delight is in the Word of God, and I believe the Spirit of God is speaking to him and helping him day and night.

Please pray for his upcoming surgery on his hip tomorrow, that the Spirit of God will give comfort to his traumatized body and that the Holy Spirit would speak to his mind and help him to rest as he works through these very tough days.

Please pray against the powers of darkness that lurk and long to destroy God's people. Please pray for extended families, their travels and also for the room Craig resides in. Please also pray for the staff as they continue to serve Craig and this community.

The following day I was prepped for another of what would be many more long and difficult surgeries to follow. This time they would address the shattered and dislocated left femur head and hip joint. Hours later, with thanks to God, the family was able to report on the success of this surgery.

The Lord has heard our prayers! Dad just got out of hip surgery. It went very well. The doctor said he got a total hip replacement. His breathing, blood pressure, and heart rate were stable throughout the surgery. His blood count went down a little so they gave him about two units of blood. Even Dad's nurse was astounded at how well he took it.

They will leave the breathing tube/vent in for a few more days and will keep him sedated so he can rest for his upcoming pelvic surgery on Thursday.

We are grateful for the staff here. They have been very accommodating and caring. Please continue to pray for the staff and keep Dad in prayer for continued strength and that his kidney function will continue to improve. Please continue to pray for Mom, as her neck and knee are still very sore. Please also pray for Zane as his body is still in a lot of pain.

Thanks—Nizhoni

The following day was a long one for the family as the vigil continued and my body started responding to the effects of the surgeries.

From Shandiin:

Tuesday, June 16, 2009 9:06 p.m., MST

Friends and Family,

Today the doctors and nurses took out a fluid line to the heart and replaced it with another. Fevers can cause bacteria to form in and around tubes within the body, so they wanted to make sure there was no infection. Replacing the old tube with a new one can reduce that risk of infection.

Praise the Lord that they are slowly weaning Dad off his ventilator! Dad has been really working hard at initiating his own breathing.

Grandpa Jeep, Uncle Scott, Uncle Joel, and I spent the day with Dad. When we got there, they had completely taken him off his sedation medications to try and raise his blood pressure. His eyes were open and he was able to give a weak "thumbs up" at the doctors request. Praise the Lord!! They even took his neck brace off for a while. We give God ALL the praise and glory for His continued work in Dad's life.

From Nizhoni:

Mom's knee was really sore yesterday and this morning. Shandiin, Jeep and I made a decision to keep her on bed rest today. As much as she wanted to be with Dad, I know she NEEDED rest.

There are so many things I have always taken for granted, but after helping my mom with some everyday activities, I am so grateful for a fully functioning body.

From LaDonna:

Craig and I love to fix a good strong cup of coffee each morning and read our devotions together. *Streams in the*

Desert is among our favorites, and it continues to be mine at this time.

We often talk about strong trees being planted by rivers of water, but there is so much to be said about small streams that run in the desert. It is good to know that God provides refreshing water to our souls no matter where we are or what we are going through.

Thank you for refreshing our family's hearts by your encouraging notes of prayer and praise for what God is doing and is going to do in these coming days.

We love you much,

LaDonna

One of the great things about the CaringBridge website is the ability for friends and family to respond with words of encouragement. Thousands of posts have come in throughout our ordeal. We were sustained, especially in the early days of this experience, just knowing we had many folks standing with us in the journey. Some of the early responses included these:

June 14, 2009, 8:35 a.m.

Know that John and I are praying that God will continue His grace on Craig in his healing. We know that the angels are caring for him. May God also continue to heal LaDonna and Zane in whatever trauma the accident caused to their bodies. Nizhoni, Dallas, Elizabeth, Shandiin, Stefan and Lydia—your care and love are evident and God is pleased.

Love you all, John and Yan Ng

Hi, Friends,   June 14, 2009, 3:59 p.m.

You all have been in our thoughts and prayers along with many we have shared your accident with. We pray for you all daily as well as family members. You are loved with an everlasting love. May you feel God's arms around you as you go through this difficult time.

Love,

Jim & Sally Wildman

                                          June 14, 2009, 6:41 p.m.

We're praying for you—Craig, LaDonna, and Zane.

We are so thankful you are recovering. Craig, you will be in our prayers as you have your surgery tomorrow. Although you are not able to keep your plans for ministry this summer, God's plan for you will be made known when it's time. During this difficult time, your strong faith in the Lord is an inspiration to us.

Love, prayers, and hugs from The Selb Family Five: Jim, Stephi, Sammy, Jakob & Noah.

Stephanie Selb

Andover, MN

Chapter 6

MY DARKEST DAYS

Things seemed to be going along well, all things considered. I had survived the most challenging week of my life. It seemed like the doctors were making good progress as they repaired and planned for further remodeling to "this ole' house." The family was encouraged, though still under incredible stress and pain as they saw LaDonna and me in such bad condition. While still bad, things could have been much worse. It seemed the future looked promising and I would recover, over time.

Two days after my hip replacement surgery, I was scheduled to go back in the operating room for what the doctors told the family would be my next and hopefully final "major" surgical procedure. It was to repair the open-book pelvic fracture by attaching an external fixator device across my belt line.

The surgeons do this by drilling two very long screws into the pelvis (each about a foot long), on each side. These rods would then be secured to each other by metal crosspieces that would be clamped together in the middle right about where my belt buckle would be. Those two crosspieces were about two inches above my skin, crisscrossing my hip region. It looks like an old-fashioned television antenna. It was to be one of the more unusual items sticking out of me that I saw many weeks later when I emerged out of the coma.

One of the big challenges facing me at the time was consistently low blood pressure and trouble sustaining normal kidney function. Shandiin put a quick post on Caringbridge, asking for prayer before I was to go into this next surgery.

We are so thankful to the Lord for answering our prayers on Dad's blood pressure. Since I had requested prayer for this, Dad has NOT required fluid to sustain a normal reading! The Lord has allowed Dad to maintain a stable rate on his own! Also, Dad's kidney function is maintaining stability and he is not requiring help from medication!

Our prayer requests at this time would be that the Lord would protect Dad against infection of the heart and blood. Also, please pray for fevers to subside and for the upcoming surgery.

I am currently writing this at Dad's bedside. Mom is here with me. I'm smiling as I'm writing, because Mom is so cute—sitting in her wheelchair with her neck brace, sharing her faith in the Lord with the respiratory therapist. Could this moment be one of the reasons why all this has happened, so that Mom could share her hope to the staff? Only the Lord knows, maybe one day we will, too!

With Love, Shandiin

As our family was soon to learn, not everything goes as planned, even in a highly organized, regimented and structured world of a major hospital. My planned surgery got put on hold because of scheduling difficulties as they struggled to find an open operating room.

Being a level-one Trauma Center, UNM Hospital is required to have one operating room available at all times for trauma patients. That affects other surgery scheduling. All non-life-threatening procedures, even mine, can and did end up being delayed.

This brought much concern to my family. They soon found out that those concerns would only grow worse as the next few hours and days unfolded.

Trauma is brutal not only on the patient, but also for their loved ones. There are huge peaks and deep valleys of emotions.

A year after the accident I read for the first time all the Caringbridge posts my family had written. Emotionally I had to brace myself for what life must have been like for them as I spent nearly two months in an induced coma.

The following posts tore at my heart as I came to understand what my family was going through *above ground* as I lived in a crazy *underground* after the miracle at mile marker 313.

Friends and Family,   Friday, June 19, 2009 12:53 a.m., MST
    What a roller coaster day of emotions.

    We were told Dad's surgery would be today. However, as the day progressed, we were told that it might be held off until possibly Monday or Tuesday of next week. They are going to prep Dad tonight just in case there is an opening tomorrow. But they told us not to count on it. I must admit the family was disappointed with the news. We were so eager to get this final surgery out of the way, so that Dad can focus on his recovery.

They are giving Dad antibiotics to fight fevers and infections; however, the fevers persist. Our hearts desire would be that the Lord would cause any infection to be stopped and that Dad would NOT maintain these mid to high fevers.

Other than that, Dad's numbers are looking good. I'm still convinced that Dad has one of the sweetest faces I've ever seen. He opened his eyes again for a few seconds. Oh, how we cherish those moments!!

Thank you brothers and sisters! We are encouraged by His faithfulness. We are clinging to Him moment by moment.

Love,

Shandiin

Little did the doctors or we know the severity of that persistent fever. Infection is the deadly enemy of any trauma patient and can lie lurking down deep.

That possibility didn't slip by Dallas and Elizabeth. Elizabeth had been serving as a nurse with an infectious disease (ID) physician in the Phoenix area, and my symptoms were concerning to her and shared by her physician assistant husband, Dallas.

As they shared their concerns with the staff at UNM, they, unfortunately, didn't take their concerns seriously enough. They assured them they were controlling my condition in accordance with their standard operating procedures.

Somewhat exasperated, Elizabeth shared her concerns with the ID doctor she worked with back in Arizona. He told them to insist on an ID consult right away, and not to take "no" for an answer!

How thankful I am they did! Having survived death's door once, I didn't want to go back there anytime soon. Being comatose, I was dependent on the advocacy of a loving wife, and deeply concerned children to fight on my behalf, and fight they did! Had they not persisted, I could very well have survived the initial accident, only to die at the hands of a lurking infection that, to that point, remained undetected.

Friday, June 19, 2009 11:38 p.m., MST

Oh how our hearts ache.

Just when we thought we were almost over his final surgery, we were told some disconcerting news from doctors. I have been requesting prayer for Dad's continued infections and fevers. Dallas, as well as his wife, Elizabeth, went back to Phoenix this last week. They are currently on the road as I write to meet up with us here in Albuquerque.

As they were gone, they were in constant communication with the doctors and nurses. Because Dad has been running these consistent fevers, they have been pressing the staff hard to consult with an infectious disease specialist. Dallas and Elizabeth pushed hard for this request, and the doctors and nurses finally agreed to the consult, which resulted in a CT scan. The CT scan revealed significant infection to Dad's colon—something they were not able to detect prior to this day. They believe these injuries to the colon were a result of the broken pelvis. We feel so tired and weak right now. We are hiding ourselves in Him.

This is a risky situation. There are two options. One would be a less invasive surgery to drain the abscess with needles, but it might not do the trick. And in the long run, they would have to attempt the second option some time down the road anyway.

This second, most invasive option is surgery to cut out the infected part of the colon. They would then staple the colon back together. After that, the colon might be outside of his body (colostomy) for the rest of his life. They would also have to keep the abdomen open for an extended amount of time to continue cleaning out the site.

So, with that said, Dad's pelvic surgery is not even on the radar. Nor does that seem like a big deal anymore. This is a pressing issue and the doctors and nurses don't want to operate tonight, but will do it first thing in the morning. I do not think this surgery will be delayed due to its seriousness. This is the reality that because of Dad's trauma, stapling the colon back together might not even work.

We are calling upon the name of Lord for healing. We are at Dad's side and he is opening his eyes for us now. Please pray for Mom. She has been having flashbacks of the accident and we are all so tired.

We choose to offer up our sacrifices of praise to God. He is good, and everything He does is good.

Love, Shandiin

So it was off once again to surgery, but this time for a whole new problem. They decided to open up my abdomen with an incision that started at my breastbone and went all the way down to my belt line. They went in and found damage to my colon and began to address what was initially reported by phone call to our family as a "small perforation" and they were able to repair it successfully. They told the family that I had handled the surgery well and was back in the ICU unit.

Whoever they assigned to convey that message to the family either didn't have all the information right, or decided to give a much rosier picture than was the case. When the family arrived at the hospital they were given the full report of just how serious this undetected condition was.

Sunday, June 21, 2009 3:39 p.m., MST

Although Dad's colon surgery was "successful" yesterday, the perforation was bigger than was reported to us over the phone. When we got to the hospital, the doctor told us there was a significant amount of infection they had to take out. Dad did do well during the surgery and he has remained stable since; however, we ask that you pray for blood supply to return to that part of Dad's colon. There is concern that a part of the colon is turning dark, which is indication of a lack of blood supply.

We are celebrating this Father's Day at Dad's side. As we think of the significance of this day, our hearts are thankful and we also celebrate our Abba Father. Today is another day of celebration of our Lord and Savior. We are so grateful He is our Father, and that in his gracious love, has given us our earthly father.

Happy Father's Day, Dad. We love you.

This initial surgery would begin a long and tedious process of unanticipated multiple surgeries done over the next few weeks.

These surgeries put on hold the other major orthopedic repairs, including stabilizing my pelvis with the external fixators.

My already critical condition was made worse by ten continuous days of poisoning myself with my perforated colon. There was no sense in repairing my shattered pelvis when my abdominal cavity was filled with infection that would soon take my life if not addressed.

It became clear to us all—both my family and the medical staff tasked with my care—that Dallas and Elizabeth did have it right. Had they not pressed for this consultation, the infection would have taken over my body and death would have been inevitable.

We had to prepare ourselves for daily visits back to the operating room where, through multiple surgeries, they would continue to wash out my abdominal cavity and deal with the damage done to the colon itself.

I learned one very important lesson through this experience: as much as I love Garduno's all-you-can-eat Mexican lunch buffet, the last thing you probably want to do if you're planning on perforating your colon is to have had the all-you-can-eat lunch buffet at Garduno's! In the next few weeks I would undergo ten surgeries to wash out all those refried beans!

The next day they wheeled me back into surgery for my second abdominal washout. It was in this surgery another serious issue was uncovered and cared for by the surgeons. Dallas reported the results in a Caringbridge update a day later:

Tuesday, June 23, 2009 12:32 p.m., MST
First the good news: Dad's surgery yesterday was pretty successful overall! The surgeons removed about six inches

of colon that was very unhealthy and moved the opening to his abdomen further up his body towards his rib cage. His relocated colon tissue looks much healthier now, and they were able to flush quite a bit of infection out of his abdominal cavity.

Now the not-so-good news: This morning was a bit of a scare, since Dad has had a delayed trauma injury to his right hip area, where doctors are watching for fluid buildup between his muscle layer and his adipose tissue (fat). They decided that the pressure caused by the fluid buildup was threatening blood flow to his skin in that area, so they opened the skin to allow fluid to drain.

The scare came when over two liters of fluid came pouring out immediately and continued to drain more than a liter of additional fluid over the next hour or so. Dad's blood pressure has been very dependent on the amount of fluids they've been giving him, and he has a very delicate fluid balance, so losing over three liters of fluid from there caused his blood pressure to plummet.

They gave him quite a bit of intravenous fluids and strong medication to normalize his blood pressure. He is responding well to this combination, and it seems his pressure has normalized currently. They are decreasing the amount of blood pressure meds they are giving, and we are grateful for this.

He will be going into surgery later this afternoon to once again flush any remaining infection from his abdomen and to check on the fluid collection in his right hip to see how far back that pocket goes. There may be more fluid that needs to be drained.

Along with washing out my abdomen, this second surgery revealed another serious effect of the accident: a rare but devastating injury the doctors called a *Morel-Lavallée lesion*, or simply *Morel's lesion*.

Apparently, the impact of my body slamming up against the ceiling and then back down onto the floorboard multiple times caused the skin and fat layer of my right hip to become separated internally from the muscle layer below. That created a void that became a collection place for blood and all the fluids that were being given me through IVs, etc. Over time that void was filled up with these fluids, and the blood supply from the muscles up to the skin were cut off, resulting in the skin dying though still connected to my body.

Once all that fluid drained, they had to cut away a huge chunk of my skin from my right pelvic region. They then found muscle below the skin that was damaged beyond repair and they had to remove a good amount of the top portion of my right buttock. The damage was extensive enough that they removed muscle all the way down to the pelvic bone itself. I have affectionately come to call this wound my *shark bite*, because when you see it, it really does look like a shark took a big old chunk out of my right side and back.

They told LaDonna after this unexpected surgical find that had the damage gone any deeper, they would have had to remove my whole right leg—a total amputation. But, thanks be to God the damage went so far, but not one bit more, giving me the blessing of having my leg still with me!

It's not often we look down at our extremities and thank God for them, but when I realize how close I came to having that happen, I'm greatly moved by the goodness of my Lord!

Friends and Family,   Thursday, June 25, 2009
                                        11:08 a.m., MST

Dad is going into surgery again today. They will continue to clean out his abdominal cavity, and assess any further steps needed to address his Morel's lesion on his right thigh/flank area.

He has been intubated [had a breathing tube inserted] for over two weeks now. It is a delicate balance of keeping the tube in for his much-needed surgeries (pelvic repair, colon and Morel's lesion cleanings, etc.), but it also carries the risk of Dad developing pneumonia.

Dad has also developed some irregular heart readings. They are monitoring them.

Thursday, June 25, 2009 10:51 p.m., MST

Thank you all for praying for Dad's surgery today. It went well and Dad seemed to have a good day of rest. They still saw some pockets of infection near his pelvis, so they were able to clean that area out. He will still need to go back to the operating room for frequent "clean-outs," but the surgeon did say there was not as much infection found as there was last time. Praise the Lord. We are continuing to pray for that infection to stop. Once the infection is cleared, they will place a mesh over the opening.

With Dad's Morel's lesion, they debrided [removed dead tissue from] a small area and they said the muscle tissue looks really healthy. Yet again, we are thankful to God for his faithfulness in all this! Dad has a few wound vacs on that pull fluid out so as not to harbor infection.

They have been changing his vent/breathing settings as an attempt to wean him off of support. Thankfully he is initiating his own breathing, but there might be a need for them to put a tracheal tube in his throat. This would only happen if Dad has a difficult time transitioning off the ventilator. At first, we were a little concerned, but Dallas and Elizabeth reassured us that a tracheal tube is less harmful to his vocal chords, and it is actually a step up from the ventilator. We are praying that they wouldn't have to put this in, but necessity trumps desire.

Our desire would be that Dad could get off that ventilator (to reduce that risk of pneumonia), but pending surgeries are causing the staff to keep it in. We are trusting in God's timing, even though we want so bad to relieve Dad of this tube.

We had a wonderful time with Dad today. Dallas decided Dad would appreciate hearing music. He placed some good ole' Southern Gospel music (The Kingsmen Quartet) up to Dad's ear. After seeing Dad's numbers go crazy, and his heart rate skyrocket, we decided we should probably hold off of the tunes for the time being. Dad was probably jiving inside and couldn't help but get excited. We had fun with that one. Maybe later, Dad.

Zane and his family were also able to stop in on their way through town. It was great reuniting with him and seeing how the Lord has protected Zane. We are so grateful.

Love, Shandiin

The family began to settle in for what was to be a long and arduous next few weeks of more surgeries, recoveries, and progressive healing. It seemed that the most serious and dangerous part of the journey was behind us now. The family had to endure the daily challenge of seeing me being repeatedly wheeled back into the operating room for more abdominal washouts and maintenance of wound vacs, etc.

They still hadn't addressed the much-needed repair of my open-book pelvic fracture. Those discussions were put on hold as a much higher priority was given to addressing the life-threatening infection still in my body.

My breathing got stronger, so in one of the abdominal washout surgeries they decided it was time to remove the ventilator that was breathing for me and give me a tracheotomy.

Instead of a tube stuck down my windpipe through my mouth, an opening was made on the outside of my neck, just below my second chin which I've used as a vocal cord bumper for most of my life. (When you are dependent on your voice to make a living, you've got to protect these valuable assets to the best of your ability; my friends know I've done a good job of padding those cords for a good chunk of my life!)

My breathing would still be assisted, but the oxygen line would be attached externally rather than internally through a plastic plug stitched to the outside of my throat.

As I began to be more stable, the kids began to set up a schedule of who would hang around Albuquerque and who would go home to get back to work. Even though LaDonna was discharged from the hospital, she was forbidden to drive and needed a lot of hands-on care. For the time being, someone needed to be with LaDonna constantly to help her.

Her heart's desire was to be with me every day at the hospital, regardless of her own discomfort and pain. The kids had difficulty in pulling her away from my bedside, but thankfully she did give in a time or two and went to whatever home available to her for much-needed rest.

We're so thankful for a number of ministry folk in the area who made their homes available to our family. Some who were complete strangers, yet brothers and sisters in Christ, became dear friends as they opened their homes up to my kinfolk. Over the five months in Albuquerque, LaDonna ended up moving about six times from one home to another, but each place was an oasis in the desert for her.

There wasn't a lot the family could do for me but be there at my bedside. I laughed a bit when I later read their Caringbridge posts: they said I would look at them, they would talk to me and I'd respond. To be honest, I knew nothing of what they say I did for almost two months; I was living in that crazy underworld of a drug-induced coma. I may have nodded to them when they spoke to me, but I'm sure most of the youth who were smoking dope, popping pills, and injecting psychedelic drugs in the '60s and '70s did the same thing when questions were posed to them.

My family lived on the topside of reality; meanwhile I was living in my own, very vivid underground world. The only thing positive I can say about it is that it helped me finally make sense of all those rock 'n' roll lyrics I remember hearing as I was growing up!

June 28 was Dallas' day to serve as Mom's chauffeur and author of the CaringBridge posts.

Sunday, June 28, 2009 3:29 p.m., MST

Well, it's just me and Mom and Uncle Joel here in Albuquerque now, since Nizhoni, Shandiin, and my wife Elizabeth had to head back to Phoenix today. It's Shandiin's birthday today, so happy birthday little sis!

Dad is looking slightly better every day. Today, he had wound care nurses change out his wound vac dressings on his left hip, right hip/flank and the one on his abdomen. That's done to keep his wounds from getting infected. Dad's Morel's lesion seems to be under control, meaning there seems to be no further dying tissue cells there, and it doesn't appear to be infected.

Dad has the tracheal tube now, and appears more comfortable without the breathing/suction tubes going into his mouth. He is still on ventilation assistance but is doing most of the breathing on his own. The docs seem pretty sure he'll be able to be off assisted ventilation within the week.

He continues to have buildups of infection in his lower abdomen/pelvic cavity. He will require several more procedures to flush out the infection before they can seal up the opening with surgical mesh. Only when the mesh is in place would surgeons consider repairing Dad's broken pelvis, since it would be a disaster if the hardware they were putting in got infected.

Dad is still on large amounts of pain meds/sedatives to keep him comfortable. He is only able to open his eyes for short periods of time. He is aware that we're there and understands most things we're saying to him, but is only able to respond with head nods or facial expressions.

Dr. West, the surgeon in charge of Dad's care, is pleased with his progress so far and states Dad is making baby steps towards recovery.

We pray that God will comfort Dad since being unable to communicate makes him visibly frustrated.

Dallas

Chapter 7

THREE WEEKS AND COUNTING

As Dallas and LaDonna settled in to another week of waiting for the next round of washout surgeries and recoveries, other life-altering events were going on around us.

Remember the family that came to see our house the day before we left? Well, they finally decided that this was the house for them and they put in an offer that, they hoped, we just couldn't refuse. But how do you consider such an offer when you are sailing in a yellow submarine in the vast ocean underneath the city of Albuquerque?

Even if the house did sell, who would pack and move our things? It had been very inconvenient to have them look at the house the day before we left on our trip, but it was even more inconvenient to have them put in the offer while I lay in a coma! Why couldn't they wait for what our real estate agent said was the normal home-selling season—five months later?

What a time for our house to sell!

Dallas wrote the following on the CaringBridge site:

Monday, June 29, 2009 5:20 p.m., MST

Well today's been hectic so far. We found out last night that Dad has been off antibiotics for two days now. This blew our minds since we understood that Dad needed to finish killing off the bacteria in his abdominal cavity so they could close up his abdomen with surgical mesh. Then he could have his pelvic surgery.

According to the docs, he's been doing pretty well without antibiotics. He's still spiking occasional high fevers, but has been pretty good temperature-wise the past few days. His white blood cell count, which would be very high if he had active infection, has been low so far. They will consider starting another course of antibiotics if his fevers worsen or white blood cell count increases.

Today wound care nurses were cleaning Dad's stoma site and noticed his colon was not adhering to the opening, as it should. As a result, there is a small amount of space between the colon and abdominal wall where waste or bacteria could fall back into the abdominal cavity and cause a new infection.

A surgeon came in and briefly explained that Dad would need to have another surgery to repair that problem. He was scarce on details, but we should know more by tomorrow, if they haven't taken him to surgery already. This will be the third time they have operated on his colon. The first two times they took out six inches of colon for a total of one foot removed. Hopefully that will be it.

On a brighter note, Mom and Dad have been trying to sell their house for a while now. Yesterday they finally got a decent bid on their home, and we spent the day having Mom sign the paperwork for the contract to be official.

Today we found out that since Dad's name is on the original sellers notice, we needed to have Dad's signature on sales contract in order for it to be legally binding. Due to Dad being pretty heavily sedated with the amount of pain medicine they are giving him, this proved to be a problem. We spent the day rushing around getting legal advice and trying to speak with social workers and other experts on these types of matters to figure out what our options were.

We got hold of a Power of Attorney document and were able to track down a social worker that was also a notary. Nurses stopped Dad's pain meds long enough for us to explain the situation to him and allow him to make a mark for a signature on the P.O.A. form. When I explained that his house would be sold for a price close to what they were hoping to get, he smiled a giant grin and made good eye contact with both Mom and I for the first time since his accident!

He showed signs of relief and extreme happiness at this news, and we're grateful for everyone who helped us through this ridiculous legal nightmare today! The sale of the home will hopefully be finalized within the next few days, so please keep that issue in prayer, as Mom and Dad will definitely need a one-level home in the future.

Thank God for delicious Rudy's Bar-B-Q, the only good thing about Albuquerque. Mom said that's not a very nice thing to say.

All along LaDonna had been so strong for our family, even though she was facing serious healing issues of her own. Seeing her husband, lying there in pain, trying to scribble an "X" on that signature line brought her to the breaking point. The trauma of the accident, combined with the emotional challenge of selling a home that was so much a part of our lives for almost fifteen years, deemed us powerless to adequately address these challenges on our own.

How LaDonna held on that long is a miracle and a testament to her faith, fortitude, and love for her husband and family.

As I put the "X" on the line, all she could do was go over to the corner of the ICU unit, cover her mouth and weep quietly as not to disturb this important conversation. Sometimes the emotional build-up inside has to spill over, much like a volcano, as internal pressure is released. Tears often flow like lava as body, soul, and spirit purge themselves in a very important healing stream. It was LaDonna's time.

Tuesday, June 30, 2009 9:50 p.m., MST

Dad had a bit of a rough night last night. Docs have him on less sedation and slightly less pain meds, as they want him to breathe on his own. Yesterday, Dad was getting used to having a tube in his trachea, and he was coughing frequently and struggling to clear a few weeks of fluid buildup from his lungs. His heart rate was higher than providers were comfortable with. They gave him a couple extra bags of IV fluids to help his heart work less hard. We left the hospital slightly worried about his condition.

This morning, he was like a brand new man! Around 8 a.m., they were able to take Dad completely off his ventilation assistance. He was breathing on his own! He was completely awake and aware of his surroundings for the first time, and was able to keep his eyes open for hours at a time without fatigue. He was making good eye contact and was trying to communicate with us.

Because the tracheotomy opening is below his vocal chords, air goes out the opening before he can form word sounds. We did our best to lip-read and he was able to ask for different things and we were able to fill him in a bit on his current status. We explained that he still had some broken bones that needed to be fixed, but he has an infection in his abdomen that the doctors need to take care of first. He seems to understand the situation and was in good spirits throughout the morning.

We left the hospital when they took Dad in for another procedure to wash infection out of his abdominal cavity. One of the doctors mentioned they would be taking a look at his stoma site during the procedure and hopefully they'd have a surgery date for the repair of the opening.

Since Dad would be in surgery through the rest of visiting hours, Mom and I checked out the movie *UP* in 3D at a nearby theater! It was Mom's first 3D movie ever, and she loved it. I miss *Captain EO* from Disneyland in the '80s, but just have to say 3D technology is a million times better than when Michael Jackson battled the cyber-alien lady in 3D when I was like eight years old.

Anyhow...

When we came back tonight for visiting hours, the nurse says Dad did quite well during his surgery. Doctors decided they will be doing another course of his previous antibiotic, which means Dad may have had more of the infection in his abdominal cavity than before. This may not be the best news that he needs antibiotics again, but I can't tell you how relieved I am that he's on at least ONE antibiotic now.

Dad is running a slight fever at this time, but that's not uncommon after a procedure like the one he had. He is still slightly sedated from the surgery, so he's temporarily back on ventilation assistance until around midnight when he'll be back to breathing on his own. As of now, Dad is starting to wake up and express some discomfort with his fever. His heart rate is high again, so we're waiting to see if they will give him more fluid or some alternative treatment.

The nurse doesn't have any information about when Dad's stoma surgery will happen, but she did note that they changed the dressing there, so they definitely did take a look at it. Will update more when we know more about this.

Dallas

The start of the fourth week of my recovery was the start of a new month as well. June 2009 will be a month not soon forgotten. The beginning of July seemed to set the stage for brighter days ahead for us all. The healing and surgeries continued, but at least I had survived three incredibly challenging weeks.

Wednesday, July 1, 2009 9:31 p.m., MST

Dad had a big day today! Like yesterday, he's very anxious to ask questions and, due to us being terrible lip readers, is not being very successful in his attempts. I asked him if it would be helpful for him to know everything that has happened to him since the time of the accident and he nodded yes.

I spent a good half hour explaining to him all of his injuries and surgeries so far. I told him that a lot of his surgical fixes are temporary, including the tracheotomy tube, which hopefully will not affect his speaking or singing voice down the line, and tried to anticipate any possible questions he might have about strange sensations (for example, the wound vac over the Morel's lesion feels very wet to Dad), or possible complications to his care.

Between every piece of information I asked Dad if he understood what I was telling him, and he nodded yes. Hopefully having this knowledge will make the process a little less scary for him. Doctors routinely pop in and out and talk about testing various things, and with less pain medication and sedation, Dad is more aware of discomfort in some of the surgical areas—at least now he'll know why.

Dad seems to be most concerned about his current inability to move his feet when doctors ask him to. I explained that off and on throughout the past few weeks he has moved his feet on request. Trauma docs and orthopedic docs all agree his inability to do so at this time is probably due to continued inflammation around the area of his still-broken pelvis. They are fairly certain he will regain his ability to feel sensations and move his feet in the future, but are calling in a neurology consultation to figure out other possible explanations for his come-and-go control and sensations of his feet.

Shortly after that discussion with the doctors about a neurological consult, the nurse came in to flex Dad's feet a bit to prevent something called "drop foot." The bad news was that this caused Dad a tremendous amount of pain. The good news is that he can FEEL pain down there. This is more evidence that hopefully his occasional lack of sensation is a result of inflammation in his pelvis, where a lot of nerves in the feet and legs come off the spinal cord. We'll hopefully know more about this after Dad has his neurological consult, and we'll update when more is known.

Because Dad felt so much pain from the manipulation of his ankles, nurses called for physical therapy to come in and start helping Dad move his legs. He seemed to like most of the movements and responded well to a special boot they put on to help prevent drop foot.

We have been able to give Dad some water in his mouth via a small sponge on a stick. Up to this point, all of Dad's hydration has come via IV fluids. He definitely likes the water, and asks for it frequently, which we are happy to oblige him with!

Dad was surprised when Mom told him that three weeks have passed already since the accident. He seems to be in pretty good spirits, and nurses all comment that he always wakes up smiling and seems very patient when they or we try to figure out what he's trying to tell us. One nurse said, "most people would be very angry, but your Dad seems to be different."

We're proud of him, especially for keeping his trademark attitude throughout this lousy situation!

The doctor who performed yesterday's abdominal washout procedure checked the stoma site. Since the antibiotics had stopped infection there and the site looked clean, he feels they will not have to revise the surgery! Wound care nurses say that the colon is adhering to the wall at least a little, and everything looks healthy! Awesome, awesome to the max!

We continue to pray for emotional strength and perseverance for both Mom and Dad, especially now that Dad's alert and expressing his discomfort more. It's really hard to witness Dad in pain, and this may wear on Mom over time.

Thanks again for guestbook love! It's really nice to hear from people who have known and supported Mom and Dad for years, and for all friends and relatives who drop us a line. Again, Mom loves reading them and finds lots of encouragement from them.

Dallas

One of the most significant long-term effects of my injuries was not an issue in the first few weeks of my recovery. According to the updates the kids would post, I had the ability, early on, to move my feet without any problem. Simple procedures like pushing down with the foot as you would on a gas pedal and pulling the foot up as in taking a step were doable, as I'd respond to the doctor's commands. But something happened in those early weeks that caused me to lose the ability to move my feet at all. They just weren't responding, though my brain was sending the signals to them to do so. Something dramatically had changed, and with it, hope for full recovery apart from another one of those miracles of God.

Thursday, July 2, 2009 9:51 p.m., MST

Dad had mostly a restful day. Nurses are giving him pain meds through his feeding tube in an effort to try and wean him off the IV pain meds he's currently on. He was in a comfortable and sleepy state for most of the day and got some much-needed rest.

We've been waiting all day for Dad to go in for today's abdominal washout procedure, but he keeps getting bumped for what they feel are more pressing trauma surgeries. As of now, Dad is scheduled to go in for that procedure around 11pm.

A doctor came in about 20 minutes ago to discuss his Neurologist consult from earlier today. The doc said that they would like to get an MRI of Dad's spine to see if there may have been any trauma to the spinal cord that may be caused by the force of the accident. We know Dad doesn't have any breaks in his spinal column that would threaten the spinal cord, but they want a better picture of his soft tissues to figure out what exactly is causing Dad's occasional lack of sensation in his feet and inability to move his feet at times when asked to do so.

The MRI is scheduled for the morning, barring any problems with the hardware they installed in his hip during his hip replacement or the metal rod they placed in his right femur to repair the break there. For those that don't know, an MRI uses high-powered magnets to create a picture of the body in cross sections. Usually magnets + metal = bad situation if the metal is inside your body, but some surgical parts are MRI safe. They will be checking Dad's chart closely to see exactly which make and model of hardware they used during surgery to see if it's safe to turn a giant magnet on around him.

Obviously we are concerned about any potential soft tissue damage to the spinal cord or nerve roots there. We know that an MRI is much better than a CT scan to assess soft tissue damage. Hopefully they'll be able to do the MRI without any problems tomorrow and maybe we'll have more answers. They should also be able to view his cervical spine to finally clear him from any injuries there. He occasionally has to wear a neck brace when they have his bed above a certain angle, since he hasn't been cleared medically via MRI of his cervical spine. If it looks clear, Dad won't have to wear the neck brace anymore, which would be a good thing.

I don't know if it's been mentioned before, but for a while there, they were unable to shave Dad's upper lip due to the ventilator he was on at the time. They left the growth, and over time, follicles turned to stubble, stubble turned bristles, and bristles bloomed into the most spectacular super-Tom Selleck-MAN- mustache the world has ever known! The reason I bring this up is now that Dad is more awake, he's starting to itch his upper lip and he has requested that the glorious mustache be shaved tonight. "Sigh!"

Seriously, this mustache is more worthy of a public viewing at the Staples Center in LA than certain other unnamed celebrity figures. I will miss it, for sure, as I'm such a fan of good mustaches.

I digress . . .

People have been asking about Mom and Zane's current status as well. Mom's broken C-1 vertebra is healing without surgery. She is currently wearing a neck brace, and will need to do so for an additional twelve weeks, but should recover well.

She has a sore hand and knee that occasionally swell up, but doctors are encouraging her to walk around, so she is doing as much as she can with her current injuries. She is able to tolerate pain using only Ibuprofen, which is awesome!

My uncle Zane was the least injured out of the three people involved in the accident and was released from the hospital a day after the accident. He will be coming out to help Mom this coming week, as all of us kids have to return to work then.

Mom requested I continue writing the updates so I'll do my best to get the information from whoever is helping Mom and write it down for this site as best as I can.

Thanks again for the notes of encouragement. I know we'll all miss Dad's mustache, but let's try to make the best of it.

Dallas

I love my kids so much. Each have amazing personalities, which bleed through their Caringbridge postings.

My girls are more serious and conservative than their crazy brother, Dallas. His medical expertise, combined with his off-the-wall sense of humor began to emerge as he continued to write the updates that were now going out worldwide to family, friends, ministry colleagues, and even complete strangers who somehow found their way to the site. It sure made for some interesting responses from people in the guestbook section.

In the days that followed, I went back in for yet another abdominal wash out. This time no signs of infection were present, and that was encouraging to both doctors and family. I was cleared for the MRI of my spine, and thankfully those powerful magnets didn't attract my metal implants, and I got through the 5 a.m. procedure well. I continued to have difficulty breathing on my own, so I continued to depend on assistive breathing through the ventilator.

Though I don't recall them being there, it was helpful to LaDonna to have Nizhoni, Stefan and Shandiin, and our little granddaughter, Lydia, visit over the July 4th holiday. I couldn't see them, but they could see me, and it was an encouragement to them to just be there for us. I was touched by one of the postings our firstborn, Nizhoni, put on Caringbridge about this visit:

Sunday, July 5, 2009 1:15 p.m., MST

Shandiin, her husband, Stefan, and I were so glad to see Mom and Dad today. Mom was happy that little Lydia was able to make the trip as well. It was hard for Shandiin and I to go back to Phoenix this past week as our hearts were still and continue to be with our parents. I am so glad we have a God we can turn to in time of need. It is during this time that I am learning to trust, trust, trust in the Lord as never before. I'm reminded of Psalm 121, "Our help comes from the Lord, the Maker of heaven and earth."

It's so comforting to know who's helping Dad when it feels like we can't—One who knows his thoughts and very being more than anyone else because of who He is. This truth is what I cling to at this time.

Just a quick update on Dad:

I have not been able to see him open his eyes since he started doing it the past few days. Finally this morning he did open his eyes and gave me a great big smile! Shandiin, Stefan, Lydia and I are leaving in a few minutes to go back to Phoenix. I'm so glad I got to see him alert, awake and smiling before we have to leave.

He is scheduled to go into the OR within an hour for another abdominal flushing. There is still concern of infection in the old and new stoma site, so they will check on that during that procedure as well. It's hard for them to tell without opening it up to further assessments, but hopefully they can pinpoint what's going on without any further delay.

Doctors are still a little concerned about his high blood pressure. I'm near his bedside and he's having an EKG performed right now.

Thanks!

Nizhoni

As Christians and serving the Lord most of our lives, LaDonna and I have prayed diligently for our children, even before they were ever born. We had faith, but it's not automatic, that the next generation will have a heart after God. Often it has been said, "God doesn't have any grandchildren!"

Our faith must be personal and not based on the faith of our parents or those who have preceded us. Nobody will ever get to heaven based on the faith of a mom or dad. We each stand accountable to God for the spiritual decisions we make—or choose not to make.

Severe trauma has such an emotional and physical toll on patient and family alike. These life-altering events have the potential of either driving us away from God or to God. How thankful we are that the deep pain we've experienced as a family has driven us closer to the Lord, not away from Him!

Once the kids left, LaDonna's brother, Zane took his turn being there for LaDonna. Their days continued to be filled with daily trips back and forth from her temporary home to the ICU unit, often staying well past visiting hours.

As my incredibly damaged abdomen was just about cleared of infection, the doctors could now begin turning their attention to repairing all the damage done from the open-book pelvic fracture that had been one of the major issues all along. LaDonna communicated the update to Dallas back in Phoenix, and he began once again to, let's just say, do his thing, on the Caringbridge website:

Sunday, July 5, 2009 10:37 p.m., MST

Dad is back from his routine abdominal procedure. They continue to wash pockets of infection out of his abdominal cavity. His last cleaning was pretty encouraging and docs are seeing very minimal infection at this time! Mom was not able to talk to the surgeon who performed the surgery, but there is a chance they may not have to do very many more of these.

Mom did talk to the orthopedic surgeon who told her that Dad is on their schedule for repair of his broken pelvis tomorrow! Based on what previous providers have said, they would have been unable to perform this operation if there were still infection in his pelvic region, due to risk of infected hardware. I can only assume this means Dad's abdominal washouts are almost over with, and they may have already closed his abdomen with surgical mesh.

So, Dad may have his external pelvic fixation procedure done soon.

This involves a large external halo around his pelvis with several brackets that brace the pelvis in the correct position for healing via screws in several areas. This is a preferred, non-invasive surgery, compared to the traditional instillation of metal plates and rods. Those require quite a bit more open surgery to perform. The orthopedic surgeon is pretty sure they will be able to use the external pelvic fixator vs. the open surgery. The possibility for the more invasive procedure still exists, though. It's dependent on how much Dad's pelvis has healed already.

One of Mom's main concerns at this time is with Dad's blood pressure, which has been high for the past week. It seemed to be lower when he was on the ventilation assistance. He was working harder to breathe on his own without the vent, therefore increasing his heart activity. Now, even when he's back on the vent, Dad is still running high BP. This along with some anomalies on Dad's heart rhythm monitor led docs to do a 12-lead ECG test.

They wanted to rule out any cardiac muscle damage. A blood test indicated he probably doesn't have any cardiac muscle damage at this time. Phew. That's one less thing to worry about. Dad is back on BP meds, but according to Mom, it is still running high most of the time.

Dad's stoma site is still looking good. They did find an abscess around the opening that they were going to drain today during an abdominal washout procedure.

Dad also has a couple of abscesses around the area of his left hip replacement. They had removed two staples and inserted a wick in the area to help the infection be drawn out from the area and to allow the wound to heal from the inside out. That prevents the skin from healing over any infection pockets, which would seal them inside the skin, as that would be bad.

All these pockets of infection haven't seemed to bother Dad too much. His vital signs are good, other than his high blood pressure. According to Mom, Dad doesn't have a fever at this time. This is a good sign that his antibiotics are working well.

Hopefully that is an accurate summary of the goings on in Albuquerque, at least for today. We should have more info once Mom talks to surgeons tomorrow.

I think it was Martha Stewart who once said, "Secondhand information is like a flaky, crumbly pastry tart . . . just don't use it for insider trading. You'll go to jail."*

Dallas

*Martha Stewart may or may not have ever said that.

Tuesday, July 7, 2009 5:00 p.m., MST

Dad's surgery to repair his pelvis went very well, and they were able to do it the less invasive way by inserting an external fixation device.

Since he has a halo-like support system outside his body they are unable to sit Dad up higher than a twenty-degree angle at any time. This is good for healing but a potential problem when it comes to things like developing pneumonia. So far Dad is still coughing up fluid from his lungs every so often, which minimizes the risk of infection. Dad is currently running a bit of a fever, but nothing extremely concerning.

In the last report, I was guessing that they may have been able to seal Dad's abdominal cavity with surgical mesh, and Mom was able to confirm that they have done this! This means the last time they did an abdominal washout procedure, they did not find any infection there and were able to put this stuff called *vicromesh* over his open abdomen, creating a sterile environment again, keeping bacteria out.

Dad still has the wound vac above the mesh. Surgeons will be unable to completely close his abdominal musculature and skin layers for several more weeks. For the time being, however, his abdominal infection is pretty much taken care of.

Now that Dad's pelvis is fixed, physical therapy is swinging by daily to help Dad move his legs, both to keep blood clots from forming and to retain his normal range of motion in his limbs. Being bedridden for a month will definitely prevent anyone from doing an aerial cartwheel into the splits. As you well know, this is Dad's trademark move at speaking engagements. Dad is still in the special boot that prevents foot drop, and seems to be responding well to the movements the physical therapists are doing, which is another reason for praise.

Mom and Dad are currently in the process of selling their home here in Glendale, AZ Currently, the house has an offer and a contract on it, but the appraisal came back less than the buyers were offering originally. This puts Mom and Dad in a position where they need wisdom on whether to accept the lower offer or attempt to get more appraisals.

Dallas

P.S.—One area of embellishment I need to clarify: Dad does NOT do cartwheels into the splits at speaking engagements— at least not without several back handsprings through a ring of fire first.

Just when it seemed that things were looking brighter, another challenge hit me and hit me hard. Two days after Dallas' encouraging update, LaDonna asked the kids to rally our prayer warriors once again to help pray us through another emergency situation:

Friday, July 10, 2009 9:44 p.m., MST

Dad's had a rough couple of nights. His breathing has been labored and his blood pressure continues to remain very high. Yesterday on chest X-ray doctors noticed some fluid that he's been coughing up prior to now has been accumulating down in the lung to the point where it is keeping that area from inflating with air. After they saw this, they put Dad back on higher ventilation assistance to help force that lobe of the lung open again. This seems to have worked pretty well over the past day. Mom now reports they have taken Dad back off the ventilator and he is breathing on his own through his tracheal opening without assistance!

Dad was running a four-day fever of about 102+ degrees, and Mom has been extremely concerned about this. People with a collapsed lung will sometimes run a low-grade fever, but we're still worried about infection of his other wound sites and possible pneumonia, which could all also cause a fever. They took a sample of the fluid Dad's been coughing up to see if any bacteria grow from it. So far, there has been none, which means no pneumonia as of yet. They will need to give any bacteria another day or two to grow before they can know for sure that his lungs are pneumonia-free, however.

Getting back to Dad's fever, the good news is that today Dad's temp is finally dropping back to normal range, which hopefully is a good sign that his body is successfully fighting off the infection. Dad finished his second course of antibiotics a few days ago and doctors say they will not add another one unless they absolutely have to. For now, Dad's immune system is on its own to fight off infection.

Mom has not gotten a detailed report about the MRI Dad had done several days ago, but doctors were able to tell her they did not see any spinal cord damage of any kind on the MRI! Doctors still think Dad's swelling around his broken bones in his legs and pelvis are pinching off nerves, preventing him from moving and feeling sensations in his feet.

The next step that's necessary in this medical mystery is to do an electromyogram (EMG) study. This involves a special needle that senses electrical activity in muscles when the body is at rest and then when the muscles are contracted.

This can show if there are any problems getting the electrical signals from the spinal cord to the muscles and from the skin back to the spinal cord.

They will be unable to do this study until the swelling Dad has around his legs start to subside. They are giving Dad medication to help his body remove some of the excess fluid, which includes the areas of swelling. Once the swelling goes down enough, they will be able to get accurate readings from the EMG study. This may be several days in the future before this happens, so no concrete answers yet regarding this issue.

Wound care nurses replaced the wound vac over Dad's Morel's lesion today, and it is reportedly healing quite well! One of the trauma surgeons estimates they should be able to close that wound with a skin graft by late next week.

Dallas

P.S.—Thanks again for words of encouragement in the guestbook, and for the prayers and emotional support you've all provided for our family! If it were up to me, I'd take all of you on a quaint horse-and-buggy ride through Amish country and we could watch people with rugged, spectacular neck beards churning their own butter and whatnot. (I guess that could be a reward OR a punishment depending on whether you're a fan of hand churned butter, neck beards, or fun things that are awesome in every way.)

Monday, July 13, 2009 4:52 p.m., MST

Well, all right! Dad is doing quite a bit better the past couple days than he was doing at the time of the last update! Mom states his vital signs are good, with blood pressure under control, no fevers currently, and he seems to be a little better rested. Dad still has his night and day schedule backwards, where he sleeps most of the day and is up all night, but as long as he's getting rest, nurses are letting him do so.

A parade of various therapists are traipsing in and out of Dad's room at all hours these days to help Dad along the road to recovery. Physical therapists are still moving his legs and arms around to keep his muscles limber. Dad is getting a visit from the speech therapist as I write this update. The speech therapist did a test of the muscles used in swallowing. Dad passed that test, so they may be able to change Dad's nutrition to solid food in the next day or so.

Mom says Dad is now on a smaller trache size, so it's easier for him to form words! Usually in order to understand someone with a trache opening, the opening has to be covered to force air over the vocal cords. Mom says Dad has been able to speak intelligibly without having to cover the trache opening! This means he's getting stronger and will hopefully have less frustration when he's trying to communicate with everyone. They possibly may even put a vocalization piece over his trache opening so he can communicate with ease. They may do this as early as this evening if all goes well with the speech therapist.

Last report I mentioned that Dad was having some problems with lung inflation due to fluid buildup. Since then, respiratory therapists have had Dad on a special machine that vibrates his rib cage in order to break up the fluid in his lungs. After twenty-four hours of that treatment, and some good hearty coughing, Dad's chest X-ray is looking good and his lungs are clearing of fluid!

I was afraid they'd have to use the hospital's top scientists to shrink a small space-age dirigible piloted by a miniaturized Mom and have her navigate into Dad's lung and break up that stuff via high-powered heat-seeking explosive weaponry! This is a totally American Medical Association-approved treatment for atelectasis, but not very practical, plus Mom can't drive with her neck brace on right now. The moral of this ridiculousness is that Dad's lungs are clearing up! Excellent.

Mom is also still doing pretty well, and she has a couple appointments this week. Her left knee has been extremely sore and swelling up since the accident. She has an MRI scheduled to make sure there is no soft tissue damage or ligament injury in her knee, as X-rays have cleared her of any fractures of her knee already.

The other thing that has been bothering her is her right hand, which also swells up and is sore fairly regularly. On Wednesday, she has some physical therapy. She has a follow up orthopedic visit to check on the fracture of her C-1 vertebrae sometime next week.

My grandfather, Jeep, is back out in Albuquerque for a couple more weeks, and has been helping Mom out as well as spending time with his sons.

Dallas

Can anything else go wrong as this old bag of bones tries to heal? It seemed our family all boarded a continuously running roller coaster on June 9th, and it hadn't stopped yet. One day there would be encouraging progress, quickly followed by a new and greater challenge.

Wednesday, July 15, 2009 9:25 p.m., MST

Just when you think everything's going quite well, and you post a good report on your Dad's health status, things seem to go haywire for a while. This proved to be true yet again, and this time around, Dad started having an abnormally fast heart rate and some disconcerting changes to his EKG. This led docs to do another 12-lead EKG test that came back normal.

It turns out Dad has been dehydrated from the medication they are giving him to get rid of excess fluid in his legs. If you lose too much fluid from your body, blood pressure lowers, and the body tries to compensate by having your heart beat faster to pump the smaller amount of blood volume through the circulatory system. Dad turned out to be very dehydrated, so his heart rate was through the roof for a while. It was an easy fix by adding some IV fluids and backing off on the medication, but was quite a scare for us for a little while there. His heart rate continues to be slightly high, but nowhere near what it was up to earlier.

Trauma surgeons inspected his Morel's lesion today. They would like it to heal for an additional month before they attempt to seal it with a skin graft. This will allow the wound to grow much smaller in size and minimize scarring and the amount of skin graft they will need to use.

Dad still has a small amount of infection around his stoma site, which they are cleaning routinely. Dad's original stoma site is looking healthy and is healing well. He continues to be fever-free.

Dad will need extensive amounts of physical therapy to regain full function of his lower limbs, and some of his docs are concerned that the hospital he's in may not be able to fully meet his needs from the physical therapy side of things. The problem is that there are only one or two physical therapists for an entire huge hospital. They may be unable to give Dad all the attention he will need for his recovery process. There will be a meeting of all his doctors to evaluate the possibility of moving Dad to a facility that would be more intensive in physical rehab.

Dad had a series of X-rays performed on his legs and pelvis to make sure he is healing nicely. Docs would prefer multiple angles of X-rays, but due to the nature of Dad's injuries, they were only able to get one or two views of the bones, since they can't be rolling him on his side while his pelvis is healing. Hopefully the X-rays they were able to get will show good bone alignment, and areas of new bone beginning to form over the fracture sites.

Dad asked to watch some baseball before he got tuckered out and had to turn off the TV. We're excited he's starting to gain interest in things that he enjoyed before! We take it as a good sign.

We're pretty sure he'll want the Gaither Family Singers to parachute through his hospital window amid large pyro-technic explosions, with amplifiers strapped to their backs to give him a personal southern gospel-a-thon performance in his room at some point in the future soon.

Mom and Dad have officially sold their house and it closes at the end of July. We will be moving their stuff into storage until they can find a new house here in Phoenix.

Continue praying for our entire family, as we all seem to be having rough patches on top of everything going on with Dad's current situation. When it rains, it pours, and we're definitely in need of prayer for strength and perseverance, too.

Dallas

Right around this time I emerged from my deep, dark venture into the underworld of a drug-induced coma. I'll never forget the moment when I finally felt like I could understand all that was going on around me.

Chapter 8

MY CRAZY COMATOSE WORLD

While the medical staff, family, and friends dealt with the real-world happenings on the topside of consciousness, my experience was quite different as I sailed along the currents of an underworld so vivid and yet so unbelievable. All I can say is, in the years following; I still have a very clear recollection of a world that never quite made sense at the time.

When you're in a coma they say you are "unconscious," but in reality my comatose world was anything but undetectable. Those weeks were filled with the most vivid, crazy, stunning, scary, and disjointed experiences I'd ever had in my life!

After I came back to the topside and began to ponder it all, I realized many of those happenings were, in one way or another, tied to the real world events that were going on around me. My family and I were traveling on two totally different parallel tracts. Eventually, and thankfully, those two tracks merged as I climbed back to the top and joined my loved ones in the land of the living.

None of these events seemed to have a distinguishable time frame, and I seemed to join in as they were already in progress. It was as if you were pulled into a theatrical play that you hadn't bought tickets for, nor planned to attend. You had no idea of the plot or ending, but were jerked out of the audience onto the stage as the play was in progress and you were expected to know your lines and your role.

Act One—The Rescue Mission

My first cameo appearance happened in a small desert town, similar to many of the communities dotting the landscape across northern Arizona and New Mexico, much like the ones I've visited many times on the Navajo reservation.

You can still see to this day the remnants of old lodges and motor inns in towns that used to be filled with activity when old Route 66 highway was the main artery connecting the American West to the rest of the country.

The curtain opened and the scene unfolded, as I was bed-ridden in what seemed to be an old motel. It was run-down and dingy. There was no air conditioning to cool you in the desert heat of the day. A coin repository on the nightstand where a quarter could be dropped would activate an old bed massager to soothe those aching joints and muscles. The heat was overpowering and all I could do was sweat it out and wish for my old homeland in northern Minnesota where the cool winds would make even a hot summer day tolerable. It was a motel I checked into, not of my own will, and didn't have a checkout day to look forward to.

I could look out the window and see a lot of pickup trucks driving by, loaded down with what seemed to be primarily Navajo Indians (my wife's tribe, by the way). Many of these four-wheel drive mammoths had the truck-bed sized fresh water containers in the back, which they would fill routinely at a nearby windmill for home and livestock usage. Some were pulling horse trailers. Kids were running around outside my window, laughing, playing, and getting into all kinds of mischief.

The summer heat in the desert often produces "dust devils," which look like mini-tornadoes. I'd often see these swirling clouds of dust pass by the dirty window that was my only outlet to the outside world. Tumbleweeds would roll by on a frequent basis. All I could do was look out the window and watch it all happen.

For most of the time I thought I was in an old motel, but then the scene changed to what seemed like an old Indian missionary compound that I now called home. I would see various missionaries coming and going, all wearing their cute little name badges that had not only their names but also hometowns from which they hailed. Along with these career non-Native workers, there was a handful of what seemed to be Native gals serving as interns, learning the ropes of ministry from their experienced cross-cultural counterparts.

I remember this mission being run much like an inner-city rescue mission, where a good hot meal could be had, but only if you sat through an evangelistic service. At that rollicking service the old hymns were sung, testimonies given, and a fireball preacher would bring down heaven's wrath on sin just before the salad, roast beef, and mashed potatoes were served.

I distinctly remember interns being given the assignment of taking care of me and getting me ready for the gospel services. I got a bed bath, and then they wheeled me into the sanctuary where yet another service would be held. I recall feeling very sick and not wanting to go back to that meeting room. Regardless of how I felt, the wheels of the bed would move as they rolled me up alongside the back bench for what seemed to be an unending number of revival services that would last for hours on end.

Once I started reading the postings of my children a year after the accident, I began to see strong similarities to the real-life happenings and these crazy comatose experiences. The real irony of this first comatose experience is that this is what I primarily do for a living! I'm one of those preachers who conduct good old-fashioned revival services all over North America and beyond! It was like a microcosm of my life, work, and what I love. But this time, I was the reluctant soul that had to go. It was the last place I wanted to be!

When I read Shandiin's post about my high temperature early on and putting cold washcloths on my body to try and cool me down, I saw the dusty hot motel room I had recently checked into.

Young ministry interns were actually Certified Nursing Assistants (CNAs) who had to bathe me and care for me in the Trauma ICU Unit.

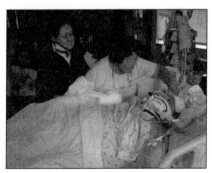

LaDonna and Auntie Nonabah visiting me.

Early visitors to my bedside were LaDonna's Navajo aunties, Marjorie, Nonabah, and Rosie, who live in communities much like the one I was seeing in my coma.

Could it be that the frustration I had of *not wanting to go* to another revival service was actually my frustration in *not being able to go* to the numerous revival services we had in the schedule book because of my pain? Hmmm.

Act Two—Off to War . . . Submarine Style

The next scene ended up being stranger than the first, and it involved dear friends of ours from back home in the Phoenix area.

Our SUV was a trusty vehicle that we had logged many thousands of miles in until it took its last breath at mile marker 313. It was an Eddie Bauer Edition Ford Explorer that had served us well for so long.

These dear friends own the largest Ford dealership in Arizona—Sanderson Ford, in the city of Glendale. Dave and Sue Kimmerle have run the business ever since Sue's father, Don Sanderson, the founder and patriarch, passed away. Their kids and our kids went to the same Christian high school, Northwest Community Christian School, and that's how our friendship began.

Dave and Sue are some of the finest people we've ever met, and they have a heart of gold demonstrated in the many ways they help encourage and support many worthwhile charitable causes in the Phoenix area and beyond.

We are all big sports fans and often we'd be invited to join the Kimmerles at either the Phoenix Suns basketball or Coyotes hockey games. They've grown to be very special friends to us and have encouraged us in our recovery and rehab.

I can only surmise how they became so prominently involved in the crazy underworld I was living in. My best guess is the connection between the make of our SUV, and they being Ford dealers themselves.

I'm sure there were many conversations going on in my ICU room in the early days about what happened in the accident. Discussions would, no doubt, include our now totally destroyed Ford Explorer. At least I think that's why they showed up in my comatose dream world. It makes sense, though; since they've showed up so many times in my conscious world, why wouldn't they be available to come see me "downstairs" in my underworld experience?

Dave and Sue have a beautiful home in Phoenix, complete with a menagerie of exotic animals not normally seen in the Southwest desert of America: emus, llamas (or are they alpacas?) and even a camel. Other farm animals can be seen from the road that borders their home as well.

One thing I never knew about their home, though, was revealed to me in my comatose state. Lying deep below their beautifully landscaped property is a very special underground "Bat cave" just like the one Bruce Wayne would go down to as he prepared for another superhero excursion in his Batmobile. You'd think Dave would have a souped-up Ford equivalent, but he didn't have a car—he had a submarine!

This excursion was painful in several ways; I actually felt physical pain in this dream. The dream was repeated multiple times.

Both LaDonna and I were involved. We were strapped down onto gurneys and placed in the hull of the sub. The Kimmerle's kids, who were now grown up, were assigned to our care. They did all the nursing duties needed to keep us going while this submarine was sent out on numerous highly classified missions for the good old U.S.A.

Not only did they have a submarine—it was a top secret one. It got its orders directly from the White House. Numerous times we were sent out on covert missions around the world. It would seem like we'd just get back to port only to leave the very next day for the next mission. The ride would get bumpy and dangerous as we kept on the run from the enemy who seemed to keep finding out our location. They desperately tried to take us out with their powerful depth charges. When exploded, our broken bodies would shake in those gurneys as we cried out in pain.

I can clearly recall the Kimmerle girls caring for us with great grace and dignity, but oh, was it painful. I remember asking Sue time and time again, "Can't we stay home this time? We don't want to go back into these battles!" She was under strict orders from the Oval Office, apparently, and we'd head out for yet another undersea, highly classified mission.

Looking back now, I can only laugh at how unimaginable it would be for any of this to actually happen. First, Dave and Sue are some of the kindest and most gracious folks we've ever met. Second, that submarine would have to travel a long way under the Sonoran Desert to reach the ocean. It only goes to show you that which seems implausible in real life can actually happen when you get enough happy juice flowing through your IV lines!

Once again, reality met fantasy when I read the kids' postings about my perforated colon. My multiple journeys back down to the "Bat cave," I believe, were linked to the multiple daily trips to the operating room to have my abdominal cavity washed out.

Act Three—Stay Thirsty, My Friends! ®

As my happy juice continued to flow, Dave and Sue were once again front and center. This time, my dream included a new supporting actor: my father, Ray Smith. I was later to find that this dream coincided with the time Dad returned from his summer home in Wisconsin to help LaDonna out.

For some odd reason, Dad and I were working with a host of migrant workers in fields that Dave and Sue seemed to own (which, if they do in real life, they sure do keep secret!). It was clear we were working for Dave, and the working conditions were hot and uncomfortable.

Occasionally we would be asked to help the family inside the house rather than the fields, which Dad and I were grateful for as the desert heat can wear you down quickly in those cotton-pickin' fields.

On one occasion a visitor came to meet with Dave and Sue. He was tall, bearded and walked with an air.

In some way he represented the Mexican government and was there to talk about a special trade deal. Boy, was he a smooth talker.

He was working hard at convincing Dave to help expand his business. This new business plan would be one in which he would play a very prominent role, of course.

He was all about helping Dave become more powerful, wealthy, and influential across the Americas. It seemed that Dave saw the potential in this merger and began buying into the ideas the visitor was espousing.

It was big stuff Dad and I were hearing. After all, you couldn't help but overhear their loud and intense conversations.

The only problem was, Sue didn't buy into it and saw Mr. Suave as someone who wasn't about to help the business, but rather to weasel his way in and take over. Peaceably if he could, forcibly if he must.

There were some pretty long and intense conversations going on between Dave and Sue for what seemed to be days on end.

It all culminated with a huge party that they threw for honored guests from both the U.S. and Mexican governments. Dad and I were eyewitnesses to a huge drama that unfolded as we were wrapping the burritos and making the enchiladas for this big shindig.

Our fellow workers were dressed in their service tuxedos. I recall Dad and I carrying big round serving trays like the ones the waitresses carried at truck stops we've frequented over the years. This was a lavish affair with a menu that also included tacos, and refried beans.

The Mariachi singers sang extremely loud throughout the festivity.

Dad and I kept muttering to each other, "They better not sign that trade deal tonight. Come on, Dave, listen to Sue, for crying out loud!"

It all came down to that fateful moment when the table was set with the legal documents that would change Sanderson Ford for either good or bad. Mr. Suave was doing his thing. Glad handing, toasting, and celebrating what soon would be his, if only his evil sugar coated plan was enough to keep the blinders on Mr. David Kimmerle! What would he do?

As Dave approached the documents it seemed like time stood still. He looked them over intently, picking them up, putting them down, looking over at Sue, and at times, even looking over at Dad and me.

Finally, he looked Mr. Don Juan straight in the eyes, along with all the other dignitaries assembled, and said, "No!" and tore the documents up. A brawl almost broke out, and all the staff was called upon to help usher out the scoundrels, and that was it. It was all over in what seemed to be only a few short minutes!

Weeks later, when I came out of my coma, I began to hear the familiar voice of Mr. Suave coming in over the television.

A beer company, *Dos Equis,* was running a series of commercials featuring someone who they called, "The Most Interesting Man in the World!"

He'd often say, "I don't normally drink beer, but when I do, I prefer Dos Equis. . . . Stay thirsty, my friends!"®

That was HIM! That was the guy! He was the one trying to deceive Dave, but to no avail.

Apparently, as the TV commercial was heard in my ICU room, somehow it made its way into my crazy happy juice. It brought this guy, the Kimmerles, my dad, and I into another one of those stranger-than-life stories.

About a year after the accident I shared this dream with the Kimmerles. When I told them about the "Bat cave," Dave grabbed Sue's arm and said, "Oh, no—nobody's supposed to know we have all that fun stuff under our house!"

When I told them about Mr. Suave, it was Sue's turn to grab Dave by the arm. She looked him straight in the eye with one of those classic spousal looks as she commented, "How many times do I have to tell you..."

So what about the contract signing? It correlates, in my mind, to the crazy way we had to deal with the sales contract on our home in Glendale!

Act Four—Colleagues Come-a-Calling

Just when I thought things couldn't get much stranger than that, my happy juice must have gotten some sour lemons thrown in, because the experience that unfolded to me in the next episode made me incredibly sad and emotionally distraught.

The Native ministry world is a small world and most of us who've served in it long enough know just about all the players, leaders, and organizations that work among North America's aboriginal people.

This act involved an implosion of an organization because of internal squabbling, and another group coming to the rescue.

Somehow I ended up in the middle of this ordeal. I'm not quite sure how I got there, but it seemed like I was invited to speak at their annual conference. It was there that the wheels came off this organization's bus.

It's not the first time this has happened to me while speaking for a group. The other time, though, happened in real time and in real life.

My real-life experience happened a few years ago when I was asked to preach at a church in one of America's big cities. I don't recall if they were in between pastors or if the pastor was only away for the weekend, but I was asked to pinch-hit.

Equipped with a wireless lapel microphone, I took my place in the front row as the service started. All was going well as the worship team led the congregation beautifully in song. After one of the leaders introduced me, I stood and approached the steps leading to the pulpit.

Suddenly a man ran past me, commandeered the pulpit, and started ranting and raving about how ungodly this church was and how it had done him wrong. I was startled, along with the numerous others in attendance. I just stood there, right in front of this man, with one foot on the step and one on the floor, wondering what to do next. More importantly to me at the time was the question, "What was *he* going to do next?"

You hear stories these days of deranged folk going over the edge, pulling out guns and shooting people, even in churches. That thought raced through my mind as I stood only a few feet away from this man who, obviously, was not in his right mind. I was the closest body to him, and I'm sure if he were going to do something horrible, he would have started with me.

Several staff members had to rush the platform and do their best to subdue this guy. After a minor scuffle behind the pulpit, they dragged him off and out of the building. I wasn't going to ask what happened to him; I was only glad to start my sermon!

As often as I've done public speaking, nothing equips you to get up and follow such an opening act. I'm notoriously a long-winded preacher, but somehow that day the Spirit moved me into fifth gear, and my five points were done in about fifteen minutes! All this happened without an ounce of that happy juice flowing through my veins!

So, back to my other "speaking engagement"—this time in my comatose state.

During this imaginary Native ministry conference I slipped in on one of their business sessions. I was curious to see how they handled their organizational meetings. Maybe I could learn something new from how others take care of their agendas.

As the meeting progressed, out of the blue an individual stood up and made some horrific accusations against this organization's leader.

I remember the feeling of being punched in the gut when these arrows were flying in his direction. Over the next few days this issue took over the conference, and a lot of confused, angry, and bewildered folks waited to hear from this endeared leader as to the veracity of this accuser's claim.

Eventually this brother got up in front of his followers and gave a half-hearted rambling rebuttal that left you wondering who, in fact, was the real truth teller. A stunned silence settled over the place and delegates were left to try and sort out truth from lies.

The leader left the room as a heaviness of heart remained behind him. Moments later, the leader's family found him lying on the floor of his room, dead from a self-inflicted gunshot wound. I can still feel the sting of that moment as I pen these words today—despite the fact that I now know it was only a dream. It was just horrible.

Being an invited guest, I was asked to meet with the leaders to help them sort out the broken pieces of their incredibly damaged organization. There seemed to be no time for tombstones as they sought to do something to start putting the pieces back together.

This is where the nightmare turned a corner and the glimmer of a new sunrise seemed to appear. The consensus among their leaders was that another organization be brought in to help manage and care for this crippled ship. They decided to call in one of the leading Christian Native organizations in North America, CHIEF Ministries, to help.

One of the closest friends I have in the world is my brother in Christ–Huron Claus. He is the president and CEO of CHIEF, which is located in Phoenix, Arizona. He and his dear wife, Lois, are great friends to LaDonna and me. The scenario in which they were called upon to help was terrible, but their arrival on scene was as equally comical. I guess that's what happy juice does to you.

Back at the conference center we got word that Huron and Lois understood the urgency of the moment. Huron and Lois determined to get there as quickly as possible, so they would be flying in. They wouldn't be flying commercially, though, because they were coming to the rescue in their ministry's corporate jet!

Now CHIEF Ministries using a private jet is totally off the charts when it comes to Native ministries. Of course, in the real world they don't own one, and are never likely to. But in the fantasy world of IV-infused medications, nothing seemed impossible. In fact, the impossible was more the norm in this counter-world of make-believe.

In real life, most of us in Native ministries can barely get to our commercial flights because we have to get from home to the airport in our "Indian" cars. They usually are held together with duct tape and plastic; some are still equipped with eight-track tape players. The only GPS instructions we have in our Indian cars are barked out by a real, live female passenger: "Golly, how come you didn't turn left back at the Wal-Mart? I knew my cuzzin' should have taken us over dere to the airport!"

Well, Huron and Lois arrived, and out of curiosity (and maybe a little envy) I went to the airport to pick them up. Somehow they seemed like rock stars as I drove them "over dere" in my loaned Indian car.

They met with the leaders over what seemed several days. They ended up entering an agreement to take over the administration of this organization until they could reestablish themselves. And that was it. This very unusual and painful underground experience passed, but not without my incredible sadness at the events, and amazement at my good friends' new mode of transportation.

Later, I read in our kids' postings that somewhere during this time frame Huron and Lois Claus planned to fly into Albuquerque to visit me while in my comatose state.

If I can tell you anything from these experiences it would be this – take your conversations outside the Trauma ICU unit unless you want your loved one to go on a tour of crazy town based on what he or she hears around the bed!

Act Five—Submarine Voyage, Minnesota Style

The next excursion found me back in a submarine again, but this time my hometown in northern Minnesota and the neighboring town of Grand Rapids were the settings. Grand Rapids has a sign identifying its claim to fame as the birthplace of actress and singer, Judy Garland. (Cass Lake is the birthplace of Craig Stephen Smith, but I've noticed they don't have a sign.)

Why these two communities were so prominent in the dream was a mystery to me at the time. I can understand Cass Lake, because that's my home, my roots, but Grand Rapids? I didn't spend much time there growing up so it didn't seem to be relevant. Later on, however, it started to make sense.

Most of my journey was under water, and we seemed to navigate back and forth between the two communities in the Land of 10,000 Lakes. I remember once, though, surfacing and I was topside with the captain of the ship. The identity of "Captain Who" was a mystery to me then and still is now.

My ship eventually got to Grand Rapids and docked at a marina. Supplies were offloaded to bring aid to hurting people in the community. We then went back down underneath the earth and made our way to my hometown, emerging topside at, of all places, Sailstar Marina. (Yes, there actually is a Sailstar Marina in Cass Lake.)

Somehow I was mobile enough to be up walking, but not without assistance. We made our way into town and found ourselves smack in the middle of what used to be Cass Lake's biggest annual summer celebration, the Water Carnival. Local stores had set up on the streets to sell food, clothing, and other merchandise at rock-bottom prices. The smell of hotdogs and hamburgers on charcoal grills filled the air, and snow cone vendors were out in full force.

Even the old red popcorn wagon I knew from my childhood, Herb's Popcorn Stand, was pulled over from its moorings at 4th Street and Beltrami Avenue in nearby Bemidji and was doing great business that day. The streets were packed with locals and summer visitors, all having a great time. Live music was flowing from the open stage next to the Big Tap Tavern. As I listened more closely, I heard familiar sounds and familiar voices, but something just didn't seem to be quite right.

Walking to the microphone was a steady stream of old friends and fellow classmates from decades ago. They were all singing the gospel music songs our family has sung in our many years of music ministry. That was totally out of character for most of them, at least in a public setting. Yet these were guys belting out, many with cold beers in both hands, those great old gospel standards like "Why Me Lord," "Ten Thousand Years," and "Glory Road."

I found myself both confused and rattled that they were singing "our" songs!

"Hey, that's what we do and you're stealing our songs!"

As much as I tried to get up and in line to take over and do it the right way, I kept being pushed aside.

Many of them were looking at me like, "Who is this guy? We've never seen him around here before." I felt so alone—like a stranger in my own hometown.

I can still feel the emotional pain from that part of my coma experience. It was so weird and unnerving. To this day I still can't tie this part of the journey to anything plausible. It just must be one of those strange happenings that clinging to life in a trauma ICU bed in Albuquerque, New Mexico can do to you. Maybe it's different in Amarillo.

Many months later I did seem to find correlation to the Grand Rapids portion of the journey. In the weeks that followed our accident, LaDonna heard from our organization's national office about another great tragedy that struck the Christian and Missionary Alliance family that month. No doubt it was a discussion she had with other family members in my room. Long after I regained consciousness LaDonna then shared with me the details.

We have dear ministry colleagues in that city that suffered a great loss that June. My friend Randy Junker is pastor of the C&MA Church in Grand Rapids. I've known this brother in the Lord for many years. We've had the privilege of ministering to his congregation many times in our years on the road.

Randy's son, Nathan, was a youth pastor at another church in that community. Nathan was thirty years old, married and a daddy.

Nathan and a sixty-year-old layman took the youth on an outing. They were on a pontoon boat on a local lake when a violent storm came up out of nowhere. It was much like a microburst storm that can hit quickly and cause great damage. A fun summer outing turned tragic and it didn't take many minutes for the scene to unfold. The kids were swimming around the pontoon when the storm came upon them. Most were able to get back safely, but one was unable to get out of the water in time. Soon the waves were overtaking him, and he needed to be rescued. The two chaperones jumped into the lake to rescue the struggling teen, and got him safely back on the boat, but the waves overtook the two rescuers and they both drowned. It was a devastating loss to their families, their congregations, community, and our whole national church family.

I'm sure that was the mission we were on that day as we sailed that submarine from Cass Lake to Grand Rapids, bringing much-needed help to that hurting community. It, too, stands out yet today as so vivid and real, even these many years later.

Act Six—An International Incident

So what else could these crazy drugs do to me? What other exciting adventures lay ahead? I was soon to find out—this roller coaster ride wasn't ending anytime soon!

My next experience found me halfway around the globe on another one of my world travels. In real life I've had the privilege of visiting North, Central and South America, Europe, the Middle East, Asia and Australia.

I normally love the intrigue of international travel, but this time it was an experience I wish I could forget. I found myself traveling with another unidentifiable ministry colleague and we happened to be going to a very isolated third-world country that was in many ways hostile to the gospel message we were bringing.

Our trip through their customs and immigration was seemingly uneventful, but all the while I felt uneasiness about our surroundings and circumstances. Nothing done by the border officials involved a single computer. It was all handwritten on very thin paper that reminded me of those papery breath mints that immediately disintegrate when you put them on your tongue.

We met the host workers who had invited us to come and minister. Much of it was to be done in covert locations. You could tell they served Jesus Christ under very difficult situations with their lives constantly in danger. I felt I was among giants of the faith and was honored and incredibly humbled to even be in their presence.

Somehow, as the trip unfolded, government officials got wind of why we were in the country—to proclaim the gospel—and immediately sent a rogue band of trigger-happy militants to capture or kill us. Word came to us through an informant. You could see the concern on the faces of our hosts.

We ended up being whisked away by them, barely escaping this militia's first attempt to subdue us. We were told there was a bounty on our heads, and we were more valuable to our pursuers dead than alive.

With the spine-tingling intensity of a Hollywood spy movie, we moved from place to place with our pursuers hot on our trail. Sometimes we'd evade them only by mere minutes or even seconds. It seemed at times that we'd never get out alive. We were constantly on the run, always looking over our shoulders. We never quite knew how close these aggressors were to us.

This game of hide-and-seek went on for what seemed to be several days until we finally reached a remote corner of the country. Freedom was just over a huge wall totally covered in razor wire. Our only hope of escape, we were told, would be if we climbed to the top of the vehicle and were somehow launched over the wall. It would have to be done in such a way that we'd fly far enough in mid-air to clear the razor wire— which could tear us to shreds.

There was no time to consider other options; we could see dust clouds from approaching vehicles coming closer. Our pursuers were ready to make a final attempt to stop us on their side of the fence.

Our hosts said their plan, if successful, would get us over safely but at the sacrifice of their own lives. There wasn't any time to protest or look for another way out. We were quickly being cornered and would all be dead if something wasn't done immediately.

Before we could say anything more, our hosts demanded we stand on top of the truck cab. They put the vehicle into gear and started accelerating faster and faster towards that razor-wired cement wall. They would crash the vehicle into the wall. The front of the vehicle would take the brunt of the razor wire, while the impact of the vehicle hitting the wall would launch us safely up and over into our new Promised Land.

The sound of the vehicle hitting the wall was eerily familiar. It was the same sound I heard only weeks before at mile marker 313, as our vehicle crashed and rolled. But this vehicle didn't roll. It came to an instant stop as it crashed headlong into that wall, immediately bursting into flames.

The plan worked. We were launched end over end for what seemed to be hundreds of feet. We both landed hard on the ground as our bodies rolled along that grassy meadow that seemed to soften the blow.

Out of the corner of my eye I could see the explosion as these amazing indigenous hosts sacrificed their lives to save ours.

The attackers could only stand atop their vehicles beside the burning truck, shouting their vile obscenities at us as we found the strength to get up on our feet, brushing off the dirt and mud. Both parties seemed to just stand there, frozen in time, for what seemed to be quite a while looking at each other across that wall. We were saved, but it came at such a high cost.

Once again, it took months for the significance of this experience to have its full impact on me. There were actually several real events that happened at about the same time I was experiencing this vivid action thriller of my own.

Back in the real world, in another corner of the globe, a group of missionaries had gathered for a regional conference in Thailand. Along with all the regular business sessions, worship and preaching, they were later taken to a park that featured performances by exotic animals of the region.

As part of the regular program, elephants were brought in to perform stunts for the crowd. But that day, something went terribly wrong: A few elephants got out of control and stormed the crowd. Several were grabbed by the animals, violently thrown about and trampled. They had to be evacuated for high-level emergency medical care. Whether they would survive was unclear for days.

LaDonna got word about this real-life tragedy right about the time I was having my own drug-laced third world experience.

Also, in real life, other very strange, unexplainable events occurred right before LaDonna's eyes as I was clinging to life. These supernatural events were happening to a wide-awake, normal and conscious person. These can't be explained in the natural. But real they were. It was part of the story she told me after I came back to the topside in one of our daily conversations.

These two experiences happened over the course of a few short days. The first took place when she was alone in the room with me. The second incident was witnessed not only by LaDonna but also my father and our friends Huron and Lois Claus.

In the scientific-based world we live in what I'm about to share will be passed off as untrue, superstition, or maybe a first time to hear of such things. It may cause some readers to question the veracity of everything else shared in this book. I understand that possibility. It would be much easier, and would probably make this book more believable and marketable if I simply left this part out. But I can't, and I won't. It's a part—an important part—of the real miracle at mile marker 313.

Western culture is science-based. Unless you can touch, taste, feel, or smell something, it doesn't exist. There is little room for the supernatural in the worldview embraced by the West.

Native American culture, though, is more aligned with an Eastern worldview, which it shares with many cultures world-wide. That worldview embraces the supernatural as much as the natural. In fact, it's only through an understanding of the super-natural that life in the natural can be explained or understood to the fullest.

No matter what worldview you have been raised in—Eastern or Western—when you become a true follower of Jesus Christ, your worldview must become subject to and reshaped by biblical Truth.

As followers of Jesus Christ, LaDonna and I embrace without question the existence of the spirit world. Why? Because the Bible says it exists.

Ojibwe and Navajo cultures believe strongly that there is a spirit world and that manifestations of the unseen can show up in the seen world. That is a fairly normal part of life in the Native community.

In the Native world, spiritual activity is *overt*. In the Western world, where the existence of the spiritual is jettisoned, the influence of the spirit world is *covert*. The reason is simple: why would Satan need to manifest himself to a world that doesn't believe in the existence of the very world he operates from? There's no need. He influences that world, but he prowls about undetected by a mindset that excuses or rationalizes for unexplainable behavior or occurrences.

"Superstition" is the term often given by the "enlightened" world to describe what less "intelligent" cultures would call spiritual activity as it crosses over into the natural world.

In our Native world, however, if you go to a medicine man, and he performs ceremonies and calls on the spirits to do his bidding, those spirits are ready, willing, and able to comply at great cost. They do his bidding, and often leave their calling cards when they want to get your attention.

The great challenge for many people being raised in the Western culture in places like America, Europe, etc., is when you become a follower of Jesus Christ, you have to embrace the existence of the supernatural as the foundation of your faith and belief system.

God's Word says, "God is spirit, and his worshipers must worship in Spirit and in truth" (John 4:24).

Scripture goes on to say, "The person without the Spirit does not accept the things that come from the Spirit of God, but considers them foolishness, and cannot understand them because they are discerned only through the Spirit" (1 Corinthians 2:14).

I know my fellow Christ-followers will have no problem accepting the reality of these supernatural manifestations I'm about to share. The real question is, what do they mean? What was the message being sent to us from the region beyond the veil at this darkest point in our lives?

So here's what really happened.

All of a sudden, as she was by my bedside, LaDonna began to hear the distinct sound of Indian drums beating in the corner of my ICU room. The steady drumbeat was clearly distinguishable. She went over to that corner of the room as they continued unabated. Just to make sure, she went outside the room to see if someone was playing a CD of pow-wow music next door or in the hallway. There wasn't a next door; I was in a corner room. The hallway was empty. Immediately she called several godly men who know and understand spiritual warfare.

This isn't the first time LaDonna or her family has heard the unusual sounds of drums beating inside a room.

As a young child, LaDonna and her family were living on a Sioux reservation in South Dakota. Her father was serving as the pastor of a local Native Alliance congregation.

In the middle of the night, Herman and his wife, Fern, began to hear those same eerie sounds beating within one of the walls of their bedroom. It was clear and distinguishable, and confirmed by two wide-awake people. Herman searched around the rooms on the other side of this wall; there was nothing to be found, but the drumming was loud and clear.

Herman had befriended a local man who would come to the house to offer to give him haircuts from time to time. Herman was all about interacting with the local people, as he had a heart to see them come to Christ.

Not thinking anything but the best about this stranger's offer, Herman agreed, and he ended up with a much-needed haircut.

But this man wasn't there to do a good deed; he had a different motive.

When someone wants to put a curse on you through the medicine man, he needs a personal article of some sort from you. It could be a piece of clothing, or even a lock of your hair. It is that point of personal contact that is supernaturally doctored up and used to summon and send the spirits to afflict or even kill a person.

Herman began to develop difficulty breathing, similar to severe asthma attacks. In fact, the night the drums visited the wall, he was up having a difficult time breathing.

All Herman could do was to confront the spiritual power that was manifesting itself inside that wall. He began to pray and then began to speak as if the invisible drums were actually visible in front of him: "You drums, you've been sent here to torment us. We are followers of Jesus Christ, and He has all power over you!

I command you, in the name of Jesus Christ to stop immediately and to go back to where you came from!"

Just like that, the drumming stopped, his breathing returned to normal, and he was able to settle down for a good night's sleep. That sleep was interrupted one more time, early the next morning, with a knock on their door.

"Pastor Williams, could you please come with me? Something terrible has happened, and we don't know what to do."

Herman got dressed and followed them to a home. Upon entering, he looked over on a makeshift bed and there, curled up in a ball, was someone he did not at first recognize because his face and body was all twisted. The man made eye contact with Herman. Dad prayed for this man, not knowing that he was the medicine man that had tried to take his life. The next day, the same lady knocked at the door to tell Herman the man had passed away.

Herman prayed and stood behind the finished work of Jesus Christ in confronting this power encounter. The incredible power of the risen Christ sent the spirits back from where they came, attacking the very one who sent them Herman's way in the first place. That day that man died a horrible, painful death. Herman and his family were restored to health, all because they rested in the protecting keeping hand of the *God who answers by fire*!

Here we were, a generation later, encountering again the same powers of this unseen world.

Around the same time this occurred, our friends, Huron and Lois Claus, visited us. They had flown in from Phoenix (commercially, I should add), and were there in the room with LaDonna and my dad, keeping vigil on this old, beat-up bag of bones.

Even the best of friends and my closest family members get hungry, so they decided to let me rest and go out for a bite to eat. Huron and Lois climbed into the front seats of their rental car and Dad and LaDonna sat in the back seat. But something strange happened on their way to the restaurant.

When Dad and LaDonna entered the vehicle, they didn't have to move or rearrange anything on the rear seat. Nothing was between Dad and LaDonna. But that changed by the time they arrived at the restaurant.

As LaDonna was exiting the rear, she put her hand down on the seat and felt something strange. Looking down she picked up an object in her hand and said, "Oh, what's this?"

A traditional Indian medicine pouch was the answer to her question. These are used as a mediatory object to the spirit world.

"Huron, did you bring a medicine pouch with you from Phoenix?" she somewhat jokingly asked.

"How did that get there?" they said. "When we picked up the car there was nothing there!"

When these kinds of manifestations happen in our Native world, you are told to watch out, because someone is trying to harm you through supernatural means.

It became very clear to Dad and LaDonna that the legions of hell had been unleashed against us at this most vulnerable time. It was coming from the animistic dark side of our own Native world.

I was clinging to life by a thread, and LaDonna was overwhelmed with the pressure of being there with me every day, seeing me unresponsive, all while battling the physical and emotional trauma of her serious injuries.

These manifestations hit her especially hard in body, soul, and spirit. I thank God for the spiritual fortitude, sensitivity, and understanding of my beloved wife, who has been such an encouragement to me all the years I've known her. She didn't take these attacks lying down. She trusted in the strength of our Sovereign Savior, taking on the enemy of our souls.

She did what she had to do. She picked up the phone and called several very close and trusted ministry colleagues who understood clearer than most the realities of these supernatural battles. This elite force of intercessors joined with her in committed prayer against the forces of darkness. As the demons of hell were trying to capitalize on the moment, especially as I was so close to death, they were met by the awesome power of the resurrected Christ!

I guess you know the outcome. Here I sit, several years later, recounting the goodness and gracious favor that the God above all gods has lavished on us with such abundance. To Him be the glory and honor!

Act Seven—Indigenous Games and Pains

There was one more excursion I was to take in my journey to the comatose side of life. This time I was, it seemed, above ground and in some old familiar surroundings. I was back with the OEW Native youth ministry at the 2008 North American Indigenous Games on Vancouver Island off the coast of British Columbia.

This is an event that goes on every few years for North America's Native youth. These Indian Olympics feature representatives from many of the hundreds of sovereign Native nations in the U.S. and Canada. The games rotate between a Canadian and

American venue. It is always exciting to see the youth compete for medals, just like in the World Olympic games. Many of the events held in the World Olympics are found at the Indigenous Games. Also included are contests unique to some of our Native cultures and people.

The last time we were at the games was a year or so prior to our accident. At that time LaDonna and I were leading the OEW Native youth ministry.

Every summer we'd travel with this team of young Native Christians, visiting Native communities throughout North America.

Our experience with OEW was one of the most incredible chapters in our many years of gospel ministry. What a joy it was to stand together with local ministry leaders who had never seen such a team of positive, energetic, and hope-filled young Native adults.

That hope was contagious, and many local youth, for the first time in their lives, heard from one of their peers that drugs, alcohol, and suicide do not lead to happiness and fulfillment. We were and are created by our Creator, the Lord Jesus Christ, for something more special than that.

OEW was quite a traveling troupe. We resembled a traveling carnival group, complete with several motor homes, support vehicles with huge trailers, and a forty-five-foot-long charter bus that the team would call home for those summer journeys.

OEW had volunteered to do some events at the Games to entertain the athletes. We weren't there for the crowds attending the Games, though. We were there to help bring hope to the participants, many of whom lived in very painful and difficult surroundings back in their home communities.

We would do daily events that included games, and great Native Christian hip-hop artists, like my good buddy, Marcus Guinn, aka Emcee One. Interspersed throughout were the hope stories of our team members, many of whom came from the same pain-filled environments that these athletes were getting away from, be it for a few days at least. Our once broken youth had found a new and living hope through a personal relationship with Jesus Christ. They were not ashamed to tell others of the healing work He had done in their lives.

In my coma dream, I was on the OEW bus, but I was once again strapped to a bed. Actually, it was more like a very uncomfortable ambulance stretcher. Several seats had been removed from the back of the bus to accommodate me.

If you've ever been on this kind of bus tour, you'd know pretty fast that being next to the bathroom was, without question, the very last place you'd want to be! You'd probably prefer curling up into one of your suitcases and being tossed into the lower storage compartment than to be that close to a bus bathroom frequented by these young folk!

There I was, strapped to the stretcher, watching the bus pull into the venue where the sporting events were being held. A number of the big strong guys we had with us unhooked me from my tied-down position and carried me out the front side door.

They rolled me down a long corridor until we came to a balcony area overlooking a huge basketball complex. There were three full courts, all being used simultaneously. Someone was assigned to stay with me. But, as in real life, the OEW team members did not always listen to their leaders!

I ended up being pushed against the railing of the balcony along a very busy path where spectators came and went in a steady stream of bodies. Some of them bumped into my stretcher, and the jostling was very painful. Hours seemed to pass; yet I did not see any OEW team members at all. I remember getting more and more concerned that I had been left there and forgotten. My breathing became more labored, and it was made even worse by the people passing by me, most of whom were smoking cigarettes—some even intentionally blew smoke in my face as they passed by!

I tried to reach out for help, but no one would listen. I felt all alone. I didn't even know where LaDonna was. I was filled with pain, extremely exhausted, confused, and afraid that if I was left here, I might not live to see tomorrow.

That all changed in a moment when someone out of the blue came to my stretcher and pulled me violently up by the shoulders. I remember screaming out in pain as my pelvis and hip region paid the highest price.

Whoever lifted my torso stuck some kind of machine under my back, then threw my body back down on whatever it was they had put under me. But the worst was yet to come.

Whatever they had stuck under my back began to vibrate violently and rapidly. My whole upper body shook for what seemed to be an eternity. It was so painful, yet I was powerless to move or get away. It was a pain that I ended up having to surrender to as it continued unabated.

Finally, after what seemed to be days, the machine stopped and my body tried to relax after the incredible pain I had just experienced. All the while this was going on, people continued to file by me, unaware or uninterested in my predicament. No one responded to my cries for help.

Later I spotted one of the OEW team members. I cried out her name at the top of my voice, hoping she could hear me over all the noise. Thankfully she did and came to my side.

"Where is everyone?" I emphatically asked.

"We've been busy all day with our outreach events," she replied. "Everyone's coming back now, so the guys will get you and put you back on the bus."

Months later, as I read the CaringBridge updates, another correlation between my coma dreams and reality took place in my frazzled mind. Dallas had posted on July 13 that specialists had put me on a vibrating machine for twenty-four hours, to address the problems associated with my collapsed lung. I didn't have to read any further to know where this dream came from!

Thankfully, this crazy underworld experience, so vivid and weirdly entertaining, was soon to come to an end. I was improving enough for the doctors to back off the medications, and bring me back to the land of the living. Of all the places I visited in those almost two months, the journey back to the real world was the one I appreciated the most.

Chapter 9

HERE IN THE REAL WORLD

When my eyes finally opened I gazed upon my precious wife standing over me, wearing a huge rigid neck collar, stroking my hair and smiling as I came back to consciousness.

She lovingly said to me, "Hon, I don't know if you remember what happened, but we were in a horrible auto accident weeks ago. We all survived, and we continue to get better. You've gone through quite a few surgeries, and your body has taken a great beating. The doctors have kept you in a drug-induced coma, but now they think you can handle things better if you're more conscious. I'm so thankful you are still here! We're going to make it through, and God's name will continue to be praised through it all!"

She told me how the kids, other family and friends rallied and took time to be with us and helped to get her back and forth to the hospital. Many wonderful people opened their homes, brought meals, and prayed as I clung to life.

All that she shared that day captivated me. Thinking back about the accident and trying to remember what I had experienced and could recall caused me to ponder the goodness of God in keeping us alive. Taking inventory of my injuries came next.

As I heard about the kids updating a growing number of family and friends via Caringbridge I wanted to have them convey a message from me. On Sunday, July 19th, nearly a month and a half after the accident, Nizhoni posted this Caringbridge update from my heart to those who helped pray for us.

The following message is from my dad:
Dear Family and Friends,   Sunday, July 19, 2009
                                                    2:04 p.m., MST

Greetings from Craig. It is hard to imagine, let alone explain, how difficult these past few weeks have been. I'm just now learning some of the things I have been through since the accident. The doctors explained to me the many injuries I am now recovering from.

I first want to give God the thanks for His care and keeping. I thank the Lord that the doctors tell me I could make a full recovery. We are going through the healing and rehabilitation process, and we will continue to seek God for His healing.

This has thrown our lives into an unexpected journey. We are going to continue to trust Him. While I remember very little about the events that followed the accident, I stand amazed that, in God's Sovereignty, He has allowed me to see another day.

Thank you for your kind words and expressions of love and concern. LaDonna and I appreciate it. We will continue to do our best to update you on how we are doing. Please keep praying for us.

In Christ,
Craig

It was so wonderful to finally be back in the land of the living!

Dallas helped clarify my current condition in another one of his classic postings after I shared from my heart.

Monday, July 20, 2009 4:34 p.m., MST

Well, if you've read Dad's message to everybody yesterday, you can see that he is making leaps and bounds in his recovery process!

Several days ago, docs were able to remove Dad's food and breathing tubes. They also repaired the tracheotomy opening in his throat. He's now able to talk and express himself freely!

The speech therapist performed another swallow test yesterday, which Dad passed easily. He is now able to eat most solid foods. Dad's appetite is still pretty low, so they combine his meals with nutrition supplement shakes, which he is tolerating well.

During the surgery to repair Dad's fractured pelvis, surgeons had secured an external fixating device to the bones using several screws at points on the pelvis to allow them to heal correctly in alignment. Due to the location of Dad's Morel's lesion, they were unable to attach screws on the posterior portion of his pelvis. They will be doing another procedure to complete the pelvic fixation, including adding the posterior screws, sometime next week.

Speaking of Dad's Morel's lesion, there was talk last report about waiting a month before closing the wound with a skin graft. Trauma surgeons have now decided if they wait a full month, Dad will have larger areas of tissue they would have to remove before attaching the graft, leaving him more at risk for infection. To minimize this, they are scheduling him for a skin grafting of the Morel's lesion this Friday.

Once Dad has these surgical procedures, he will need more intense physical therapy. There is now discussion about transferring Dad to an inpatient care center where he could get three to four hours of physical therapy every day. He would return to the current hospital for any scheduled surgeries that would need to be done. The move is looking more and more likely, and this may happen fairly soon, possibly as early as next week.

Dad is now scheduled for an EMG study. This means the swelling in his legs has subsided enough to do the test! It should happen early next week.

Wound care nurses changed out Dad's wound vac over the Morel's lesion today, and they say the skin is looking good and healing well. Dad's other wound sites are also healing nicely. They removed most of his surgical staples on his hip earlier today. He's has had some mild fevers, and there are tests being run to figure out the cause.

Dad currently has a central line in place, which gives the doctors direct access to large veins for drawing blood, adding IV fluids quickly, etc. They will be removing this and going back to the traditional arm or wrist IV line. That means there's one less site for infection to attack.

We got to hear Dad's voice on Sunday for the first time since the accident. His voice sounds pretty strong despite his current situation, and he's still got his sense of humor. He's interacting with everyone, asking lots of questions, and seems to be without memory deficits.

Nizhoni, Shandiin, and my parent's home church are in the process of packing up their stuff at their house for storage. There is a contract on the house, and they close at the end of the month.

Thanks again for messages, prayer, and all other support you've generously lavished upon our family through this process!

As Franklin Delano Roosevelt so elegantly orated in one of his famous fireside chats, "May your hobo fires be blessed with ridiculous amounts of delicious, delicious hobo stew."*

Well, my friends, you've all delivered the hobo stew of love and fellowship directly into the stomach of our hearts.

Dallas

*FDR may or may not have ever said this.

As I returned back to a better state of consciousness the mood in the room turned much lighter and happier. LaDonna began to share with me how the family had been communicating with an ever-growing list of friends and family through the CaringBridge website. She began reading a few of the recent posts, and it did me good to hear the funny way Dallas began entertaining the prayer troops!

The postings of the friends responding in the guestbook portion of the site was equally encouraging as comments were coming in literally from around the globe.

Written July 20, 2009, 2:53 a.m.
What an exciting moment—to hear from you personally, Craig! It's a real answer to all our prayers. We keep praying.

It will encourage you to know that yesterday I had the task of not only preaching in my home church (Duke Street Evangelical Church, Sutton Coldfield) but also of leading the church in a time of prayer for our WAM ministry. I focused on four things, the first and foremost being you, Craig, and your continuing recovery. Even though people here have never met you (although they know your Dad!) they prayed fervently for your continuing recovery and full healing in God's will. So many people are praying for you. We send you our greetings again from WAM/CHIEF here in the United Kingdom and hope that one of these days you'll be able to come here with LaDonna and testify in person to God's gracious healing touch on your life at this time.

Blessings!

Phil South and team

Written July 20, 2009 8:21 p.m.

Dear Ones,

We rejoice with you over Craig's recovery process. May the Healing Right Hand of the Lord continue to work adjusting and readjusting—causing the Blood of Jesus to flow through both Craig and LaDonna's veins for new life and health. We pray for the fevers to cease in Craig, in Jesus Name.

Dear Lord, please continue to give the trauma surgeons, nurses changing the bandages, wisdom, and please provide the perfect rehab facility for Craig's physical therapy treatment. Please cause the swelling in his legs to go down even more—and have mercy that there would be NO nerve damage, and the feeling of his toes will return.

Thank you all for being a living testimony of God's grace being greater than a tragic accident ... and wounds ... and emotional trauma. You all have blessed us so much.

May the Lord continue to bless you and strengthen you all, seeing you through this process of healing in VICTORY.

With love,

Shelly and June Volk

Written July 20, 2009 9:25 p.m.

Hi, Craig and LaDonna,

You are daily in our prayers and we rejoice in God's healing of you.

We are also making plans to come and see you in a couple of weeks. We will give you details when they are finalized.

With you, with Him,

Jay and Lynda Letey

Written July 20, 2009 10:40 p.m.

Craig, I met you years ago when you came to Los Alamos, NM and spoke at Trinity Bible Church, which was renamed Crossroads Bible Church ten years ago. You had come when Doug and Cathy Haskins were ministering to the Pueblo Indians in our area. I remember what a dynamic speaker you were and your wonderful singing voice. So I was alarmed when I saw the prayer request for you and your wife on the Alliance Prayer List. Last week I learned that your accident happened just outside Santa Fe! I have been praying for healing and will continue to pray for a full recovery. "Cast all of your cares upon Him."

Your sister in Christ, Leilani Christensen

Written July 21, 2009 5:11 a.m.

Dear Craig and LaDonna,

You won't remember us, but we remember you starting with the Smith Family's first visit to Parkside Bible Church (then called Parkside Alliance Church) in Watertown, NY, many moons ago. Now we attend an affiliated Alliance Church in Deferiet, about 12 miles east of Parkside.

Now we are praying daily for your complete recovery at home and at church in our Sunday morning Missions Update. We were pleased that you (Craig) were able to write a few days ago. May the Lord continue to bless you with His healing touch along with His grace and peace in your hearts.

Know that you and your needs will continue to be remembered before the Lord.

Blessings,

Hope and Arthur Marston

Thursday, July 23, 2009 4:46 p.m., MST

Dad has been moved out of the trauma/surgical ICU into a sub-acute care wing of the hospital, which is an upgrade progress-wise. He is settling in well to his new room. Surgeons and nurses from the ICU are coming to check in on him and see how he's progressing.

Mom says she senses an air of amazement when they see how Dad is healing, especially those who were there when Dad was first brought into the hospital over a month ago. They have seen his journey and are very excited about his progress. They are noticing an abnormally quick healing process, which is an exciting answer to prayer!

Dad is still losing a lot of fluid from his multiple wound sites. As a result it's harder to maintain a normal electrolyte balance. He has been given some IV electrolyte-rich fluids to fix this problem. He seems to be more energetic and upbeat on the days when he has the fluid replacement than on the other days.

Wound care nurses are trying to keep on top of all of Dad's open wounds, but the pelvic fixation pin sites seem to be not healing as well as the other sites have. Doctors have placed orders for those dressings to be changed more often to promote healing and cleanliness of the area. This will prevent infection and allow the healthy tissue to adhere better.

Dad is scheduled for a skin grafting of both his Morel's lesion and his abdominal wound tomorrow. This procedure involves taking a donor graft from another area of the body and placing it over the open wounds. There is a fair amount of discomfort associated with this procedure, which also involves removing extra unhealthy tissue. The hope is that Dad's body will accept the donor grafts and that blood supply would develop quickly to keep the skin grafts healthy, so they will not have to repeat the procedure.

Following the skin graft procedures, they will place a wound-vac over the grafts to promote blood supply growth and to remove excess fluid. The wound vacs will remain there for three days, at which time they hope to be able to remove them and let the skin grafts do their thing on their own.

Mom and Dad just wanted to thank everyone who's been helping pack their house and who are helping this Saturday to move their items into storage! Thanks to anyone who offered vehicles for us to use during the move.

Dallas

P.S.—If you were to let ME borrow your trucks and trailers, I'd probably just fill them to the brim with Styrofoam packing peanuts that I would frolic through like Scrooge McDuck swimming through his money bin: "ACK! ME MONEY BIN!!!" (Scrooge McDuck, Ducktales, 1980s)

It was great to be back in a conscious state of being. I could talk, pray, smile with and love on my amazing wife as she stood by my side.

Every day her revolving list of chauffeurs would bring her to my bedside, and as long as I was awake, her tender touch was always a hand squeeze away. I love seeing the pictures of her sitting in a wheelchair by my bed, with one hand typing on her laptop and the other holding my hand! It was a precious thing to know her love for me was a demonstrable love, and it came from deep within her.

There's not a lot of thought given to the commitments people make these days to one another. The gravity and seriousness of wedding vows are not always understood in this generation. Making a vow before God is serious business, because He's listening. He hears those vows and He has an expectation that they be honored. A part of our wedding vows included the phrase, "for better or worse, in sickness and in health ..." What a comfort LaDonna was to me as I made my way back to the real world, and that commitment continues to this very day!

In my weakened condition, trying to speak seemed like climbing Mt. Everest to me, and LaDonna was having difficulty hearing what I was trying to say to her. In one of those lighter moments that we still laugh at, I tried to say words that LaDonna and the rest of the family would try and try to make sense of, but to no avail. It was both comical and frustrating, because I really did have something important to say that they needed to hear. It is serious business for a guy who has been lying almost lifeless for weeks, and now wants to talk. Finally the staff called in a nurse who was pretty successful at reading lips and understanding what people in my condition are trying to say.

The lip reading expert turned her head sideway as she leaned down close enough to my face while trying over and over to make sense of my message. Her hair was tickling my nose, and I was so weak that I couldn't even lift my arm to move her head away and scratch that horrible itch. She leaned over again as I made one more feeble attempt to tell her what was so important, and she finally figured it out. She turned to the family rather perplexed and shared my critical request: SANDWICH???

Chapter 10

OUR BIGGEST SAVE

It was a bit unnerving to awaken to the reality that not only did I already have multiple surgeries performed on my body, there were many more to come. It was beginning to sound like the worst one was the next one on the list.

Sunday, July 26, 2009 2:33 p.m., MST

The skin graft procedures turned out to be very painful. Dad says this is the most pain he's experienced in his life. Nurses are giving him good doses of pain meds to keep him more comfortable. They say within a week the pain level returns to normal, and the first day is usually the worst after skin grafts are placed. We're praying this week goes by quickly for him.

Dad was able to have a good, frank discussion with an orthopedic doctor today. He asked about how long it will take to recover from his injuries. The doctor answered "a long, long time." Dad also asked questions about possible disabilities in the future and whether his work would be impacted by his injuries.

The doctor stated that he doesn't know exactly what the future holds, and only time will tell if he'll have long-term complications from the accident. He did prepare Dad for the possibility that he may have to rethink how he does ministry, since his injuries have been so extensive.

Dad still hasn't had an EMG study done on his leg nerves to see if there is a neurological reason for his inability to move or sense his feet. The ortho doc thinks there could be damage to his sciatic nerve. The EMG study would be necessary to assess this nerve. Hopefully this will be done soon.

He also said that they would not be placing any more screws in Dad's posterior pelvic region. His pelvis should have repaired itself enough to remove the external fixator device on August 11th, pending no abnormalities on X-ray before the removal.

The ortho doc feels Dad should be able to bear weight on his left leg by now, but Dad has had little to no physical therapy since his surgery to prep him for weight bearing. The doctor ordered more sessions to strengthen his legs. There has been no further word about transferring Dad to a physical therapy facility that may better meet his needs.

Tomorrow Dad is scheduled to have the wound vacs removed from his skin graft sites. If the tissue looks healthy, they will keep the wound vacs off. If not, they will leave them there for another couple of days to promote blood flow and healing for the wound sites.

Dad seems to be in good spirits despite all the pain and uncertainty of the future. Mom says, "Only the Lord knows the outcome for Dad, and we will accept His prognosis, whatever that may be."

So that's about it for today. I wish there was more uplifting news to share, but this is a long healing process, which involves both good days and bad days.

It reminds me that if you hold an elegant seashell to your ear, you'll sometimes hear the soothing sounds of the ocean; other times, you'll get an ornery hermit crab struggling its hardest to strangle your earlobe with its tiny-but-extremely-straggly pincers of doom. This example probably doesn't fully apply to this situation, but it is one more reason I don't like seafood.

Anyhow, wherever Dad is along this healing journey, we do know he's still smiling and making the best of his situation! We love him and are grateful for all the progress he has made so far.

Dallas

One of my surgeons was a very kind man named Dr. Howdishell. He told me they would be harvesting skin from my thighs that would be used to cover the huge wounds over my right flank and across my abdomen. In much the same way new sod is cut and rolled off the ground it's planted on, the top layer of my skin would be grated from the top of my legs—in a procedure that should be banned from all operating rooms everywhere!

Not long before the accident, I had just happened to see a Discovery Channel documentary on this very procedure. I distinctly remembered patients screaming out in pain as the nurses came to do their daily cleaning and bandage changing. Dr.

Howdishell explained that this procedure would be quite painful; still, I was unprepared for the degree of pain involved.

So, it was back to the OR for yet another surgery. I wondered why this procedure was even necessary. *What a nice way to welcome me back to the land of the living*, I thought, as they wheeled me to the operating room.

I woke up from the sod-cutting surgery and looked down to see both of my thighs wrapped in huge bandages but was not in too much discomfort. The pain medications were working well, which led me to believe that maybe this wasn't going to be so bad after all. I was able to shut my eyes and drift off to sleep that night, not too worried about what lay ahead.

Then came the morning. Or perhaps I should say, then came the *moaning*!

There were two wound care nurses who were assigned the task of cleaning and redressing my legs until the grafts would heal. They came in that morning with lovely smiles on their faces, which I quickly learned was a cover, hiding what they were really there to do to me. The bandages came off, and I quickly learned just how painful this experience was going to be.

They proceeded to scrub, scrub, and scrub some more those wounds on both legs—at the very same time! It was a tag team match: they were both in the ring and I was all alone, unable to fight them off. I began to scream at the top of my lungs, because the pain was so unbearable. I had never felt that much pain anytime in my life before, or since that morning. The problem was, they would be back again tomorrow, then the next day, and then the next day until there was no more scream left in me.

I only had one very important question to ask the surgeons when they came in to visit me a few days into the torture.

"I was in a drug-induced coma for almost two months, right?"

"That's right, Craig. Almost two months."

"All I want to know is why you couldn't have left me in it for just one more week!"

This pain-filled week actually ended on a very encouraging note for both LaDonna and me, though. One morning they were wheeling me down the corridor for another test. We happened across one of the hospital's veteran nurses from the trauma/surgical Intensive Care Unit. She recognized LaDonna and me and stopped to say hi and asked how I was doing since being transferred out of their unit.

She told us that she had worked in trauma care for a long time at UNM Hospital. As the staff would talk about my progress during my time with them, they came to the consensus that I took the prize for being their unit's "biggest save ever"!

Those simple words seemed to be more effective on calming thighs on fire than any kind of happy juice flowing through my IV lines. The day ended with those words ringing over and over again in my ears.

"Jesus, you've been so good in keeping me alive. LaDonna and I both should be dead, yet we're not. I don't understand why, nor do I understand what your plans are for the rest of our lives. I don't need to know it all now, but we're really going to need your strength and healing power to get through this. In Your matchless Name I pray, Amen!"

Then I fell asleep to the familiar sounds of those medical devices and monitors keeping the night vigil with me.

Thursday, July 30, 2009 2:38 p.m., MST

The other day, Dad was able to push down with his right foot on command, which is an improvement on that side. He still has problems moving and sensing his left foot.

The wound care nurses removed his wound vacs over the skin grafts on his abdomen and Morel's lesion sites. The skin grafts looked healthy and Dad's body has accepted the donor tissue quite well!

As a result of the success of the skin grafting, docs have been focusing on increasing Dad's physical therapy. Yesterday, it was approved to discharge Dad from his current hospital, moving him over to a new physical therapy rehabilitation facility!

He is getting upgraded health-wise and will be moved to a better physical therapy care center, but there are kinks still being worked out. Mom's hanging in there and still healing from her own injuries from the accident. Nizhoni just bought her first new home, so another moving process will be starting soon! Shandiin is currently in New Mexico with my parents, helping Mom with transportation and anything else they need. ALF, the '80s sitcom about the loveable furry alien who eats cats, remains inexplicably canceled.

Dallas

Chapter 11

MOVIN' ON UP

It was a great day for us when I was finally discharged from the Trauma Center that we called home for the past two months. I was transferred to a new facility called Kindred Hospital, which is closer to downtown Albuquerque. Looking out the window of my new home I could see the downtown skyscrapers only a few short blocks away.

I had two very strong images of my transition from UNM to Kindred. The first was when the medics wheeled me outside into the desert heat for the first time since the accident. Hospitals are notoriously cold buildings and UNM had their excellent air conditioning unit running at maximum productivity. As the doors opened and my face met the sunshine and heat, I marveled at the power of the two extremes. The heat felt awesome, but the sunlight was blinding my eyes.

The jostling around in the gurney wasn't much fun, but the guys did a great job in getting me loaded up. I realized that I would be back into lanes filled with traffic for the first time since mile marker 313.

It was a bit unnerving to once again ride in the back of a vehicle, which was not under my control. When we stopped at an intersection, I watched the cars behind us through the rear window. It seemed as if the drivers didn't know we had stopped. I screamed out a time or two, thinking they would slam into us. This is a fairly normal overreaction by people who have experienced a venture like ours. At least that's what the paramedics said.

We pulled into my new home and once again I met up with the full force of the blazing sun and desert heat as we left the ambulance. Before we had a chance to go through Kindred's front doors, I was met by one of the staff with a welcome gift I was not anticipating.

"Hello Mr. Smith," the nurse said, and then she proceeded, without warning, to stick one of those long-stemmed cotton swabs up my nose. It startled me and my whole body tensed up for a moment. As quick as it was in, it was out as my new best friend explained to me that she had to check for any infectious disease that I might be bringing into their facility.

Definitely not a Welcome Wagon reception, but at least that procedure was done!

One of the "good things," if I can call it that, is that severe trauma patients have a private room to call 'home'. ICU units are for single patients and you get used to that kind of luxury not afforded on regular hospital floor rooms. I came to find out Kindred was going to be a shared experience, which was a first for me since the accident. I didn't have a problem with that, but you never know the kind of roommate you'll be matched with, and of course, they are thinking the very same thing.

I rolled into my new room and met my roommate without delay. He was a younger Hispanic man who spoke very little English.

I came to learn by now that the scariest part of my days in the hospital was when the staff had to transfer me to and from my hospital bed. There's something quite unnerving to be told, "Just cross your arms and let us do the work," as a slide board is being placed under half of your body and then moved from a wheeled stretcher to a wheeled bed.

Visions of me crashing to the floor between the two mattresses ran freely through my head as these transfers were done. Most of them were fairly uneventful, but when things didn't go quite right, with a body as broken as mine was, the pain was incredibly awful.

The transfer to the bed was fairly smooth, but the landing brought a new sensation I wasn't ready for. The Trauma ICU bed had a specialized, alternating pressure air mattress, which is a huge upgrade from the regular hospital mattress. Somehow that bit of information had not made its way over to Kindred. I landed on a bed mattress that probably was OK for the average person, but for me, with a crushed tailbone and shattered pelvis; it quickly became a very painful experience. We let the staff know right away, but the bed would not be delivered soon. This one would have to do for now.

That first night was one of the most painful nights of my life as I tried to cope with an aching pelvis that was not tamed by the prescribed amounts of pain meds my doctors had ordered. The long night dragged on, and my ordeal seemed interminable.

By morning's light I tried to adjust the head of the bed where I could sit up a bit. Perhaps that would alleviate the pressure. I almost lost it as I looked down at my legs and feet only to see them swollen more than double their normal size. It scared me silly!

I pulled the emergency cord by my bed. The staff came rushing in and saw me struggling with legs so swollen they looked more like they belonged to an elephant than a human.

They assured me not to worry, that this condition would be cared for and a rush put in for my specialized bed delivery. It was quite a start to my new "upgraded" status. Although the doctors had said I was improving and didn't have to stay at UNM, I was beginning to wonder if this transition was in my best interest.

The next morning some of the staff came in and, without much explanation, told me I was being moved to a different wing of the hospital. Strangely, they all wore yellow mesh gowns over their uniforms, and purple latex gloves. I thought back to my arrival, when the nurse shoved that long cotton swab up my nostril.

"Mr. Smith, we're moving you because your lab results show you have contracted MRSA, which is a contagious infection that hospital patients often get. Nobody can be in your room without these protective gowns and gloves."

It sounded pretty serious to me, and I had already gone through so much. I could only surrender to the reality of this new challenge, and let the staff do what they had to do to protect themselves, fellow patients, and those who would want to see me.

Emotionally, this took a huge toll on me as I struggled with yet another challenge to my body. I began to understand a bit of what lepers in biblical times must have felt: "Unclean! Unclean!" My strange new reality was becoming even more difficult to handle.

While all this was a less-than-perfect start in my new health-care home, I quickly came to love and appreciate the wonderful staff that was attending to my healing and rehab needs. We began to build relationships with those that cared for me. "Aunt Gen", a caring and awesome CNA was among them.

Kindred Hospital is what is known as a "Specialty Hospital." It's a place where you go while serious injuries continue to heal, and a more intense physical therapy routine begins. You don't need the intensive care of a Trauma/ICU Unit anymore, even though you're not quite ready for routine care, either. I guess you really can call that progress, can't you?

Wednesday, August 5, 2009 4:32 p.m., MST

Dad's been settling into Kindred Hospital pretty well so far. Although previously reported that he'd be getting three hours of physical therapy a day there, doctors are still being careful with his still-healing pelvis and are limiting his PT to one hour a day (which is still quite a bit more than he was getting at the university hospital). Whenever Dad graduates from his care at Kindred, they will move him to HealthSouth, which is a nationwide rehab facility. Once he's there, the three-to-four-hour PT will begin.

It was also previously reported that Dad might be able to be transferred at some point soon back to Phoenix. The latest is, due to insurance reasons, and continuity of care with his current physicians, the docs at Kindred want Dad to continue staying in Albuquerque for an undetermined amount of time. Boo! Mom is beginning to wonder if she needs to buy a house here!

Dad's pelvic fixation binding sites are still an issue. One of the sites is healing very well, but the other one still is open and is not adhering to the pins as well as the wound care nurses would hope. They are starting Dad on a preventative dosage of a big-gun antibiotic, to prevent infections when they attempt to remove the external pelvic fixation device. Once the device and the pins are removed, the nurses are fairly certain the wounds will close on their own and very quickly.

Speaking of wounds, Dad's trauma surgeon from university hospital came to check on his skin graft sites. He says the donor tissue is healing beautifully. Dad was able to have several bandages and an uncomfortable abdominal binder removed, since the wounds looked so good. The wounds are now healing naturally, with no coverings.

The skin graft over Dad's abdominal wound is just a temporary fix, until they can surgically close his abdominal opening. They will not do this procedure for another year, and he will be susceptible to an abdominal hernia until that time. At the same time they do that procedure, they will also reverse Dad's colostomy.

Mom is still healing from her C-1 fracture and is having more frequent headaches and some muscle discomfort in her neck. We are still waiting for MRI results from her last ortho appointment to see if there's any cause for these new symptoms.

My aunt Roberta, a registered nurse, is with Mom and Dad now, taking care of them and helping Mom with everyday stuff. We're grateful she's out there doing a great job!

Dallas

*For all those who have constructive criticisms about this update, make sure to write your observations down on standard 8 1/2 X 11 legal copy stock paper, fold them into an origami swan with at least $3.14 cents in USPS approved stamps adorning its wings, and throw your loose-leaf waterfowl high into the air. A glittering golden falcon will appear over the horizon, snatching your precious criticism cargo with a mighty CAAAWWW, and deliver the note post-haste to our "Criticism Processing Plant" in Newark, NJ. There it will be meticulously unfolded by unpaid interns and lovingly "filed" along with thousands of other constructive criticisms into the bottom of our patented "filing center deluxe" (aka giant bird cage), because hey, when you own thousands of glittering golden falcons, cage liner gets expensive.

Chapter 12

KINDRED'S CARE

M y time at Kindred was a mixed bag of encouraging progress and some emotionally difficult setbacks. Parts of my body were healing well, but other parts were not doing so good. Major wounds and broken bones seemed so far from full and final healing.

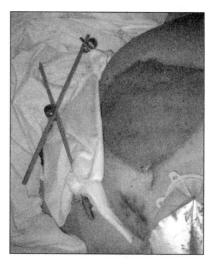

My pelvic external fixators and open abdominal wound and misplaced belly button.

Thursday, August 6, 2009
7:34 p.m., MST
Romans 6:13b says, "...but rather offer yourselves to God, as those who have been brought from death to life."

Greetings from somewhere in Albuquerque! I feel strong enough tonight to write this brief note to all of you who have prayed, supported, and loved us through this ordeal.

LaDonna and I can't thank you enough for your kind words on the CaringBridge website. We're grateful to our kids for setting this up as we have heard encouragement from so many friends and loved ones. Your prayer is still needed as we walk through more months of uncertainty.

This portion of Scripture from Romans has been my theme as I've emerged from the comas, surgeries and recovery. The Lord has never been more real and close as he is to LaDonna and me in this chapter of our lives. A lot of ministry opportunities scheduled for these months have had to be cancelled, but God has given us great doors of opportunity to share our faith and hope with doctors, nurses, techs, and all who have come to visit. Praise the Lord!

I've never been that close to death before, and LaDonna tells me that she wasn't sure I'd make it in those early days after the accident. In God's providence, we're here to live another day. I want every day to count for Him until I do take my final breath.

Dallas (can you believe his humor?) will continue to update you on our progress, and we thank you for responding back. We read every posting you send us, and they bring great encouragement to us.

One of the challenges involved a very unique piece of hardware that I was introduced to when I emerged out of my coma at UNM Hospital: my external fixator device.

It was often the center of conversation as family and friends would stop by to see me at Kindred. I was proud to show off my after market add ons, and even turned the cross pieces into imaginary guitar strings once as I attempted my best Jimmy Hendrix impersonation.

I was so looking forward to my scheduled appointment back at UNM on August 11th to get these items removed once and for all. As cool looking as they were, they really limited how much movement the therapists could give me as they attempted to move those weakened legs.

Wednesday, August 12, 2009 4:20 p.m., MST

Dad had his appointment at UNM medical center yesterday to evaluate whether or not they would remove his external pelvic fixation device. After a series of X-rays, they determined his pelvis hasn't healed fully enough to remove the device. Docs want to give his bones 6 more weeks to heal until they can remove the external fixator. His new date for removal of the device is now September 16th. Dad and Mom are a little disheartened by this setback, but they understand it's important for the bones to heal more before taking out the pins.

Dad was able to meet some of his UNM docs yesterday and they were pleased with his progress with his abdominal and Morel's lesion healing. One doc said "you were a very sick man when you came in! It's great to see you doing so well."

Dad had another assessment of his legs and feet. He did have some sensation and tingling when they tested them. The Neuro doc said "You'll be up doing the Charleston in no time!"

UNM docs ordered a six-week course of big gun antibiotics to prevent Dad's pin sites from becoming infected. His Kindred doc ordered an infectious disease consult to make sure that's the right antibiotic for him to be on prophylactically.

Dad can now receive visitors, but he's still limited on how much time he can spend with everyone, as he's still recovering.

Dallas

Wednesday, August 19, 2009 7:02 p.m., MST

Since the day of the accident, Craig has been in one position, on his back and allowed to sit up no higher than a thirty-degree angle. As of today, that has changed!

Craig's physical therapists determined that it was time to get him out of bed and into a specialized chair that would stretch his range of motion beyond what he has been able to do up to this point. It was one of those mile marker moments in his recovery process.

Back outside for the first time in months.

After they transferred him from the bed to the chair they then wheeled him out into the courtyard where he was able to drink in the sun for a bit. He had on his new sunglasses, a Pepsi in hand, and enjoyed the company of his granddaughter, Lydia, Shandiin, a family friend (who had delivered a package of some of northern Minnesota's best wild rice), and myself. Craig said 92 degrees has never felt so good!

This will become a regular part of his therapy.

Muscles that haven't been used are now getting a new level of workout. The only discomfort was the loosening of sleepy muscles! He hinted around to the PT's that he would love to be wheeled out tomorrow morning when it's super cool outside.

We are encouraged about all this great news but are still waiting for the nerves to catch up and recover. Thank you for your continued prayer and encouragement.

Some have asked about my recovery. I have four more weeks to be in the neck brace. I can't wait to sleep on my side once again! I am receiving steroid treatments to break up the scar tissue in my right hand.

Also, Craig and I will be celebrating another mile marker in our life. Tomorrow is our 32nd wedding anniversary. The best gift we can give each other is the realization that we are alive to celebrate it together!

I don't have quite the great imagination that our son, Dallas, has so all I can do is sign off for now. We will keep you posted.

LaDonna

"I will extol thee at all times; his praise will always be on my lips. My soul will boast in the Lord; let the afflicted hear and rejoice. Glorify the Lord with me; let us exalt his name together."

(Psalms 34:1–3)

Days turned into weeks and weeks turned into a month as I slowly began the long and painful rehabilitation of my body. I never had worked with physical therapists in my life, and never ever dreamed of needing that kind of help. I quickly came to learn how important they are to the healing process and how patient they have to be with patients who can make their lives miserable! Sometimes you love them, but sometimes you just want to harm them!

Kindred had some wonderful therapists, and the one who worked on me the most was a wonderful gal named Alison. She always met me with a smile and helped me understand all the crazy things they were attempting to do to me to help me get back on my feet.

She started her visits with simple leg exercises in bed, and eventually transferred me onto a device called a tilt table. That was an interesting experience that helped me realize just how messed up I really was.

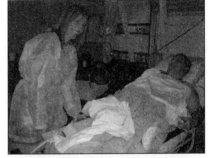

Kindred's Physical Therapist, Alison, working my damaged legs.

How simple is it to stand upright? I've done it all my life, except for those past few months. Should be an easy thing to get back in the vertical position, right? I found out really fast it wasn't as easy as I thought.

The first time I got on that tilt table she set it horizontal, and then moved it at ten-degree increments. At each ten-degree position, she assessed my physical reaction, including my blood pressure. I was amazed at how light-headed I became at any position past thirty to forty degrees. The scary part came as we moved up to fifty, sixty and eventually seventy degrees. The pressure on my lower legs was intense.

I was never more thankful that my body was strapped securely as the first time they moved the tilt table toward vertical! It was scary; I had the sensation that I was going to fall forward and land face first on the ground, even though I was far from being upright. It was another one of those strange feelings as I attempted the simple task of standing on my feet.

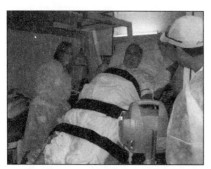

Alison getting me up on the tilt table as my brother Joel looks on.

It actually took several days and several attempts before I was finally able to reach the eighty and ninety-degree tilt! It felt so good, yet so weird, as Alison and her team kept me for a period of time in a locked and upright position. It felt almost awkward to be back at a position I had been accustomed to. I could make eye contact with my brother and Auntie Barb as they stood by my side, celebrating this step forward for me.

I patiently (and sometimes not so patiently) waited for my bones and wounds to heal. The great day came when the ambulance came by to take me back to UNM Hospital to visit the Ortho clinic and see my surgeon, Dr. Gehlert, about getting the "TV antenna" (the external fixators) removed from my pelvis.

We got to UNM Hospital in time for my appointment, and they wheeled me into one of the exam rooms. I asked the paramedics how the doctor removes the long screws embedded so deeply in my pelvis. "Do I need to transfer onto that exam bed?" I asked. "What kind of tools do they use? Do they put me under again?"

Time seemed to drag on as we waited for a very busy surgeon to finally get to me. I was still on the somewhat uncomfortable ambulance stretcher, pushed up against a wall of cabinets and drawers. Inquisitive me started opening up some of the drawers that were within my reach. I know I wasn't supposed to be digging around, but if it was going to take that long to be seen, I thought it would be OK to snoop around.

I came to realize that an orthopedic surgeon's toolkit is surprisingly familiar to most of us. I'm sure they also use very specialized equipment, but my venture into those drawers revealed tools found in the garages of most homes in America: saws, drills, hammers, chisels and the like. It looked more like an episode of *This Old House* than a doctor's office. I began to wonder what he'd pull out of the drawer to use on me.

My questions were soon answered as he came in and started talking with me. He leaned over, took out what seemed to be an Allen wrench, and started to loosen the cross pieces. Soon only the foot-long screws that had been drilled deep into my body were left.

Reaching into the drawer, he took out what can only be described as a simple socket wrench. As we talked, he put the socket over the top of the screw, and without any further words to prepare me, started turning the rod like a mechanic loosening a bolt from the underside of a car.

Deep in my pelvis I felt the turning of the screw, yet there wasn't a lot of pain to the extraction. Once the screw was loose from the bone, he simply pulled it all the way out and, *voilà*, there it was!

He continued in conversation with me as he reached over the gurney and started the same process on the other side. I thought to myself, *Hey, the first one wasn't so bad; this will be a piece of cake!*

But this time, I could feel, *really* feel, that hardware spinning around deep in my pelvis—and oh, did it hurt! It felt like a giant toothache running all the way down my leg to my foot. A weird sensation since I had lost almost all feeling in that leg from nerve damage.

But it didn't last long. In what seemed to be just moments after starting the procedure, he was done. It was another major step forward for me, especially in the battlefield of my mind. Having that hardware out of my body meant I was getting better, and my road to recovery was moving full speed ahead!

"What do you do with those things, Dr. Gehlert?" I asked, looking at the fixators.

"You want them?" he replied.

"Sure do!" I said.

They cleaned them up and handed me the prized possession. I asked LaDonna if there was a way we could mount these things somehow, like the horns of a trophy bighorn sheep, on my office wall. The best I could do was to get a picture with her and my "rack of honor!"

After a long delay my pelvic external fixators finally came out.

My experience with Alison and her PT skills introduced me to one of the realities of every physical therapist. If you show them some kind of accomplishment, they'll celebrate it with you for sure, but it does something to their psyche and they have to immediately move the bar up even higher and get you on to the next challenging level of activity.

My next feat, according to Alison, was to see if I could actually stand on my own. My core muscles were still split in half. Thankfully the skin graft was keeping my innards from falling out on my lap. When they tried to sit me up at the side of the bed, one of the assistants had to sit behind me, back to back, to support me from tipping over.

By this time I was able to transfer to a wheelchair though painful and difficult. They wheeled me down to the rehab room. Two parallel bars would help me from falling flat on my face. With one therapist in front, one in back and one on either side of me, they started the countdown to my first launch on my feet. My job was to lean forward and pull on the bars to help elevate me up to the upright and locked position.

Pull as I might, my best efforts were met with only great pain and greater disappointment. For some reason my left hip cried out in pain. *I have a new hip now, so why should it be so painful to try and move it*, I thought to myself. After several efforts, Alison and the crew would have to try another day to meet that all-important goal of standing on my own two feet.

Recovering from my injuries was hard enough, but we faced other challenges during my time at Kindred that were emotionally draining for both LaDonna and me. We had to battle our insurance company over what they would pay for. Sometimes we were living with mixed messages that the doctors would give us. It all added to the stresses we were going through.

LaDonna was living with the reality of a badly injured husband and trying to cope with a fractured neck at the same time.

We were hundreds of miles from home—and now we didn't even have a home to go home to! Others had to open their homes to LaDonna and various chauffeurs that rotated in to help out. Our kids had to make regular trips between Phoenix and Albuquerque. We could see the emotional toll it was taking on them.

We had been away from home for three months when the insurance company, as we were led to believe, agreed to get us back to Arizona. We welcomed this news with great excitement and anticipation.

Tuesday, September 15, 2009 4:34 p.m., MST

Mom has asked me to update the site with some good news!

Dad was able to have his pelvic fixation device removed today, which means he will be transferred back to the HealthSouth rehabilitation facility here in Glendale, AZ! This is a huge answer to prayer and we're excited that Dad will be able to heal and complete his recovery journey back home here in the Phoenix area!

Mom also had her cervical collar removed today, which is another answer to prayer. She will become more self-sufficient and able to do more day-to-day activities on her own, such as driving, as a result! Mom says it's nice to have her neck back again.

We're excited by the good news today and we appreciate all the support you've shown our family! If I know my American history (and I definitely do not), it was Dwight D. Eisenhower who once said,

Dwight D. Eisenhower: "Recovery is never so complete as when you're back in the warm confines of your own home surrounded by the ones you love, isn't that right Mamie?"

Mamie Eisenhower: "I don't care if you ARE the president of the United States, Dwight! Leave the toilet seat up again and you're toast!"

Secretary of Defense Charles Erwin Wilson: "Ziiiiiiiiing!"*

*This exchange may or may not have ever happened.

The point is, Eisenhower dropped the bomb and we won the war of 1812.

What was the question again?

Dallas

Friday, September 25, 2009 8:22 p.m., MST

Friends and Family;

Dallas had mentioned previously that we were getting ready to be transferred to an acute rehab facility in Glendale, AZ.

That was the plan, and all the staff and doctors who have worked with me here at Kindred Hospital seemed to be in agreement that I was ready to go once the fixators were removed.

We've hit a glitch in that process in that our insurance has balked at approving the transfer. They state that they don't think I'm ready for the acute level of rehab, even though those who are giving me the on-site care and evaluations have no hesitation in saying I'm ready.

Our doctor is presently going through an appeal process with the insurance company and we're waiting to hear the result of that appeal.

On the positive side, the additional days at Kindred have allowed me to receive more intense physical therapy, upping me from one to two hours a day. I'm showing encouraging improvement in the stretching of dormant muscles and more strength coming to my extremities. I know there's still a long road ahead, but it's been a blessing to see the improvements, which we're measuring by the inches rather than the miles.

Please pray with us for a successful resolution to this appeal. Our heart's desire is to get back home as soon as possible, but we continue to pray, as Jesus prayed, "Nevertheless, not my will but Thine be done."

We've seen our assignment as His ambassadors to the staff and people of Kindred Hospital in Albuquerque, and will continue with "orders unchanged" until God allows different. Keep praying!

Craig and LaDonna

Thursday, October 8, 2009 6:56 p.m., MST

Dear friends and family,

We've been waiting for several weeks while the medical staff at Kindred Hospital and our insurance is working out the details of where I should be transferred. After days of waiting, all of a sudden today was a buzz of activity.

Our insurance rendered its final verdict that we needed to be transferred to a Skilled Nursing Facility (SNF) at this point. Also, because there are a number of SNFs in the Albuquerque area, they would not cover the ambulance costs to move us back to Arizona.

We have accepted this decision, and the good news is God opened up a door for us at a new SNF facility that is only six months old, has state-of-the-art rehab equipment, and is also opening another facility in the Glendale, AZ area within a month. The possibility exists that when I progress to the level of being able to transfer from bed to wheelchair to vehicle, I could possibly be driven back to Phoenix to continue rehab at the new facility opening there.

One of the concerns we had about going to a SNF was that the level of daily rehab I would receive would not be as intense and long as an acute rehab facility. This facility will work with me up to the same level as an acute rehab, so that concern has been alleviated.

We've trusted in God's leading every step of the way, and that hasn't changed. This facility is beautiful, the staff already has made us feel welcome, and I'll be looking forward to working with their physical therapists to progress in my rehab. The Lord continues to give us peace, even when plan A is replaced by plan B.

I'll step aside so LaDonna can share her thoughts with you as well.

Whew! What a day! The news that we were to be transferred "someplace" new today or tomorrow and that it wasn't going to be back home put us in a high gear search for a facility.

We are so grateful for all of your prayers for us during this time of waiting. Your and our prayers have been answered! We are to hang out here for a bit longer. Craig and I are thankful for the care that our Kindred Family gave us during these last eight weeks. We have built relationships that will continue long after we leave.

As we were packing up, friends from the area came to visit us. How awesome for the Lord to send them to us for fellowship and also for them to offer to help us make the move to Craig's next "home." When we arrived here all our stuff was waiting for us. Thanks so much, Chuck, Lucinda, and James for helping us out!

Craig's new room faces the beautiful Sandia Mountains. Just below that is a Super Wal-Mart!

We love you all! Again, thanks for walking and trusting with us each day for God's purposes to be carried out. To God be the glory, great things He has and is doing.

LaDonna

Chapter 13

ADVANCING MY CARE AT ADVANCED HEALTHCARE

I t was a bittersweet day for us as the ambulance took us to our new 'home'. Our heart's desire was to get back home, as it had already been four long months since our sudden stop in New Mexico. It was also going to be difficult for us to leave the staff at Kindred Hospital, who took such good care of us.

The bottom line for health insurance companies is always the bottom line, so why should they pay the rather expensive costs of a medical transport from Albuquerque to Phoenix when there are adequate facilities right there in that fair city? It saves them money, but in doing so, they don't consider the impact on the patient being so far from home and family.

It meant LaDonna would have to continue to live off the generosity of friends, who continued to provide housing and transportation for her. If our family and friends wanted to visit us, they had to take time off from work to make the fourteen-hour round trip. Some even hopped a plane to help out.

Thankfully, we had some wonderful friends who treated LaDonna just as their own and made their home hers. Cris and

Cindy Kinney were truly a blessing to us as their home was the one LaDonna was finally able to settle into after bouncing from one great place to another.

Two of the greatest people on earth, Cris and Cindy Kinney.

I was impressed as the ambulance crew wheeled me into the lobby of this brand-new facility. It looked like I was checking into a five-star resort. My new room had a little kitchenette and a flat screen TV with satellite reception. And the best part? It was a single room—I didn't have to share it with some old snoring codger. They told LaDonna that whenever she wanted to spend the night, she could stretch out in the reclining chair. It seemed too good to be true.

Once again my specialized air mattress somehow didn't get included in the relocation orders, so my first night was another rough one. But by the next day, they were sliding me onto my new mattress and my outlook was much improved.

They had a gourmet chef named Lupe who prepared incredibly delicious meals every day. My appetite had finally returned after a long hiatus, and I began to really enjoy settling into this very nice place.

Not only was the facility great, I came to find that the staff was equally great as well. The physicians, nurses, CNA's, techs and therapists were very friendly and helpful. On my first day there, a therapist explained my routine and their expectations of me.

"I want to remind you to take your pain medications ahead of our therapy sessions," she said.

"I've heard of people getting hooked on these things," I said in reply. "I'm not planning on taking any pain pills unless it's really necessary."

She looked me straight in the eyes like only a mother can and said, "Oh, yes, you *will* take your pain medications, young man!"

When Momma tells you something in that tone of voice, you're left with only one option: you take your medications as ordered! Plus, she called me a *young man*! There was no way I was about to argue with a woman of such wisdom and insight!

Thursday, October 22, 2009 10:03 p.m., MST

There's been entirely too much proper punctuation and grammatical structure the past few posts, so Mom asked me to write the new update in order to give all our eyes a break from those big, irksome capital letters we all despise so much. anyway, here it goes...

dad has been at the advanced care center of albuquerque for two weeks now. both of them feel that one of the best perks is the extremely delicious food they serve there! most hospital food looks and tastes like those nature shows where mother eagles feed their screeching, ungrateful eaglets via regurgitation, so dad is especially grateful for Lupe, the skilled chef at the care center.

physical therapy has been intense and extremely painful for dad, but he is making slow and steady progress. he is experiencing the most pain in his left hip, but x-rays show that all the bones are in good alignment, so the pain may be a result of scar tissue from the surgery. hopefully this tissue will loosen up as physical therapy continues. mom also still needs therapy for her injured neck. she has been able to do her rehab alongside dad and they have the same physical therapist currently, which is pretty sweet.

mom says they are enjoying the cool fall weather. she says she's taken a liking to the climate and "small" big town feel of albuquerque. she loves waking up to cindy kinney's home-made bread, and she cherishes their neighborhood walks and prayer times.

there is still a long road of recovery ahead for both mom and dad, but they are continuing to approach struggles one day at a time.

although dad is having problems with his intense work-outs, we rest in the knowledge that as a result of his hard work, his biceps shall soon become the size of honeydew melons! how we long for the day when the sticky lids of our many sealed mason jars—their precious jams, jellies, and preserves forever trapped within—shall be freed by a simple movement of dad's powerful, vice-like forearms! oh, the joy we shall feel as the jams, jellies, and preserves pour forth like rushing mountain streams flowing from majestic alpine glaciers in spring's warm thaw! you will all be invited!

bring some peanut butter.

dallas

For the most part, the incremental steps forward I was making in my daily physical and occupational therapy sessions encouraged me. Dr. Sarah, Amy, Julie, Tanya, and the rest of the staff were such an encouragement—but oh, did they push me to the limits!

Dallas made mention of a lot of pain I was experiencing in my left hip. It kept getting worse the more they tried to manipulate the joint. Dr. Amy recommended I go back and see my ortho surgeon to discuss this problem.

A new series of X-rays were ordered during my visit with Dr. Gehlert. It didn't take long for him to let me know what was happening. "You've got a pretty serious case of what we call *heterotopic ossification* in your left hip joint, Craig," he said, point blank.

He then went on to describe just what that is. When a bone is broken doctors do their best to realign the broken pieces and splint or cast the area to hold it in place while it heals, usually in four to six weeks. The broken edges begin to form new bone that starts out like wet cement. The cement fuses the edges of the broken pieces together, it hardens over time and the bone heals.

In severe trauma patients, the brain goes into overdrive, telling the affected area to keep making more and more cement. The overgrowth of bone starts hardening and getting in the way of normal joint movement. That's what was happening with my metal hip implant.

The remedy is to surgically remove the excess bone, usually with a hammer and chisel. The only problem, he noted, is that they need to give the bone adequate time to harden before they can effectively remove it. "And that," he said, "Takes at least a year or more!"

"You mean I have to live with this excruciating pain in my hip for at least another eight months?"

"At least that long, Craig. I wish I had better news for you."

I had a real battle with disappointment as I realized just how long it might be before I was back on my feet. My heart sank as the wheelchair van rolled me back to that beautiful new facility that all of a sudden didn't look quite so good any more.

The doctor wrote new therapy orders that limited the staff from doing anything extensive to my left leg from then on. (They really couldn't do much anyway, due to the incredible pain I was experiencing.)

It was another war of the mind that had to be fought, and it usually raged in the late night hours, when all was quiet. My biggest battles happened when LaDonna was at the Kinney's resting up for her next daily visit to the front lines.

I did a lot of praying during those nighttime skirmishes. The trauma to my body had been horrific, but it had occurred many months ago. *Why am I not getting better?* I thought. *Why is it taking so long, and why, oh Lord, is it going to take even longer? Why can't we just go home?*

The questions seemed to keep coming like a scrolling marquee in my mind. Every thought had to be taken captive and surrendered over to the Sovereignty of God, sometimes a hundred times over.

How many times had I told an audience, "No matter what you go through, no matter how dark the valley, if you put your hope and trust totally in the finished work of Jesus Christ, He will not disappoint"? The thought kept coming back to me, "Are the things I've preached, taught, and sung about to so many others in so many places for so long really, really real?"

As I fought those battles on a daily (and nightly) basis, I'd fall asleep totally surrendering my situation back over to the very One who, according to my understanding of Him through His Word, allowed this accident to happen.

Believers in Jesus are called upon to trust, rest, and surrender ourselves to the God we love in total abandonment. Thankfully, those daily battles were being won as I clung to the truths of the gospel message that had shaped my whole life and sustained me through even this deep dark valley.

Two things sustained me during those days. The first was my daily time with the Lord in His Word, with LaDonna at my side. We'd read the daily devotions found in the old classic *Streams in the Desert*. The second was the amazing truths found in the dusty pages of an old-time hymnal.

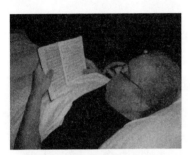

Getting blessed from the pages of the old hymnal, Hymns of the Christian Life

As a musician, I have great appreciation for many different styles of music. But nothing compares to the depth of truth found in those great old hymns of the faith. LaDonna brought me a hymnal on one of her visits, and what an encouragement it was as I'd get lost in its pages, rehearsing the deeper things of the Lord.

Some progress you measure in miles, some in inches. What was impossible for me at Kindred finally became possible for me at Advanced Healthcare.

As the weeks progressed, I kept eying the parallel bars over against the wall. Dr. Amy kept challenging me by saying, "It won't be long before we get you standing, Craig!"

Around me I saw fellow patients, most of whom were older, getting up and walking around after their hip or knee replacements. In fact, the gym was laid out with equipment lining the four walls, and in the middle of the room it looked like a makeshift version of a NASCAR track.

Some were out there on crutches, some with walkers, and some all on their own, with minimal assistance. Round and round they'd go, while I could only watch, and mutter to myself, "Hey, if these seniors can do it, I can too! Keep on pushing, keep on pushing."

One day, as these silver-haired survivors paraded before me, I burst out, "Looks like we've got our own version of *Antiques Roadshow* going on around here!" Oops! I probably shouldn't have said that, but say it I did.

It made me more determined than ever to take on Mt. Parallel Bars. The pressure was on me now more than ever. It was time to put up or shut up, and put up I did!

Dr. Amy (in front) and Julie, spotting my first stand in months.

It was a painful yet incredible feeling to be finally up on my feet, though it lasted only seconds. The sensations were both exhilarating and frightening as I thought I'd crumple down into a pile of goo at any moment.

The return to the sitting position on the table behind me reminded me of the heterotopic bone that raised serious objections to letting me sit down in comfort. My dismount usually was accompanied by animated screams loud enough to clear out the gym. I'd land painfully down on a tailbone and pelvis that still cried out in pain when resting on anything but my precious specialty air mattress.

Progress? I'd have to say yes, but it only reminded me about how far I still had to go and how long this road to recovery would evidently take.

I have nothing but high praise for all the people who had been a part of the miracle at mile marker 313: the first responders, the staff that revived me in Santa Fe, the helicopter crew that kept me alive and got me to the trauma center, and the staff at UNM that received me that fateful night. They all were awesome. The Trauma/ICU staff and folks at Kindred and Advanced Healthcare were incredible professionals with hearts of gold as well.

Monday, November 9, 2009 1:28 p.m., MST

"Whoever is wise, let him heed these things, and consider the great love of the Lord." (Ps. 107:43)

This was one of the verses we were reading as we had our morning devotions together today, November 9, 2009. Five months ago was the date of the accident that changed our lives, and now here we are, compelled by His Word to consider and share the great love the Lord has for us.

He demonstrated His love by protecting LaDonna from more serious injuries as she fractured her C-1 vertebrae. Just a little bit more pressure on her neck during the rollover could have changed the outcome of this most serious of neck fractures. LaDonna could have become a paraplegic, or been killed, but today she is walking, driving, and continuing to rehab from this neck fracture. THANKS BE TO GOD!

He demonstrated His love by allowing off-duty firemen and a nurse to be right behind our vehicle when the accident happened. They stopped to render aid until the ambulance and fire rescue arrived. Their swift and careful aid prevented further injuries. Was it just a coincidence that they were there? Nope! THANKS BE TO GOD!

He demonstrated His love by bringing me back from death at St. Vincent ER in Santa Fe, NM. I suffered cardiac arrest, and they had to resuscitate me before being transported by helicopter to the level-one Trauma Center in Albuquerque. THANKS BE TO GOD!

He demonstrated His love by encouraging and impressing on our daughter-in-law, who is a nurse and was at my side within days of the accident, to push the doctors to get a consultation from an infectious disease doctor. They finally found that I had perforated my bowel and was becoming toxic. After almost a dozen surgeries within the next three and a half weeks, I pulled through another life-threatening situation. Had they not found the source of the poisoning in my system, I would not have survived. THANKS BE TO GOD!

He demonstrates His love by allowing us to receive wonderful rehabilitation care at Kindred Hospital and Advanced Healthcare of Albuquerque. The progress we have made from five months ago is truly remarkable. Therapists support me in my efforts to stand on my feet and to see life return to my lower extremities. I'm reminded of how far I have come in such a short amount of time. THANKS BE TO GOD!

He demonstrates His love by allowing us to see the possibility of returning to the Phoenix area in the near future. We are discussing with the staff how I could safely and conveniently transfer to another one of their facilities in the Phoenix area, possibly even before Thanksgiving. While nothing is confirmed, we continue to trust the Lord for His provision to finally return home. THANKS BE TO GOD!

We continue to consider the great love of the Lord as we mark this fifth month of our lives being extended for His good purposes. Thankfully, throughout this ordeal I've never had to ask the Lord, "Why?"

What I continue to ask Him is, "Lord, what do You want to do in us and through us from this that will bring the greatest glory to Your name and help many more find the hope we've found in You?"

That's what this is all about!

Expectantly,

Craig

So, why not just settle down here and make Albuquerque our new home? We didn't have one to go back to in Phoenix anyway! While that thought never crossed my mind, LaDonna seriously considered looking for a home to buy there, because it seemed like a great place to live.

In reality, Phoenix was home, and we had so many reasons to get back to where our hearts were for so many years. Our children, grandchildren, and parents lived there, as well as so many dear friends.

LaDonna's Dad, Herman Williams, was in failing health. Many times over the past few years we had to rush LaDonna back home from somewhere on the road, because we thought her Daddy was on his deathbed. He'd always rebound and then another one of those calls to us would start the process all over again.

Home kept calling, and the longing never left me to want to go back as soon as possible. In fact, a friend of our daughter offered to drive their motor home out to get me and let me sleep in the back bedroom on the seven-hour trek west.

The only question was, how would they get this immovable object up and into such a small tight entrance door? After taking one of my very high-powered happy pills just prior to therapy I came up with the answer! Why not rent an appliance dolly from U-Haul, pad it, then strap me in? I'm sure I could squeeze through, and then they could roll me back and somehow flip me over and onto the mattress. Not a problem!

Once the happy pills wore off, I began to wonder how my body would handle a much firmer RV mattress when I was comfortable only on a specialty air mattress. It wasn't the best scenario, but it sure sounded appealing.

Determined to get home, we kept working with the administrative staff to petition the insurance to let us transfer. Our continued attempts were met with a firm "no" every time.

An Advanced Healthcare Center was getting ready to open less than two miles from our former home in Glendale. I could go to an acute facility for a month or so until it opened, then transition over there. It made sense to us but didn't make sense to the folks in some corporate office somewhere in downtown Pittsburgh.

In the middle of the night, as we were all sleeping, LaDonna called me from the Kinney's home. I could tell by her voice something wasn't right. Something must have happened back home.

"Craig, I just got word. My daddy went home to be with Jesus!"

Oh, how my heart ached, both for my precious wife, and for the tremendous sense of loss that I, too, had just experienced.

Herman Williams was like a second father to me. He was a lifelong mentor, friend, and ministry colleague. We had worked in The Christian and Missionary Alliance all our lives and shared so many things in common, especially the love of his only daughter, LaDonna.

My pain for LaDonna was that she wasn't able to be there with him this time, of all times. Though expected at some point, his passing that night caught us all off guard. No one in the family was at his side when he died, which made it even more difficult and painful for everyone. Later, Rockford, LaDonna's younger brother, and her mom, Fern, remembered how his face shined so brightly during their hospital visit the night before he went to be with the Lord.

I remember my Auntie Barb and LaDonna coming to my room early the next morning. LaDonna fell into my arms. We wept together, prayed together, and began to grieve his passing. At the same time we celebrated the incredible life of this very unique Navajo Christian leader, our dad.

LaDonna was torn with her desire to stay with me and the need to return home to be with her family. I assured her I would be well cared for. Everything in me wanted to get on that plane with her, but only one ticket was purchased that day—and it was in her name. She had to go back to the Kinney's, pack up as best she could, and leave the rest in the capable hands of Aunt Barb, my brother Joel, and the staff here in Albuquerque. As quickly as she showed up to see me, she was gone—gone home to grieve with her family and help plan the celebration of a long and well-lived life.

My heart ached all the more, knowing that my wife was far away, and all that she would be going through in the days to come.

I began to come to grips with another reality that only added to my grief. I would not be there to say goodbye to one of the most influential men in my life. It was going to be a tough day, and an even tougher night.

Thursday, November 19, 2009 6:49 p.m., MST

Wow, what an amazing few days!!!

Sunday night I couldn't sleep, partially as I was grieving the home going of my father-in-law, and partially because I would not be able to be there with LaDonna and the family to say goodbye to him. I began to think about what it would be like to be able to be there with them.

Monday morning I determined to ask my therapist one more time to see if my insurance had had a change of heart and would let me go home to Arizona. Maybe, just maybe, they might relent, and maybe, just maybe, I could get back in time for the funeral. I asked her that morning and she said she'd at least try. Later that day she came to my room with the bad news.

She said the insurance called them back and basically said, "Why are you even asking this as we've already denied this transfer. The answer is no!"

God helped me to accept this news, as disappointing as it was, and that day I died to that idea once and for all. I would carry out my assigned days at this level of rehab and never ask again for an early transfer or even to go back to Arizona. It looked like we'd be New Mexicans for an indefinite period of time.

The next day I reluctantly went to my morning therapy session. Before lunch I went back to my room to work on my computer and get ready to do something technically challenging for me.

The family had wanted me to do the eulogy, and we were going out on a limb to do it from Albuquerque using Skype and the Internet. With the help of my laptop's webcam and video projector at the church, I would be beamed in, if it all worked out.

Right then the nursing supervisor came in and said, "Craig, I can't believe what just happened. This never happens! I just got off the phone with your insurance company, and by the way, THEY CALLED ME! They told me they had reversed their decision and have authorized you to move to the next level of care. The facility in Glendale has space, and if you can get there by tomorrow, they can receive you! WOW!"

I immediately went to the Internet and found a flight that would get me back, if there were no delays or glitches, just in time to go to the funeral. There was one challenge, though. Could I even handle a flight in my condition? Dr. Amy came in and I had a somewhat hyper conversation with her. I asked her if she'd be willing to fly with me to make sure I made the transfers ok from wheelchair to airplane seat, etc.

Without hesitation she said, "Sure, I'll go!"

Amazingly, the management gave her the green light, and the flights were booked!

My brother Joel and Aunt Barb helped pack the belongings LaDonna had left behind in the home we were staying in, then helped pack my room.

By 5:30 a.m. Wednesday I was loaded into the wheelchair van, and it was off to the airport. We boarded well, and the flight arrived in Phoenix early.

A medical transport van met us. As I transferred to their wheelchair I gave Amy the biggest bear hug I could. As Amy returned to Albuquerque I arrived at the church about fifteen minutes before the scheduled start time for the funeral!

What a blessing it was to sit next to LaDonna as we and several hundred others said goodbye to Herman in a wonderful funeral service. I was so blessed to be able to deliver the eulogy in person. What an honor it was for me.

From there the van took me to my new home, HealthSouth Valley of the Sun Rehabilitation Hospital in Glendale, Arizona.

I got checked in, and the rehab staff has already gotten me up on the parallel bar! I was able to take three steps today, with very little assistance from them! Praise the Lord!

The day was topped off by a visit with family and friends. What made my day, though, was when my grandbaby, Lydia, came by. She jumped up on Popio's bed and her little head rested on my chest! In some small way, at least compared to Herman's home going, I can sure say, "It's good to be finally home!" To God be the glory!

Delivering the eulogy at Herman Williams' funeral.

Chapter 14

FINALLY HOME

Tuesday, December 1, 2009 4:58 p.m., MST

Well, Dad's back in the Phoenix area! He is now residing at a facility called HealthSouth, and he's adjusting to the change well. Physical therapists are working him hard, and he's rising to every challenge they set for him. Over the past week or so, Dad has gone from barely being able to stand from his wheelchair to walking the length of the 15-foot parallel bars he uses for support, not only once, but THREE TIMES.

This is a huge improvement in a short amount of time, and we can only give God credit for these leaps and bounds! Although Dad's therapist states it will still be months before Dad walks normally, we are definitely grateful for his progress so far.

Not only has Dad been working extra hard at his ambulatory awesomeness, but he's also been able to spend some good quality time with friends and family now that he's back home! Along with being here to give the eulogy at grandpa Herman's funeral, he was also granted an eight-hour "get out of jail free" card this Thanksgiving from his care center.

He was able to join our family at my Grandma Fern's home for Thanksgiving dinner. We were overjoyed to be able to spend it with Dad, and we all ate turkey and stuffing until we could no longer bear the relentless onslaught to our cerebral turkey cortexes.

Dad said Thanksgiving was his first day of true "normalcy" since the accident and the subsequent six months of hospitals and rehab facilities. This has made him all the more determined to work hard at accomplishing his physical therapy goals in order to return to normal life as quickly as possible.

Although the timing of Dad's return has been bittersweet with the loss of grandpa Herman, it's nice to report some good news regarding Dad's situation for a change. I'm grateful to have him back in Phoenix! I think it was Simon and Garfunkel who once sang in their classic 1970s anthem:

Both (in perfect harmony): Like a bridge over troubled water, I will lay . . .
Paul Simon: No, no, you missed the E minor, Garfunkel!
Art Garfunkel: Whatever Paul, your E-minor chord is stupid.
Paul Simon: No, your AFRO is stupid!
(Simon and Garfunkel's fist fight)

The point is, Art Garfunkel's hair WAS terrible and Dad's recovery is excellent.
Dallas

Thursday, December 3, 2009 10:43 p.m., MST

One of the lessons I've learned in this journey is that when things happen, sometimes they happen fast. Just two days ago I got a hint from one of my therapists that they were working on my discharge from this facility and it could happen within days!

Today it was confirmed that tomorrow, Friday, December 4th, I will be discharged from HealthSouth to finally go home! All I can say is, "PRAISE THE LORD!"

I have progressed well enough in my rehab to enable me to finally, just five days short of six months in trauma centers, hospitals and rehab facilities, move to the next level of care. That will include home health services and outpatient rehabilitation!

One of the last major hurdles I needed to overcome was transferring in and out of a vehicle. It reminds me of our dear friend, Dr. Keith Bailey's great story of the two old folks in the nursing home, one 95 and the other 93 who fell in love, got married and spent their honeymoon trying to get out of the car!

Well, I could sure relate to that yesterday as my therapist Josh, LaDonna, Shandiin, little Lydia, and Grandpa Ray cheered me on. I slid from the wheelchair into Grandpa's front seat and wiggled around enough to get my slowly improving legs bent enough to finish the transfer and officially qualify as a passenger! Once that hurdle was crossed, I met all the requirements to finally go home!

Along with great excitement has come a flurry of activity for LaDonna and the family. Our friends worked all day today getting Nizhoni's home ready to receive "Chief Weak-in-the-Knees."

Words are hard to come by for me as I think of what tomorrow holds for LaDonna, my family, and me.

We've prayed and dreamed about this day coming, and it has come much faster than we anticipated, especially being in this facility for only several weeks. But what a great day tomorrow will be for us! I GET TO GO HOME!

Thank you for being with us in the journey! Wow!

Once I was discharged and officially became an outpatient, things started moving ahead. My new nurse case manager, Theresa Coleman, helped us find the right doctors and specialists who would continue our care. She was an incredible help in navigating our healing ships through the new waters of the old home place.

LaDonna was scheduled as an outpatient and started receiving physical therapy for her neck. Her primary care doctor told her that her broken neck has healed incredibly well. They couldn't even tell on the most recent MRI where the breaks were!

Her neck muscles continue to need therapy to get back into shape. She was getting therapy in New Mexico, but when her father Herman passed away that came to a screeching halt after she returned to Arizona. I was pleased she was starting again to receive much-needed therapy on her miracle neck.

In her initial visits to the therapists she was beginning to see improvement. She got in to see a hand doctor who set out a course of action for further treatments of her right hand. She continued to have limited movement in the knuckle area.

I began my outpatient therapy in early January at a facility in Phoenix called Touchstone Rehabilitation. This group specializes in spinal cord and nerve injury rehabilitation and was recommended by my new PM&R (Physical Medical and Rehab) physician who was now serving as my overseeing physician.

When I heard about this group I googled them and found their website. I went to their homepage and prominently displayed the Bible verse, *Jeremiah 29:11*! I was thrilled to be in the care of a Christian owned rehab facility.

Touchstone Rehabilitation was started and is run by a wonderful Christian man named Dan Bonarati. He has a great heart for the handicapped. In his professional career, Dan and his company have helped numerous people.

A month had passed before I began rehab with Dan. It seemed like I needed to start all over again with my muscles and ligaments. Things turned around for me during the month of January, though, as I began to show encouraging progress.

I continued to walk with the use of parallel bars and was able to be in a standing frame device for twenty to thirty minutes at a time. By the week of January 27, I was able to get up from a therapy mat to standing position (with the help of a walker) and then to pivot enough to successfully land without crashing back down on my wheelchair! I had graduated from the stable world of parallel bars to the uncertain world of walkers! The very next day I took my first eight steps with the walker.

With every day that progressed, things that seemed impossible became possible. For LaDonna and me, words just couldn't describe the joy that came with these small but big steps of progress. It gave us all renewed hope that one day I would be able to walk again.

Friday, January 29, 2010 4:20 p.m., MST

Both Mom and Dad are thrilled with their new PM&R (Physical, Medical & Rehab) doctor, Mary Merkel. She has been right on top of their care. She ordered some MRI tests for Dad to try and identify the source of his nerve damage. While the tests were inconclusive, she did tell us that Dad suffers from what she called "maturing issues" in his bones and nerve passageways. Yup, you guessed it. What that means is Dad is showing signs that he's not as young as he used to be and is now leaning to the side of qualifying as an old wise Indian elder, and/or Methuselah's shuffleboard partner.

One of Dad's referral visits was to a wound care clinic affiliated with Good Samaritan Hospital near downtown Phoenix. What seemed to be a rather normal doctor visit for some preventive wound care turned into connecting with well-respected Dr. Marc Gottlieb, who told us he could help with some important follow-up care. He is able to help surgically reconnect Dad's core abdominal muscles and reverse his colostomy when the time comes. Dad say's he'd like to have his belly button back where it used to be so he's excited about that.

He also specializes in surgically repairing damaged nerves, which is one of the primary areas of concern for Dad's long-term recovery. He's anxious to look at Dad's MRI's and see if there's anything he can do to help bring sensation and movement back to Dad's legs.

In looking back over these months, Mom says every day seems like Christmas, with special blessings, answers to prayer, and even little "stocking stuffer" reminders from the Lord that He's in control and taking care of them. For all of us, we can't help but agree!

Mom and Dad are starting this year off with encouraging progress on all fronts; the Lord has been faithful, He continues to meet their needs, and we're all along for the ride! Thanks for hanging on with us!

It reminds me that when Mozart was composing his classic *Flight of the Bumblebee* sonata in Erroneous Minor, he would often stop and blow air horns into his neighbors beehives and, utilizing the latest in beekeeping technologies of the day, harvest the sweet, sweet honey within. The parallel to this current situation should be so blatantly obvious that I won't insult your intelligence by explaining it.

Dallas

Chapter 15

SETTLING IN ON THAT LONG HIGHWAY 50

I was excited to meet Dr. Gottlieb and to hear the positive view he took on the potential for me to regain the use of my legs. We still weren't clear as to the extent of the nerve damage, but knew both legs were severely affected. To know the possibility exists to have some of the nerves compressed by scar tissue reopen in a highly specialized "nerve decompression surgery" was exciting for me.

In order to prepare for such a procedure, a number of tests would need to be ordered—another round of MRIs, CT scans and finally, an EMG study. These tests would help give the doctors a better picture of the current layout of my recently rearranged insides.

We were a bit disappointed with the first attempt at my EMG study. I was unable to transfer from my wheelchair to that uncomfortable-looking exam table, so we had to cancel.

A new EMG was ordered, but this time in a big city hospital. They gave us the assurance they could meet my mobility needs without a problem.

Wednesday, March 17, 2010 10:18 p.m., MST

Greetings! Thank you all for praying for us for the EMG studies. Other than being electrocuted about seventy-five times in all my extremities and then stuck with needles in places needles were never intended to go, it was a rather uneventful outing! Seriously, while I'm glad the tests are over, things went relatively smooth.

Two different tests were done on me that day. In the first, electrodes were placed from my head to my feet and various intensities of electric shocks were given to attempt to see how the muscles responded to those stimulations.

The phrase they used was to see if they could "evoke potentials." After about ten minutes, I couldn't be 'evoked' due to the severity of my nerve damage. Early into the tests he knew there wasn't going to be a lot of response, and he decided to stop the process rather than continue to put me through the ongoing electrical shocks.

From there we went to another part of the campus and got set up for the actual EMG study, which included more electric stimulus and then those wonderful needles.

Though it's a painful process, it really is amazing how these tests can identify how the body is working, what areas in the nerves are damaged, and which muscles the damage nerves affect.

Dan, my physical therapist, joined me for this study. He wanted to have some specific muscle groups checked that he felt were suspiciously not working like they should be. The doctor zeroed in on those muscles in question.

We met last week with our PM& R doctor who got the report and test results. She gave us some of the answers we were looking for. Her explanation of the test results indicated that the nerves damaged were located in an area in my pelvic region called the *Plexus*.

She explained that down in the lower back the spinal cord splits, becoming similar to a horse's tail, winding its way down into the midsection of our bodies. From there those strands of nerves resemble some of the freeway interchanges in southern California, going this way and that and mixing up similar to a macramé weaving. It's in that web of nerves where the damage is, and it affects each of my legs differently.

I have better sensation in my left leg than in my right. Some muscles are working in one leg but not in the other. In my left leg my hamstring, a major muscle, isn't firing. The smaller muscles adjacent are picking up the slack and working overtime as I try to walk. In one leg some of the calf muscles that control my feet are working, while others aren't. In the other leg, there are even more muscles that are not working, resulting in an inability to either pull up on my foot or press down with it.

All these injuries makes it difficult for me to walk, even though I'm taking more steps and seeing more smoothness to my stride, thanks in part to some special foot and ankle orthotics (AFOs).

To top it all off, I found out that my gleutial muscles are not firing as well as they should. I never knew this, but apparently my heiney is there for a very important reason: it serves a crucial role in standing. Because my "glutes" are weak it's not easy for me to stand straight as I attempt to walk. Some of that weakness is probably a result of nerve damage, but also I have a huge chunk of my right buttock gone from the Morel's lesion. The best part of the day was when the doctor administering the test commented that the nerves that work the glutes do show some signs of regrowth.

Dr. Mary Merkel told us that nerves can regrow, but it takes time. Normally, it takes about two years to find out how much nerve regeneration will occur through normal regrowth. We're about nine months out from the accident, so another year or so would give us an indication of my long-term mobility, if we were dependent only on the normal regrowth estimates.

I mentioned that our visit with our primary doctor gave us only part of the answers we were looking for. I say that because we meet soon with the surgeon who does nerve repair and transplant surgeries with some amazing results. We're hoping that he will be able to let us know if there's anything he can do surgically to repair or bypass the damaged nerves. That could result in some major steps forward in bringing sensation and motor function to my legs.

Craig

Later, Dan told me that the doctors estimate only about thirty-five percent of my leg muscles are working. That's why walking is so difficult and why my legs continue to be very weak as I attempt to use the walker. Stability continued to be a problem as well because my core muscles still have not been reconnected.

I ran into another challenge in this season of my care. As I attempted to climb stairs, I found increasing amounts of pain to my left knee; it just wouldn't bend. My new ortho surgeon, Dr. Sherwood Duhon, took an X-ray of the knee and explained to me what the problem was.

In the early days of my time at UNM, the trauma surgeons had to off-load the pressure on my dislocated hip until they could surgically repair it and give me my new metal implant. They drilled a hole just above my knee from the outside to the inside of my leg and inserted a rod through that opening, attaching a pulley system to that rod and hung weights over the end of my bed, providing much-needed traction to the hip.

"When they drilled through your bone, bone dust came out the other end just like when a drill is sent through wood, sawdust collects around the exit hole. There are bone-fragments that have collected and calcified in your muscles. As those muscles move, sharp shrouds of bone are causing your pain," said Dr. Duhon.

They could go in and try and clean it out, but only if and when they were in surgery doing something more productive than just that. Or, he noted, with continued stretching at PT, it could remedy itself. Either way it sounded painful. We chose the less invasive course, thinking that another surgery was not what I was ready for.

Wednesday, March 24, 2010 5:48 p.m., MST
Yesterday was an important day in the overall recovery process. We met with the surgeon regarding potential repair of my damaged nerves.

Our son, Dallas, as always, gave a thorough overview of the issues, breaking down the medical process in words we all can understand.

After reviewing my MRIs and EMG studies, his conclusion was that there was a good possibility surgery could help repair the nerves. If we wanted to go that route, he'd be ready to help us.

He explained that if nerves have been severed, they could be reconnected and sutured back together. If scar tissue is pressing on nerves and blocking them from functioning properly, that scar tissue can be taken out, thus relieving the pressure. The only way they can know what's causing my issues is to get in there and look around. They have to carefully make their way through a lot of tissue and objects to get to the nerves. Then they will identify and tag them, evaluate their levels of function, and do whatever is necessary to repair them.

It could be done in one long surgery, or, he said, it might take two surgeries, done over a two-day period.

He also said that while they were doing this surgery, they could also reconnect my abdominal muscles and get my belly back to normal, and even reverse the temporary colostomy. I asked if they could throw in a tummy tuck and a chin lift as well, but it doesn't look too hopeful for that.

I'm also scheduled to meet with a hip specialist to get a second opinion on the heterotopic ossification issue in my left hip. One doctor feels we need to wait a while to let the extra bone growth mature around the hip replacement joint. My nurse case manager wants to see if another doctor concurs.

I continue, five days a week, to visit the physical therapists as they help me stretch, bend, sit, stand, walk, and climb steps.

We continue down this road, given to us by our Sovereign Lord, who has sustained us through it all. During these days, LaDonna and I have been greatly encouraged by our times in the great devotional book, *Streams in the Desert.* Yesterday's reading included this anonymous poem, which for me, says it all:

> He placed me in a little cage away from gardens fair,
> But I must sing the sweetest song because He placed me there,
> Not beat my wings against the cage if it is my Maker's will,
> But raise my voice towards Heaven's gate and sing the louder still.

Craig

By now, all the months that had flown by since the accident were catching up on me emotionally and physically. The pain I was in was constant and at times overwhelming.

I remember so clearly what was going through my mind eight months prior as I emerged out of the coma. I was convinced that within a few months, all this would be over, I'd be healed up, and back home in Phoenix.

I remember one of my trauma surgeons scheduling me for a follow-up appointment way out in November 2009 and that seemed so far away. I was certain that I'd have to drive all the way back from Arizona to Albuquerque to meet that appointment. Little did I realize that come November 2009 I would still be in New Mexico trying to get home. Now, many months later, the reality hit me that my road to recovery was going to be way longer than I had anticipated or hoped for.

It was another one of those moments for me when my own prayer life and faith was put to the test, simply because I was so tired and weary, without any good options to consider.

If I were going to overcome this adversity and win this fight, I would have to win it on the battlefield in my mind. I was struggling with the reality that I may never walk normal again and be confined to a wheelchair for the rest of my life. My traveling days surely were over; who would ever want to hear an old crippled man talk about the goodness and grace of a loving God?

The reality hit me like a ton of bricks that things would never be the same as before. My life had changed dramatically, and I wasn't sure what it would all look like in the end. I now knew life and ministry would be different than it was prior to mile marker 313. It led me to share my heart with our wonderful CaringBridge family.

Wednesday, April 14, 2010 10:28 p.m., MST

I've traveled down many roads in my lifetime but none as boring as a stretch of US Highway 50 in Nevada. It's a barren stretch of asphalt that is as straight as an arrow. If it's a clear day you can see that road stretching all the way to the horizon way off in the distance. Once you reach that point in your journey you're rewarded with more of the same. That boring road goes on for well over a hundred miles.

Sometimes that picture comes up in my mind as I journey through this long road of rehab and therapy. Please don't get me wrong, I have come to love and appreciate the wonderful folks who are working with me. They are great and we're seeing great progress.

As far as I've come, I just realize that I've got so far to go. Something happened last week that brought me to the realization that the road will continue to be long and challenging, with very little change in the scenery.

I had asked my therapist, Dan, why, after walking now for almost a month, is it not getting any easier. You'd think that my walking would be less painful than when I started and that with all the stretching and exercises, my joints and ligaments would be more limber.

Dan gave me my reality check when he stated, "Craig, remember, you only have about thirty to thirty-five percent of your leg muscles working!"

That's when it hit me. Unless the Lord allows me to regain nerve functions, walking will continue to be something very difficult for me to do. That's why we're coming into a season that is very important for my long-term recovery.

Things are moving forward in plans to have me return to the surgery table, possibly in May, to see if my damaged nerves can be repaired. In conjunction with that surgery I will probably get my stomach muscles stitched back together again, which would be a real step forward for me. If anything, at least I'll be able to see my feet better!

Next week I'll be having several CT scans of my pelvis and abdomen done in preparation for those surgeries. We'll be meeting soon with a general surgeon who will do the stomach surgery, then back again with the surgeon who will work on the nerves, all in anticipation of that major event.

We're excited about one of the rest stops on that long highway that is coming up for us this weekend. We are planning to venture out for the first time since the accident on a major trip. We will be flying to Chicago, where we'll be joining a number of other Native ministry personnel promoting Native ministry to the greater Chicago area. These ministry leaders will be speaking in a variety of schools, universities, churches, doing radio and other media interviews, culminating in a rally at the Billy Graham Center at Wheaton College on Sunday evening.

The organizers are including a tribute to our ministry work and the impact the accident has had on us, and on others through us. It will be a great encouragement to us just to see our dear friends and ministry colleagues who have been praying for us through these challenging days.

LaDonna continues to receive regular therapy on her neck and hand and we do see some ongoing improvements in her overall condition. I continue to stand in amazement at how God spared her life, and now, how she demonstrates such a godly love for me as she tirelessly cares for our family and me.

We continue to praise the Lord through it all, and continue to appreciate the prayers and words of encouragement that come to us through your replies on this site and through direct e-mail contact.

Thanks for your continued support and prayer.

With gratitude,

Craig and LaDonna

The trip to Chicago was very difficult and challenging, yet rewarding and encouraging. As we got all packed and rolled into Sky Harbor Airport, LaDonna commented that we looked like Jed and Granny Clampett in the old TV show, *The Beverly Hillbillies*. All our carry on as well as all I needed for my care needs made for a comedy team rolling down the concourse. Imagine LaDonna pushing the wheelchair with bags around her neck, and me, sitting in the wheelchair with both arms holding roller bags. Needless to say we turned a few heads.

Getting on the plane was another exercise. I had to slide-board over to a really narrow aisle chair, with my bodily sideboards hanging off both sides, finally arriving at our bulkhead seats, which were reserved for handicapped folk like me.

Once there we found out that the armrests would not lift up and so I couldn't slide over. Two petite airport helpers thought they would try and lift me over the armrest but we told them differently. It was a full flight so to change seats was going to be tough. The row behind the bulkhead seats did have moveable armrests, so we were forced to bump a couple of folks from those seats, and we got settled in. The flight was good and I was able to manage, somewhat painfully, the three-and-a-half-hour flight to Chicago.

We stayed right at the airport hotel so getting to our room wasn't too bad. For the first time since last June, I slept in a real non-hospital bed. It was a bit of a challenge, especially waking in the morning and having LaDonna help me get out of the bed. I slept somewhat, but she spent most of the night rotating me from side to side. All that went away with a breakfast that, if we spent the same amount of money getting groceries, we could have fed the 11th cavalry for a month!

What made all the inconvenience go away was being able to be reunited with a number of Native ministry leaders, some that we've been in the trenches with for over four decades. Our dear friends, Huron Claus and Ron Hutchcraft, honored our lives and ministry that night with wonderful words. I also had the opportunity to share some thoughts with the crowd assembled.

Afterwards, nobody wanted to leave, but the security guards at the Billy Graham Center wanted us out. In a way Dr. Graham would have been pleased with, they removed us from the premises. It was a quick trip back to the hotel, then up the next morning to get back to Beverly Hills.

Both Jed and Granny suffered some sore muscles and joints, but we'd have had that even if we didn't make the trip. It was great to get home and pick up where we left off with our rehab schedules.

One of the things that stood out vividly on the Chicago trip as we left O'Hare Airport was a grove of trees that were showing their first signs of spring buds. I normally am not drawn to things like that, but after being indoors for months it really made an impression on me. It was as if the Lord was giving us a picture from nature of the work He has been doing in our lives.

The long hard winter gave way to the budding of the trees, fresh with new life and vigor and ready for the warm rays of the summer sun to help them start their new season. Maybe some budding of the trees might be ahead for us!

That prayer gave way to reality a few nights later.

199

LaDonna was massaging my feet when she asked me to try and move my toes. There had been numerous days where she asked me to do that and as hard as I would try those little sausages remained motionless. Not really expecting anything different that night, I gave it another try. For the first time in eleven months several of the toes on my right foot responded!

I was also beginning to have a bit more sensation in that foot as well. Instead of being totally numb on the bottom of my foot, I was beginning to feel something similar to needle pricks as I slid my right foot along the carpet and as LaDonna and the kids worked and massaged my feet.

Other doctors told us we could see some return of sensation and mobility as nerves regenerated and healed. It could take up to nine years to see what level they would be able to return to, though. That's why I'm glad we have a Savior who is also our Healer! We continued to trust Him for healing that would be completed in His timing and for His purposes!

As excited as we were about these new developments, we were equally challenged and much in prayer about some growing difficulties I was experiencing with my physical therapy and rehab.

Over those weeks I had a lot of pain in my ankles and knees, especially my left knee, while attempting to walk. The pain was not getting any better. Dan tried to find out why these joints were flaring up as bad as they were. It was getting so bad I was able to take only a few painful steps, compared to the seventy-foot excursions I was seeing a few weeks earlier.

As I faced these challenges, LaDonna and I would be reminded about the suffering of Christ on the cross, and how painful that experience was for Him. He was not even able to scratch his nose, or to move at all as he hung there. In some small way I was beginning to identify with His physical pain and incapacitation. I began to count it a privilege to know Him deeper and more intimately through the suffering I was experiencing.

I knew Him as all sufficient, loving, and in control but never as intimately as I was experiencing now. It made me sleep well at night, and once in a while as I moved my toes during the midnight hours I was often compelled to lift my voice in praise to Him!

I knew He was going to take me all the way through.

Chapter 16

THE LONG HOT PHOENIX SUMMER

Even though we called Phoenix home for several decades, it had been years since we had to endure the brutal summers the desert produces. For us, our traveling ministry kept us on the road almost constantly, and summers meant frequent stops at Bible camps, conferences and music festivals in more moderate climates.

We'd often find ourselves venturing into Canada, going to communities never heard of by most folk. A lot of these ministry trips I would liken to a National Geographic adventure, because many of the places were isolated and filled with incredible beauty. But the accident changed everything, including our breaks away from the desert heat.

I had almost forgotten how hot a Phoenix summer could get. Trying to hold onto the blistering hot metal rails of my wheelchair, I resembled a concert pianist tickling the ivories as I rolled down the sidewalk in 110-degree heat. The difficulties I faced with my recovery were multiplied by my inability to travel to a cooler climate.

I wanted to get my upcoming surgeries over with, and quickly, but my hopes were dashed as the doctors felt I wasn't quite ready for their scalpels and sutures. We woke one morning to find that we had reached a major mile marker of our own: the anniversary of the accident.

Wednesday, June 9, 2010 3:04 p.m., MST

It's hard to believe that right about now (late afternoon 3:00 p.m. Phoenix time), one year ago, our lives changed drastically with the accident at mile marker 313. We look back with thanks to God for the blessing of extending our lives, even though the year has been one of great difficulty and trial.

One day last week I did something I had never done before: I read through all our kids' postings, when they first started spreading the news and prayer requests on the Caringbridge website.

I was blown away by all the challenges they and our extended family faced as they saw their mom and dad trying to recover from such serious injuries. My heart ached for what they must have gone through emotionally as hours spilled into days, days into weeks, and weeks into months.

I read where they and the medical staff communicated with me, but I don't remember much of it. Not long after the accident they wrote where I signed papers giving LaDonna power of attorney to sign closing documents for the sale of our home.

My son, Dallas, walked me through the details, and told me where to put the X on the appropriate line. I then heard LaDonna go over to the corner in that ICU room and cry softly so as not to distress me. This abnormal signing away of the sale of our home overwhelmed her.

Still, so much of those early days are vague and unclear to me.

What I do know now is that we came through very deep waters, thanks to the grace and willingness of our Sovereign Lord. He heard and answered the prayers of so many people.

Today is an anniversary of remembering for us. We are reminded of the goodness of our Lord, the love of our family and friends, and the prayers of many on our behalf. We look back and see His hand, which gives us great confidence as we look forward.

Speaking of looking forward, I'm excited about tomorrow. We meet with Dr. Duhon, the orthopedic surgeon who will hopefully do the much-needed surgery on my left hip. The only thing standing in the way of this is if the bone is still actively growing. A bone scan test was done a few weeks ago. That will help Dr. Duhon determine if it's time to get the hammer and chisel out and go to work.

Along with this important visit is another one scheduled for June 15th with Dr. Gottlieb. We may know within a week about finally getting me back on his operating table.

Once again that great classic devotional *Streams in the Desert* brought God's Word to our hearts this morning. It quoted Hebrews 13:5–6: "Be content with what you have, because God has said, never will I leave you; never will I forsake you. So we say with confidence, the Lord is my helper, I will not be afraid. What can man do to me?"

He never left us or forsook us. He has helped us, and we're not afraid! We'll keep going with that confidence for His Glory!

Grateful,

Craig and LaDonna

P.S.—LaDonna here! The other day we were rushing about as we do each morning getting ready for PT. Once Craig is situated in the standing frame for an hour, we have a great cup of coffee, our daily devotional readings, sing a hymn or two, and then I get his breakfast. Well, this particular morning Craig wanted his breakfast sooner than later and skipped the singing. I said, "Craig, aren't we going to sing today?"

Then Craig said, "How about after breakfast?"

He immediately regretted saying that and opened the hymnal. It fell open to page 256, *My Savior First of All!*

Wednesday, June 16, 2010 4:35 p.m., MST

Dr. Duhon told us that the kind of hip revision surgery Dad needs is very rare, and in his seventeen years of doing surgeries he can count on one hand the number of times he's had to do this specific procedure. This is further testament to Dad's condition being unique—even the best of surgeons see this as a challenge. In order to get ready for the procedure, he ordered some specific tests (CT and X-rays), which will be done at the end of this week. There will then be one more visit with him on July 1 to set a date for that surgical procedure.

Dad also met with Dr. Gottlieb who is ready now to do the microsurgery on both sides of Dad's lumbar plexus region. He was very encouraging to us as he saw the partial movement Dad has in both his legs. He felt that because there's some movement and activity, there probably aren't nerves that have been severed or badly torn, which would require a very detailed and long surgical repair.

The best-case scenario is scar tissue pressing on the nerves and causing the blockages. If so, all that is needed is to remove the scar tissue and free up the passageway in the nerves. Even though there's a football-sized opening in Dad's abdomen, that's not the best route to go in and find these nerves—the preferred way is through the flank.

Dad's comment to Dr. Gottlieb was, "I'm so scarred up now, with my body looking more like a patchwork quilt, a few more scars wouldn't make any difference!"

The best news of this visit was seeing him sign the paperwork that put in motion the scheduling of this surgery. We're looking at probably six to eight weeks out for this procedure and a hospitalization time running anywhere from three to ten days, depending on how well the wounds heal and the abdominal repair heals.

Dad has scaled back his time at PT from five days a week to three until these surgeries are performed. The increased pain in his hip has made these sessions tougher on him. The walking process has not seen much gain because of the limited amount that his legs are responding and the increased pain in his hip, knee and ankle joints. Backing off to three a week should help keep enough activity to not go backwards but maintain his current progress until the surgeries produce their results.

It's been such a long, hard road this past year for both Dad and Mom, and they really are hoping for a break where the can take some "vacation" time to rest and relax. When these surgeries are scheduled will ultimately determine when they can get away to someplace special and cooler than the desert heat of summertime in Phoenix. Hmm? I wonder where that might be? Stay tuned to find out!*

Dallas

*Hint #1: There are lots of bloodsuckers there.**

**Hint #2: No, I'm not talking about them pasty-white, spooky kids from them there "Twilight" movies.

Chapter 17

OUR "TOUR DE THANKS"

So it was now set. My first surgical procedure since returning to Phoenix would be in early August 2010. In anticipation of that, we got ready for our much-needed vacation time somewhere other than Phoenix. The only obvious place to go would be back to where it all started for both LaDonna and me—our hometown, Cass Lake, Minnesota.

Cass Lake is a small community of less than a thousand people. It's situated on the shores of one of the most beautiful lakes anywhere and is home to the Leech Lake Band of Ojibwe Indians. I'm an enrolled member of the White Earth Band of Ojibwe, but spent my entire growing up years on the Leech Lake Reservation. It's a place that still draws us back, because there's just something special about going home.

It's not only my birthplace, but it's LaDonna's as well. We were born in the same Indian Hospital some ten short months apart. Even though she is Navajo, her parents were attending an Indian Bible Institute called Mokahum a few miles out of town when she was born. We both have strong ties to the community, people, and beauty of what many affectionately call, "Up North".

The insurance laws required me to petition the State of Arizona to leave the state if we were going to be gone for more than two weeks at a time. I almost felt like I was petitioning some parole board to let me out of the big house on good behavior. We obliged, and went through the process anyway. My *permission granted* letter came back in plenty of time for us to prepare for this major undertaking.

With all the complications of flying and renting a suitable vehicle, we chose to drive the trip and began excitedly planning for five weeks of rest and recuperation at our cabin in the northland. Other than the weekend trip to Chicago, this would be our first major venture out since the accident.

One morning as I was having my daily devotions, I came across the story in the Bible about ten lepers who were all healed by Jesus. It's recorded for us in Luke 17:11–19:

> Now on his way to Jerusalem, Jesus traveled along the border between Samaria and Galilee. As he was going into a village, ten men who had leprosy met him. They stood at a distance and called out in a loud voice, "Jesus, Master, have pity on us!" When he saw them, he said, "Go, show yourselves to the priests." And as they went, they were cleansed. One of them, when he saw he was healed, came back, praising God in a loud voice. He threw himself at Jesus' feet and thanked him—and he was a Samaritan. Jesus asked, "Were not all ten cleansed? Where are the other nine? Has no one returned to give praise to God except this foreigner?" Then he said to him, "Rise and go; your faith has made you well."

As I meditated on this story I did a heart check of my own. I came to the conclusion that I did have a heart of thankfulness to the Lord and had expressed my thankfulness to Him many times over for sparing our lives. But there seemed to be some unfinished business in this matter that was unsettling in my soul. I couldn't quite get it until one morning as my driver, John, came by to pick me up and take me to another visit with my physical terrorists—I mean, *therapists.*

"John, you've been taking me now for a number of months," I commented as he was loading me in the transport van. "I want you to know I'm really thankful for you and all you are doing to help me," I continued. He was glad to hear my words, and he later commented that it really made his day.

And then it hit me: This miracle is God's miracle, but He was using a whole lot of people who had to be at the right place at the right time in the process. It was on my heart to visit as many of the people He used and thank them for being God's hands and feet for us in our deepest time of need. I couldn't wait to tell LaDonna what I wanted to do. I went to lunch with her as I shared with her my plan.

"Hon, since we're driving back to Minnesota, I'd like to plan stops at the facilities and contact the service providers who were there to help us. I'd like to thank them and give them a gift, maybe some wild rice [what the Ojibwe are known for], and to let them know that I survived and am getting better."

She was excited about the idea. We began to make a list of the places and people we needed to visit. It would take some planning to try and connect with them. We contacted our friends, the Kinney's, to see if they would open their home again to us for a few days as we made our way back through New Mexico on what we decided to call our *Tour de Thanks.*

Saturday, July 3, 2010 2:45 p.m., MST

Greetings! We mentioned we'd be sharing with you some experiences from our much-anticipated vacation break. This is the first time since the accident we are able to get away and rest a little while.

Our nurse case manager and the insurance folk have graciously said to take time off in July for this and we welcomed it with open arms. It would be a real test for me to see how I could handle an extended road trip and life away from my specialized airbed. Since my surgeries are not going to happen until August, this was the best time to take this break.

We determined to go back home to Minnesota. Thanks to some wonderful brothers in Christ, a wheelchair ramp is being built to accommodate me at our mini-casa on the Rez [reservation]!

The journey began July 2, and oh, what a day it was! The trip started with a quick visit to Dr. Duhon. To say it was a crazy start is an understatement. We got to his office and were joined by our realtors, who have been working hard to navigate us through the world of short sales. We walked into the beautiful office building, and stepped into the elevator to go to the second floor office.

Well, there was no second floor office—they were located on the first floor. I guess I needed to pay attention to the details. When we got back to the elevator it wouldn't work.

There we were, squeezed into this box and going nowhere, and I was to see the doctor in five minutes!

We were able to pry the door open and call for help. They said help would come but who knew when? There we were, stuck on the second floor with a bad air conditioner and 110 outside, and waiting. Of course I couldn't use the stairway. Not a good way to start a cross-country trip! Help finally arrived, and I was able to get in and see the doctor.

He is looking at September or October to schedule my surgery to free up my left hip from the excessive bone growth. That will put some time between that one and the August 9 surgery for the nerve reconstruction.

We're staying at the home of some dear friends who graciously opened their home to LaDonna and those who came to help her during the months I was in the hospital/rehab facilities in Albuquerque. She's always wanted to show me where she spent her days while I was an inpatient.

What a peace-filled place this is! It's beautiful, and we want to say a great big thank you to Cris and Cindy for their amazing hospitality then and now. After another day or so here we'll be off to the great northland!

So we've started the trip by getting stuck in an elevator! I hope the rest of the journey will run a little smoother!

Thanks!

Craig and LaDonna

Thursday, July 15, 2010 5:25 a.m., MST

Greetings from "Up North," and the land of ten thousand lakes! We're enjoying one of them during this much-needed get away. Sorry for the delay in updating you but in the craziness of a cross-country trip we misplaced our Internet air card and finally found it after almost tearing the cabin apart. Guess where we found it? Stashed away in what I call my diaper bag where LaDonna keeps all the colostomy supplies. We're still trying to figure out how it got there!

What a healing time it has been just sitting out in the screen porch drinking Costco's best coffee and enjoying the Lunds, Crestliners, and pontoons passing by. We've had a steady stream of friends and family from our home area that have stopped by to say hi and enjoy brief visits. After a two-year hiatus, LaDonna finally has been able to get her hands dirty again in her much-loved flower beds around the property, followed by a pretty good dose of much-needed Advil.

We were able to share at our home church, The Cass Lake Alliance, last Sunday. It was the day they were installing our new pastor, and the somewhat rusty old Smith Family Trio even did a song. Singing is a bit tougher for me these days and I think it might be attributed to the after-effects of the tracheotomy they had to do to help me breathe. Having an open abdominal wound and a subsequent misaligned diaphragm sure doesn't help with proper breathing techniques for singing, either! We stumbled our way through, the church family endured it with a smile, and we all had a great time.

Both LaDonna and I got through the almost 2,000-mile trip reasonably well. What a blessing it was to pull up and see the new wheelchair ramp built by the men of our church. Thanks so much, Ken and crew, for your labor of love!

We have just a bit over a week left here, as time seems to fly by all too quickly. It won't be long before we have to retrace our steps back to Arizona as we anticipate the next season of surgeries looming on the horizon. August 9 is the first one, and that's going to be one of the most important ones that will help determine my ability to walk again. We're already much in prayer about that.

It's been such a blessing to have my dad here to help lift some of LaDonna's care-giving load so she can spend more time resting and renewing as well.

Thanks, Dad, for all you are doing. What a blessing you are to me!

Our hopes were that spending time here would help in our healing process. I'm here to tell you it sure is doing the trick! We are feeling rejuvenated in body, soul, and spirit. I think we'll be ready for the next long piece of road in our journey to recovery! Thanks again for being with us along the way! We love you all and appreciate all your prayers, encouragement, and support.

In Christ,

Craig and LaDonna

After a month of R&R in Minnesota, we hopped (somewhat) back into the car and headed back to the Southwest. Our first stop was at the C&MA national office in Colorado Springs.

We had the joy of sharing one morning in a staff chapel service. It was so good to see so many of our friends and ministry colleagues! They had been praying for us during those dark days. How helpful they were to us in navigating through the legal and insurance worlds we found ourselves swimming in. There was a lot of love going on that day, and it's a visit we won't soon forget.

At the end of the chapel service I asked our colleagues to remember us in prayer as we made our way down to New Mexico for this important thanksgiving tour. The first hurdle we'd have to get over is driving right past mile maker 313 again. Once we got past that spot, it would be on to the firefighters and paramedics that came to our aid.

We left Colorado Springs around noon and made the trip down I-25 into New Mexico. The mile marker numbers kept getting smaller and smaller as we drove through a mostly rainy and cloudy day. I'll never forget the image that is still vivid in my mind as we aproached that infamous mile marker 313 for the first time since the accident.

The police report indicated that we ended up in the median between the north and southbound lanes about 150 feet south of the mile marker.

As we crested a small hill, in the distance we could see the mile marker. About 100 or so feet south of it, a clear square of sunlight beamed down on the exact location where we ended up, setting it apart from the rest of the cloud-covered ground.

Our first stop was with the first responders from Pecos Valley Fire Department and Emergency Medical Services. When we pulled up to the EMS facility, we were disappointed to see the ambulance gone, apparently out on another rescue mission. We

Sunlight framing the accident scene at Mile Marker 313.

had made contact by phone with paramedic Dana Gingrich, and he was expecting us. Unfortunately, someone else was expecting him that day, and they needed him more than we did.

We decided to get a good ole' green chili cheeseburger at a local restaurant. As always, New Mexican cuisine didn't fail to amaze us! We waited a while longer and drove back to the garage. It was still empty so we decided it just wasn't going to work. We pulled out of Pecos and started heading back to I-25 and on to Santa Fe. A few miles out of town the ambulance met us as they were heading back home. LaDonna turned a 180 and we started back, trailing what was the very same vehicle I was inside fourteen months earlier.

After Dana and his partner finished parking the rig, we had an incredible visit with the man God used initially to perform the Miracle at Mile Marker 313.

Dana shared his recollections of arriving onto the scene that day. He described it as a giant 'yard sale' in between the north and southbound lanes. Our stuff was strewn everywhere and many bystanders were already there, helping to move the trailer out of the way so they could access us from the driver's side.

He told us about the challenges they faced rolling me onto the backboard and the subsequent flailing out of my legs due to the open-book pelvic fracture. They put the sheet under me and tightened it up over and around my mid-section, slowing the bleeding internally until they could get me to the hospital.

They had to dump a load of pain medications through the IV lines they had established, fearing I would not make the trip to St. Vincent Hospital. He shared also about what it was like in the

It was so much better being outside this vehicle than in it!

ER room when I coded, and how they worked to restart my heart and get me going again.

It was quite a start to our *Tour de Thanks*.

I affirmed to Dana how grateful we were for his teams' help that day. He mentioned to me that both he and his partner were Christians, and knew that we were, too, from the brief conversations we shared while in and out of consciousness. Of course, the "choir" in the front seat, singing "'Tis So Sweet to Trust in Jesus," was a giveaway as well, he noted!

"Dana, I am not sure how many people come back to say thanks."

He replied that in all his years of working as a paramedic, we were the first. You could see how thankful he was that we did.

I gave him a batch of my Ojibwe gold (in our language we call wild rice, *manoomin*), and left him my killer recipe to share with the whole crew next time they gathered for an in-service training event. He was so appreciative and said he'd be following our journey and would continue to pray for us as we moved forward in our rehabilitation. We ended our visit by praying together as I offered my thanks to God for Dana and his crew for all they had done.

Our next stop was the Santa Fe airport, where we met up with Erin, the flight nurse who took care of me that day in my transfer to UNM hospital. She gave us a tour of the helicopter and told us what the flight was like and how she didn't think I'd survive it.

I shared with her the lessons the Lord taught me from the ten lepers, and she had an interesting comment.

"There were ten lepers in the Bible and only one came back to say thanks, right? Well, we've carried literally hundreds, if not thousands, of 'lepers' in this helicopter, and no one has come back to say thanks. Craig, you and LaDonna are the first ones I've met

With my flight nurse, Erin.

who have done this, and I can't tell you how much it means to us. We hardly ever see the outcomes of the patients we deliver unless we hear about it on the nightly news, and it's normally not positive."

With each new stop, God was speaking to me about these incredible people who serve in communities across our land, faithfully showing up at work every day, but without anybody coming by to say thank you. These folk put their lives on the line in for us and deserve our thanks.

Our *Tour de Thanks* continued as we visited Dr. Raboff and the staff at St. Vincent Emergency Department. How thankful I was to meet the physician who brought me back from death's door. I'm pretty sure I slipped a bit more *manoomin* into his gift bag.

With Dr. Raboff at St. Vincent's Emergency Room.

From there it was on to the Trauma Center at UNM Hospital in Albuquerque. I was able to see two of the trauma surgeons. Dr. Stephen Lu is the head of UNM's trauma services and the surgeon who met me at the helicopter the night I was transferred. Dr. Howdishell, the doctor who did the skin grafts, could have a very successful sod-cutting business if he wasn't a trauma surgeon, based on the evidence found on both my thighs!

We also reconnected with many of the staff at the Trauma/ ICU Unit who served us while we were there. They all recognized me, but I had a harder time recognizing most of them since, at the time, I was in a drug-induced coma and off on covert White House missions. Regardless, they all heard directly from my mouth

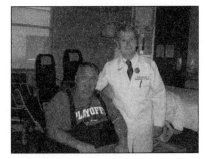

With Dr. Thomas Howdishell in the Trauma ICU unit I occupied.

how thankful I was for each of them and how God used them to perform His miracle in our lives.

When we pulled into Kindred Hospital and rolled into the building, one of the first ones we saw was my therapist, Alison. She saw us from a distance, let out a big scream, and came running down the hall to greet us. Others heard the commotion and went to see what was happening. Thankfully, it wasn't something

With Dr. Stephen Lu, Head Trauma Surgeon at UNM Hospital.

bad, but something really good for a change! We hugged them all, cried, laughed, and rehearsed some of the stories that stuck in our minds from our time there.

Our last stop was at Advanced Healthcare of Albuquerque. We were met with the very same excited welcome back from

Alison running to greet us. Oh, Happy Day!

these dear folk who took such good care of us. More laughing and crying was in order as tears of gratitude and thankfulness flowed freely from both caregivers and care receivers.

The lesson of thankfulness has not been lost to us. It's something we now do almost automatically as our lives intersect with strangers who are serving in one way or another.

People in general enjoy hearing a thankful word for what they do. Returning from death's door does that for you, I guess.

I only wish it was a lesson I would have practiced more of years ago.

How amazing would it be if a groundswell of thankfulness would break out in our country? What if people purposed to stop by a fire station, EMS garage, or Air Evac unit to express their gratefulness? Teachers, clergy, janitors, and farm workers would all have their day made a bit brighter with a random act of thankfulness. What a better place our country would be.

I do need to warn you, though, that once you decide to go on your own *Tour de Thanks,* get ready for a long trip, because it doesn't seem to have a finish line. All I know is I've been truly grateful for each and every person who has crossed my life as a result of the Miracle at Mile Marker 313.

Oh, and by the way, thank *you* for investing time out of your life to read the story of our life. We are grateful for you as well!

Chapter 18

BACK UNDER THE KNIFE

We got home exhausted but exhilarated with only a few days to prepare for surgery again. I was excited yet somewhat apprehensive because Dr. Gottlieb made it clear this was a difficult and dangerous procedure. That ended up being a very true statement.

> Thursday, August 12, 2010 8:53 p.m., MST
>
> Dear friends and family,
>
> This is day three after Craig's 16th surgery to date. I'm sitting at his bedside here at Banner Good Samaritan, just the two of us and the Lord after a pretty busy day!
>
> This surgery was a very extensive one. The incision wraps around his belt line to the tune of approximately 25 inches. I must say that I was taken aback when the bandage was removed and I saw it for the first time.
>
> Craig said he felt like a walleye fillet.
>
> As a quilter, I was impressed at the preciseness of each staple applied. But seriously, this has been a very painful surgery.

Dr. Gottlieb had hoped to send him home by now, but Craig spiked a fever last night and is still dealing with intense pain in his right flank.

Craig says, "I feel like I've been in the ring with the world champion kick boxer, who still retains his title."

The day after surgery the therapists weren't able to get him to sit at the edge of the bed, because it was too painful. He had better success yesterday and today. He sat on the edge of the bed for twenty minutes. There is concern that he is not ready to transfer from his wheelchair to his bed at home. They are recommending that he spend some time at an inpatient rehab facility until his side heals enough to safely transfer. It could be several days before he gets home. We will know more details tomorrow.

Craig had a wonderful opportunity to share the gospel with the therapists today. They were blown away that while he suffers much pain, his attitude is so different than the other patients they see. They wished he could accompany them to make the rounds to the other patients to encourage them as they face their depression, discouragement, and even anger at their conditions.

We are thankful, even through this time of suffering, that the Good News of the hope that Jesus brings is being shared. While we still don't know the outcome this surgery will have on waking up Craig's nerves, we are confident that much good is coming out of this.

Even as I am writing this, the page is going off over the intercom for the trauma team to assemble in the ER to save someone. We are reminded that another life hangs in the balance. There's a lot of hurt and pain in this world. It all comes as a result of the curse of sin. Thank God there is a remedy and there is hope in the finished work of Jesus Christ.

Thanks SO much for standing, weeping, praying, and trusting the Lord with us. We are praying for you all, too.

We will keep you posted.

LaDonna

Sunday, August 15, 2010 8:38 a.m., MST

It has been almost a week since my surgery. I want to thank LaDonna for giving you the updates while I was recovering. Boy, what a challenge it has been getting through the effects of this very major event.

Dr. Gottlieb dug deep into my body to try and free up the nerves. I sure feel the whole area where he worked in. I wasn't expecting the recovery to be so painful and difficult, but thankfully with each passing day I'm getting stronger and feeling better.

After thinking about the sixteen surgeries I've had, I jokingly told LaDonna the other day I feel like I donated my body to science but forgot to die first!

I'm now to the point where the medical staff is able to get me sitting up and transferring to my wheelchair with moderate discomfort in the process. My ability to get on the chair and back in bed will probably make my stay in this rehab facility short, and I'm anxious to get back home.

The doctors felt it was too dangerous for me to go directly home from the hospital home, so we agreed to be transferred to another facility, the Advanced Healthcare of Glendale. It's a sister facility to Advanced Healthcare of Albuquerque. They have a wonderful facility and staff.

I got checked in; the therapist came and did my initial checkup. During the exam something new happened, and it was caught on tape!

Colter, the therapist, asked me to try and move my left foot like many therapists have asked me to do in the past but to no avail. Every attempt to try and move it resulted only in frustration until yesterday! IT WOKE UP!

This is the side that Dr. Gottlieb didn't work on, and all of a sudden new movement and nerves are waking up! My calf muscles have shriveled up from inactivity. Colter and LaDonna felt my calf muscles, and a fairly strong contraction was confirmed.

Oh, how we thank the Lord for this great news. While it will take time for those muscles to strengthen, at least now the signal is finding its way home for the first time in fourteen months! Praise the Lord!

It was a wonderful encouragement to us in the wake of a very painful week. Due to the severe pain caused by any movement in my right leg, we cannot assess any new progress.

The left side reminded me again of who's really in charge! My Healer has once again proven faithful. I rest in the joy of seeing His supernatural surgery at work, and with no painful after-effect! To God be the glory!

Gratefully,

Craig

In the weeks following, my healing journey was very difficult. The big difference was that in this recovery I was awake and alert! After experiencing how painful recovery can be, all I can say is, I'm sure thankful for the almost two-month coma they kept me in!

It's hard to explain how challenging and painful this recovery was for me. The incision was over two feet long and the surgeon's blade went deep down from my right flank into the pelvic region so a lot of muscle and other tissue were affected. I told LaDonna that it hurt so much even my fat ached!

Three weeks later I had a follow-up appointment with Dr. Gottlieb. His staff removed half of the sixty-six staples that day. The other thirty-three would be removed in a couple of weeks. The good news was, the wound was healing up very well, and the deep pain and discomfort are diminishing.

I love the matter-of-fact way the doctors discuss my case and my situation.

When Dr. Gottlieb saw me, he had with him another physician. He said, "This is Mr. Smith, and he had a real bad accident over a year ago. He really should be dead . . ." and along he went with his overview.

Hearing that truth from the doctors and EMS personnel reminds me that *I'm living on borrowed time.* I really shouldn't be here, but here I am! That reality became extra special to me around this time, as our daughter, Shandiin gave birth to their second child, a beautiful baby girl named Violet. What a blessing it was when she and Stefan brought my precious granddaughter over for the first time! I'm so blessed to be alive and to be able to hold a new grand baby in my arms. I look forward to seeing her grow into a beautiful woman of God.

Saturday, September 18, 2010 4:37 p.m., MST

Greetings from the long road to recovery! LaDonna and I were talking about the need to reconnect with you about where we are at in what we are calling our *season of surgeries.*

Last week I finally got the last half of the sixty-six staples removed from my right pelvic region five long weeks after the decompression nerve surgery on August 9. It seemed to take so long for those itchy staples to be removed. What a relief to hear the long-awaited words, "That's the last one!"

Doing the honors was one of the many nursing students I've come across who, like all the others, spend time learning the hands-on patient care in real office and hospital environments. These hands-on experiences help these future nurses.

For us guinea pig patients, we sometimes try our best to surprise them. I've found that fake screams or temporary blackouts work pretty well at leaving them wondering why they ever chose the healthcare profession in the first place!

I really behaved myself this time because I was so eager to get those staples out. I took it easy on this young up-and-coming professional. I'm sure I'll make it up somewhere down the line with the next student blessed to visit my room!

The deep tissue in my flank has healed up, and there's just a little bit more needed in a small part of the incision. It took about a month to feel better, and now I look forward to the next slice and dice, which is fast approaching.

On October 4 Dr. Gottlieb will be removing the football-sized skin graft over my 'open' abdomen and attempt to use that route to go in and decompress the nerves on the left side of my pelvis. He's hoping that he will have a clear enough access through this route so he does not have to do a third surgery later on. That would replicate the two-foot incision he did on my right side in the last one.

I'm hoping he can successfully access the sleeping nerves so we can finally try and wake them up. Once he's done with that he'll close up the huge 'opening' in my abdomen. Finally, after fifteen long months, I'll get my belly button back where it belongs! Now that's something to get excited about!

The same day I had the staples removed I went in for a final CT scan of my left hip ordered by Dr. Duhon. He will be doing his surgery probably in late October. He will go into my left hip and attempt to shave down the excess bone that has grown around the new hip joint.

The CT he ordered will help him see the layout of the major blood vessels near the joint. There's concern that the extra bone has grown out near them. The possibility of accidentally cutting one of these major vessels could be life threatening. He's considering having a vascular surgeon assist him because of that.

I've already faced this reality in the last surgery. Dr. Gottlieb nicked one of the major vessels that was encased in scar tissue deep in my right side. Thankfully he was able to clamp and fix the wound right away avoiding a crisis in the OR. He told me afterwards that once that happened he realized that he could not go any further because of the danger it was putting me in.

As I've come through surgery number sixteen successfully, I realize that October will be a tough month for me, with two somewhat dangerous surgeries and subsequent recovery times. I'm grateful for the time I've had to heal up from the last one, and am now gearing up for the next rounds. We have to get through this season in order to give my body the best chance to get back on my feet.

LaDonna continues to experience pain in her neck. Our PM&R doctor got her back into physical therapy as well. She has tried a number of therapists over this past year, but most of them, she feels, were too easy on her. I guess when you show up after suffering a C-1 neck fracture, the default reaction is to go very lightly.

We decided to have her treated at the same place I'm going to. What a wonderful change this has been for her. Dan Bonarati and Touchstone Rehabilitation are an answer to prayer for us. The rehab I'm receiving is great, and now Dan's magic touch is helping LaDonna as well!

We continue down this long and somewhat painful stretch of road, facing the challenges prayerfully, and trusting in our Healer all the way. Our prayer is that He will be happy with us as His kids as we represent Him to doctors, nurses, therapists, fellow patients and their families, our family, as well as to you and anyone else He brings our way (nursing students notwithstanding).

So grateful for you, knowing we're not alone in this journey.
Craig
Psalms 57:1–2 (NIV)

Saturday, October 2, 2010 7:40 p.m., MST
Dear friends and family,
I'm sure you can see from the guestbook entries that there are folks from one end of the globe to the other who have

joined together on our behalf, storming the gates of heaven in much-appreciated prayer. I really mean this when I say I am equally grateful, not only to the Lord, who has been faithful to hear and answer your prayers, but to you, for doing the praying. You have been so encouraging to our lives through this incredibly difficult ordeal.

On Monday, October 4, I will be back in the operating room for my seventeenth surgery. This time Dr. Gottlieb will open my abdominal wound and attempt to dig down far enough to free up scar tissue in my left lumbar plexus region that is pressing on my nerves, causing my leg muscle inactivity. This is crucial to improving any level of walking in the future, so I'm anxious to see how it will all turn out.

Once he's finished trolling down at the bottom, he'll finish the surgery by reconnecting my abdominal core muscles after sixteen long months with them split right down the middle from my sternum to my beltline. I'll be so happy for that to finally get done! He has warned me that as tough as the last recovery was, this one will probably be more painful.

I found out this week that Dr. Gottlieb and Dr. Duhon spoke to each other last week about me. If they were using their cell phones I hope they have an unlimited minutes plan.

They agreed together on a strategy that will have Dr. Gottlieb also visit my new hip implant and visualize the level of heterotopic bone. He will help determine how close this runaway bone growth is to my major leg veins and arteries and give Dr. Duhon direct info that sometimes CT scans, MRIs and X-rays just can't give. That will give Dr. Duhon the best possible intel to help him prepare for surgery number eighteen, which should follow shortly after I recover from this one. It all makes me tired just thinking about it.

We've heard from many of you with wonderful affirmations on how our response to all we've gone through the past sixteen months has encouraged, blessed, and somehow spoken to your lives. We're grateful for that and thank the Lord He is being glorified in this process. We wouldn't be honest, though, if we didn't tell you we have good days and not so good days; days when the physical and emotional pain is bearable and sometimes when it's much harder.

There are days when we wish we could just pick up where we left off and be somewhere bringing the hope of the gospel in another outreach event.

That's when I'm reminded of Paul's words to the Romans where he introduces himself in Romans 1:1 as *a servant of Christ Jesus.*

I'm a servant, too. My identity and significance is not to be in my job, title, education, or anything else. A servant does not have an identity in and of himself. His identity is wrapped up in his master. A servant doesn't have a say in the jobs he is to carry out. That is reserved for the master.

Paul made it clear to the Philippians that all the things that once amounted to his significance and identity were worthless "compared to the surpassing greatness of knowing Christ Jesus my Lord" (Philippians 3:8).

The place of peace and contentment is in the center of servanthood. Our trauma is an assignment that God has given us. What turns our painful experiences into joy is to make sure we are honoring God. When I think of all He's done for me, I gladly take up my cross and follow Him! But it has to be done on a daily basis.

LaDonna and I will never be able to express adequately how much it means to have you praying for us. We leave the house Monday at 4:30 a.m. to head to Good Sam Hospital for my 7:30 appointment with the surgeon's scalpel. As he shapes my body, God is shaping my life. As the doctor does his part, may he somehow sense an unusual guiding by a blessed unseen hand!

Thanks for loving God and loving us by being with us again today.

Craig and LaDonna

Tuesday, October 5, 2010 7:14 p.m., MST

Dad had surgery to close up his abdomen yesterday. First, the skin graft/surgical mesh was removed, and the skin and muscle layers pulled together. Also, they checked the bundle of nerves that pass through his pelvis on the left side of his body to see if there was scar tissue compressing the nerves, causing lack of sensation and foot drop on his left side.

It lasted five and a half hours. When it was done, Mom and my sisters, Nizhoni and Shandiin, were sitting in the waiting area when Dad's surgeon Dr. Gottlieb came out with a big smile on his face. Mom says that he looked like he could have done cartwheels down the hall, he was so happy.

He said the surgery went well, and he was quite pleased with the results. Normally the layers of skin and muscle tissue need to be stitched together separately. You can't just stitch the top layer together and leave it that way. The inside parts would just pull apart again. In Dad's case, the different skin and muscle layers were all stuck together with scar tissue. A good part of the surgery was spent separating those layers and suturing them back together.

Before he started separating the layers like a picky kid eating granny's organic veggie meatloaf, he got a good look at Dad's lumbar plexus (the nerve bundle that passes through both sides of the pelvis and runs down the back of both legs). He says he saw much less scar tissue on the left side than he did on right side during the previous surgery a month ago. He thinks because of the minimal scar tissue, there is a good chance Dad's nerves can wake up and regenerate on their own in the future! This is why he was smiling when he came out.

The surgery was a success, but the results have been extremely painful for Dad. He is on a healthy dose of pain meds to keep him comfortable, but he still has a lot of discomfort. Dr. Gottlieb prepared Dad for this reality after the last surgery, when Dad was given a 25-inch wound around his flank.

Dr. Gottlieb told Dad at that time, "You think this pain is bad? This is nothing. Just wait until we close your abdomen back up."

The moral of the story is that the surgery went well, but Dad is dealing with a whole lotta hurtin'. Although there is good news about the future of Dad's muscle weakness and foot drop on his left side that may not require surgery, Dad has a lot of recovery to do. This surgery will further delay Dad's physical therapy as well as he recuperates.

Mom says she is doing well overall, but is putting off her physical therapy for a while until she and Dad can go back in together.

Dallas

Saturday, October 16, 2010 6:11 p.m., MST

It has been about 12 days since surgery #17. I'm now to a point where I can, hopefully, give you a clear-headed update. I've been loaded up on pain medications for quite a while and I don't think anyone around here would have trusted me telling you like it is with all that happy juice on board!

Just be glad Dallas isn't on any when he writes his updates! What a nut!

It has taken a couple weeks of painful recovery to arrive at a decent level of relief. Dr. Gottlieb told me this would be a more painful recovery than the last one, and boy was he right! He is an incredible surgeon and spot on in his explanations of how things will go. I've come to really appreciate his skills and experience as he seeks to help me in my recovery. He really did an excellent job in this last surgery. My tummy now has returned to its upright and locked position.

Dr. Gottlieb removed the twelve-by-eighteen-inch skin graft on my abdomen and attempted to access the damaged nerves on my left side. It was a good news/bad news attempt.

The good news is from what he could see, there was much less scarring around the nerves than what was found on my right side in the August 9 surgery. The bad news was that it was not a good angle to try and get deep into my lumbar plexus area, so he could not do a full examination of all the nerves and do any decompressing procedures.

He told me we would have to decide later on if he should attempt the same surgery on my left side. That could mean another two-foot incision and digging deep down into my pelvic area to try and find the damaged nerves. He thinks my left side could improve without surgery because of the lack of scar tissue evident. The nerves could rebound over time, which would be great, but that's not guaranteed.

If you can imagine it, for sixteen months I had a huge opening in my abdomen, covered with skin grafts, and it's finally been repaired! All these months my core muscles were useless as they hung out around my sides, getting smaller and weaker from inactivity. Then, there are my innards, which have been enjoying sixteen months of extra elbow room, stretched out in comfort and space!

The best analogy I can come up with is they were living in a big mansion for sixteen months, and then Dr. Gottlieb relocated them to a studio apartment!

When the wound was finally closed up, everything inside me was compressed into a very tight space. That put pressure on my diaphragm (the lining between the chest and abdomen), which pushed up on my lungs and led to difficulty breathing in the initial days of recovery.

That combined with the swelling and pain in and around the long incision made for some very difficult days. After about a week, things started to get better. After nine days in the hospital I was released to come home. It is weird, though, because two hemovac units are still attached to me. These are vacuum pumps that are about the size of a small pancake with tubes that go into my abdomen to help drain the fluids and blood that keep oozing from the wound site.

Even though I'm home, I'm not ready to take LaDonna out on a date quite yet, for fear of my pancakes falling out! I can't wait for these accessories to be removed!

It was so good to get back home. My breathing has improved and the pain in the wound area is diminishing. I'm finally feeling up to getting out of bed into the wheelchair and returning to the level of functionality that I had prior to the surgery.

Now we look ahead toward the next surgical procedure with Dr. Duhon. These are all necessary, but each one seems more challenging and more wearing on my body.

My faith and trust in the Lord has not altered a bit through it all, and while the body continues to suffer, I look beyond that to see with anticipation what eternal purposes God has through these trials.

He gave me some insight in that regard through His Word the other day. I was reading in 2 Timothy 2:1, 3, 10 and 12, where He says, "You then, my son, be strong in the grace that is in Christ Jesus... Endure hardship with us like a good soldier of Christ Jesus.... Therefore I endure everything for the sake of the elect, that they too may obtain the salvation which is in Christ Jesus, with eternal glory... If we endure, we will also reign with Him."

I was struck with the reality that one of the purposes of suffering is to impact and affect other people, especially God's people (the elect). I was moved by the reality that what I'm going through has the potential of speaking encouragement and giving hope to God's people all the while they are motivated and mobilized to pray for the one suffering.

The number of folks shared with us through e-mails, phone calls, and face-to-face discussions that God is speaking to them through this ordeal. Knowing this has touched LaDonna and me deeply. We give praise to the Lord and count it a blessing to endure these hardships.

What God is doing in my own personal life is extra special to me as well. Some of the blessings include a new anticipation of things to come when eternity is mine. I'm promised a new body and a place where there will be no more tears, pain, and sorrow. That reality has never been stronger in my life than it is now.

Another blessing is the lack of attraction to the things of this world.

I was also reminded that if we endure, we would also reign with Him. None of us can say we fully understand what that means or how it will affect us when Christ returns.

All I know is one day our suffering will be over, the pain will be gone, and the glory of Christ will be all around us. We will be able to serve Him in some capacity that He determines us worthy of. What we are going through is a small blip on the radar screen in comparison to what lies ahead.

Our heart's desire is that God's people will be challenged, encouraged, and uplifted as we journey together down this road. Also, that lost people will find hope in Christ and be rescued, and His perfect plan for our lives will unfold one day at a time.

So we'll continue on, with great hope and faith, and trust you'll continue on with us as prayer warriors and encouragers.
Craig and LaDonna

Thursday, November 4, 2010 6:16 p.m., MST
CLOTHES HANGARS, WISHBONES, TOILET SEATS and UNCLE JED . . .

Greetings! It has been over four weeks since my last surgery and the recovery continues on what seems to be quite a long and slow road. It's hard to describe just how tough this last surgery was on my body, strength, and stamina.

I'm starting to feel my strength returning to a level that enables me to return to some of my normal activity and function. My therapists have worked me over good these past few weeks. These tired bones, ligaments, and muscles are starting to fire up again and the energy is returning. Thank you, Lord!

So what's up with the hangars, wishbones, toilet seats, and Uncle Jed, you ask? Well, it all has to do with my last weekly visit to Dr. Gottlieb.

When I saw him last week he was going over some of the issues they had to deal with during my surgery. Apparently, undergoing the kind of surgery done on me two summers ago often results in an interesting change in a person's body.

In my case, an incision was made from my breastbone all the way down to my belt line. That incision opened up about an 18-inch gap in my abdomen, which was covered with skin taken from my legs. Over time, the ends of the muscle that were cut go through change and turn into what he called "boney tissue."

In some people, it's a small thin ring of bone that resembles a coat hanger. In some, it's a bit thicker and it looks like a wishbone. In others, it becomes so thick that the surgeons like to call it a "toilet seat"! All that boney tissue has to be removed before the ends can be sutured back together.

I had to ask him, "What about me?"

He just smiled and said, "Yours was a wishbone!"

All the way home I was thanking the Lord that even though I broke just about every bone from my knees up to my mid back, at least I didn't grow a toilet seat in my abdominal cavity! Now that's something to be thankful for.

I am going to ask for a moment of silence, though, at our upcoming Thanksgiving feast, when we normally snap the wishbone. I've already apologized to the well over fifty turkeys that have suffered a similar fate in my over half-century of Thanksgiving celebrations.

Now the Uncle Jed part has me a bit more queasy. I learned another lesson in the Dr. Gottlieb School of amazing facts. It dealt with another part of the surgical procedure that reminds me of LaDonna's love for making quilts.

I previously mentioned my core muscles had shriveled up after sixteen months of inactivity. When Dr. Gottlieb finished removing the wishbone and tried to reintroduce the two sides, they really didn't want to come together. Seems they were enjoying the life of ease they'd gotten accustomed to.

In order to close me back up, he had to bridge the two sides with cadaver tissue. Please, look the definition up for yourself if needed, because I just can't bring myself to explain it to you.

So I asked him, "Do you mean I've got a bit of Uncle Jed in me?"

"Not sure if it was Jed or Grandma Moses," was what I recall him saying in reply.

In about a year I will need to have that piece taken out and then the finished reconstruction of the abdomen will be done. He said that if I didn't have that surgery, I'd stand the risk of ongoing hernia problems in that area. I wasn't really excited to hear about that, but I've come to appreciate honesty over holding things back from me as we make our way through this long recovery.

And so tomorrow, I'm back to see Dr. Gottlieb for my weekly visit. I wonder what strange new stories I'll hear or see tomorrow.

I'm very anxious to meet next week with Dr. Duhon to see when my hip revision surgery will happen. Dr. Gottlieb said he didn't want any more surgery until at least after Thanksgiving, so perhaps that will come between then and Christmas. It's a much-needed surgery because the hip pain continues to get worse and is hindering my ability to walk in PT.

I tried walking yesterday for the first time since the surgery. I was able to go about fifteen feet before running out of steam. It's a good start, and look forward to a few months down the road when, hopefully, a clean hip will allow me more mobility.

In the weeks that ensued my surgical wound healed well. I had a small opening at the bottom of the wound that just didn't want to close, though.

A visit back to Dr. Gottlieb's office turned into quite an experience as he once again surprised me with something new out of his limitless bag of tricks.

He took a good look at the wound that just wouldn't heal. The he took out a pair of grabbers and proceeded to, without numbing medicine, clean out the quarter size hole at the bottom of my surgery incision. Now before you pass out, don't worry, I'm numb there anyway so I couldn't feel anything.

I asked him what he was taking out and he quite bluntly said, "Your fat!"

I gave it right back to him, as I said, "Well don't stop now!"

He told his young intern that cleaning out the wound would help, so that in about four weeks it should be totally healed up.

The results a week later seemed to confirm his statement. The leaking and bleeding slowly subsided. LaDonna said it looked much better since Dr. Gottlieb's pruning.

When I got in bed that night LaDonna noticed a softball sized red patch on right side of the incision about belly button high. When she felt it, it was rock hard and warm. I liked the rock hard abs part, but the warm to touch had us worried about potential infection.

We called our nurse case manager who told us to high tail it to Good Sam's emergency room.

I sure didn't want to go there on a Friday night. Good Sam is one of only a few level-one trauma centers in the Phoenix area. Friday nights are always one of their busiest times. Around midnight we finally were ushered back to see the ER physician.

A somewhat shy EMT student asked if she could practice taking my vital signs. Here was another chance to freak out an up-and-coming healthcare professional. Always willing to oblige, I said, "Sure, go right ahead."

She took a few steps back and stared. There, in living color, was my infamous colostomy bag.

"Ewwwww, what's THAT?" she gasped.

I told her what it was called.

"Ewwwww, what's in it?"

All I could think of saying as I tried to control my laughter was, "I think that's breakfast and lunch!"

I told her that when I fly, the airlines make me claim it as a carry-on bag, and one airline even had the audacity to charge me $25. "That's why I fly Southwest. Bags fly free!"

Needless to say, she didn't take my vitals! I never saw her again; I was hoping I would, because I wanted to ask her, "Why do you think they call this place a *Trauma Center*?"

The ER doc came in after reading some of my history stored in their files. He did a quick evaluation and all previous hilarity quickly ground to a halt.

With a real look of concern on his face, he said I would definitely need to be admitted, and blood work and a CT scan of my abdomen would be done immediately. He added that because this had appeared so quickly, it could spread rapidly and become life threatening if infection was involved.

Here we were, back at Good Sam, undergoing another barrage of tests and being admitted in the middle of the night.

LaDonna and Nizhoni got home at 4:30 a.m., as I settled back into my second home for an unplanned overnight stay.

Dr. Gottlieb's partner, Dr. Dhillon, saw me in the morning and explained that it was fluid build-up. All indications told him there were no bugs present to turn it into infection. That was the best news I could hear. He discharged me that afternoon and said he wanted to see me in the wound care clinic in a few days. That was one appointment I planned to keep.

Dr. Dhillon did a procedure during the clinic appointment where he stuck a big needle (aren't they all?) into the red spot and sucked out about eighty cc's of fluid. He planned to repeat the process in a week to see if the fluid build-up was subsiding, in which case they wouldn't have to do anything else. He said that if, in a week, the spot had the same or more fluid than the amount originally extracted, they would have to do a surgical procedure to "collapse the void" where the fluid was building up.

Along with that unscheduled weekend jubilee, I was able to see Dr. Duhon in his office in Scottsdale. He was finally ready to get the hip surgery scheduled. He hoped to have Dr. Gottlieb and possibly a vascular surgeon there as a precaution due to the proximity of major arteries and veins near the excess bone growth.

Getting two or three very busy surgeons to coordinate their schedules became an interesting process. It was nearly impossible, as I came to find out.

We continued on the long recovery road through the end of 2010. New Year's Eve arrived and the dawning of a new year was upon us, I was moved to share my heart with our friends and prayer warriors through another CaringBridge post.

Friday, December 31, 2010 11:25 p.m., MST
GOODBYE TO 2010, HELLO TO OUR FUTURE!

While the rest of the world is ringing in the New Year with celebrations and gusto, I have to say it's relatively quiet here in our neck of the cactuses.

We just said goodnight to our little grandbabies as Dad and Mom Lucas took our precious little ones home after watching our beloved Phoenix Coyotes fall to the St. Louis Blues.

LaDonna, Gramma Fern and LaDonna's brother, Rockford, are enjoying a game of Rummikub, and I've settled in for another one of my long winter naps! We've got just under an hour before this year ends, but I have to say I'm really thankful for the quiet time I'm having here in my room as I contemplate the end of this very interesting year.

Early in the year, I blogged about feeling like I was traveling on Highway 50 in Nevada. You know, that long, straight, never-ending stretch of highway in the middle of nowhere. Well, as we come to the end of the year, I really have to say it seems like we're still on that road and will be for some time to come!

It has been an amazing blend of painful yet peaceful days when the body hurts but the spirit keeps being renewed each day. I've never been in as much physical pain on a constant basis than what I have experienced in 2010. I come to the end of this year with a deeper sense of hope and confidence in the One whom I cling to more than I ever have.

There has been many a day when LaDonna and I, in our private moments, have shed tears for each other, and then later in the day found renewed strength and encouragement in a timely word from a faithful friend or prayer partner, whom God had led specifically to pray for us that day.

The physical aspect of the journey I can understand and get my arms around much easier than I can the spiritual, though I've walked with the Lord these many years. What I mean by that is we both know our bodies have been severely affected by the accident, and unless the Lord supernaturally intervenes, we will face the remaining years of our lives in pain-filled bodies.

What counters those realities, though, are the divine interventions, both big and small, that clearly indicate to us the Lord is near us and has us in His care. We don't ever know when, how, or through whom these divine visits will show up. I can tell you for sure they've shown up on a regular basis and for that we're extremely grateful! He often uses people in the process of manifesting Himself to us. Whether it is an act of kindness, a phone call of encouragement, a special visit or even special provisions, we see His hand clearly on a daily basis.

This blog really isn't about doctor appointments or upcoming surgeries. There will be time for that next year. What I wanted to do is spend some of these last few minutes of the year with you, our praying friends and family who mean so much to us, to just say thanks for rolling down this long highway with us.

We're grateful for you, and know as we turn this New Year corner, we do so living in the expectation of those continued divine interventions!

Happy New Year to you and yours!

Craig and LaDonna

As I noted in a subsequent CaringBridge post around this time, "So that's the news from Lake Painbegone, where all the joints are sore, the muscles are letting me know they are not happy, and all my pain medicines are above average!"

Only staunch Minnesotans and listeners to National Public Radio will understand what I just said.

Chapter 19

HIP HIP HORRAY

After months and months of waiting for one of the most important surgeries in my recovery, I finally had a date set from Dr. Duhon and Dr. Erickson—March 8.

We were told that, along with these two surgeons, a second ortho surgeon and a second vascular assistant would be involved as well. I guess my hips were something extra special that needed extra hands on deck! I'm not sure if I should have been happy about that or embarrassed.

Dr. Erickson's role as a vascular surgeon was to assist Dr. Duhon as he cut and removed the excess bone. Dr. Erickson would be ready to repair any potential tears to these important vessels.

I was reminded about what Erin, the flight nurse told me months ago. I was bleeding out in the pelvic region from bone fragments that had cut into veins and arteries in the legs. I was at death's door then, and thankfully God providentially spared my life. It gave me great confidence to look at what was coming up next knowing my Sovereign Lord was fully in control of it all.

We reached another milestone in early 2011 when the doctors determined that LaDonna had reached *maximum medical improvement.* This was a determination that had both medical and legal ramifications.

Insurance laws require this designation be made in order to allow an injured employee to return to work. It doesn't mean the patient is pain-free or will not need medical care in the future.

It does mean enough progress has been made that the patient is capable of returning to the duties prior to the accident. LaDonna had progressed remarkably well, in light of the injuries she had sustained. She was alive and walking, though after-effects still linger, including neck stiffness, pain, and short-term memory loss.

I was happy for all the progress she had made, but cautious in my exuberance, knowing that there were still issues she had to deal with, both physically and emotionally.

She was committed to caring for me, despite her own challenges and also took on the care of her aging mother after her father died. Three generations were now living in our daughter's house, and our lives were nothing close to normal anymore. Still, with all that pressure on her, she returned to work.

The time was fast approaching for the hip revision surgery. Dr. Duhon had me running all over the Valley of the Sun getting preoperative tests, cardiac clearances, X-rays, etc. that took several weeks to complete. Thankfully, all the tests got done, and I was cleared for this much-needed surgery.

I didn't want anything to stand in the way of getting this surgery. The anticipation of remedying this issue has been with me since first being diagnosed with *heterotopic ossification* in October of 2009! A year and a half of pain and limitations in mobility could soon be history. That would be wonderful!

I had some incredible times with the Lord during this season, and His Word continued to bring great encouragement and comfort. I affirm what King David said in Psalms 119:92–93, "If your law had not been my delight, I would have perished in my affliction. I will never forget your precepts, for by them you have preserved my life."

It's hard to describe the sustaining grace and peace the Lord continued to give me, even in this weakened condition. Some brothers came by to visit and pray with me. As I looked at my situation, all I could say was, "It's OK; I'm in good hands."

The goodness of the Lord was like a blanket that covered my being, and His peace was like a pillow that I laid my head on as I did my best to simply rest in Him.

I remembered old Jake Hess, who spent a lifetime singing gospel music and was a singer Elvis Presley wanted to emulate. One of the classic songs he'd sing is, "Death Ain't No Big Deal." I smiled whenever I heard him sing it, because those lyrics are so true. I can say that now, having been at death's door, that death really ain't no big deal!

I came to this surgery, knowing it was a potentially dangerous one. A team of surgeons would be in the room in case something went wrong. I had to be ready to face whatever outcome surgery would bring.

For the first time in our marriage, LaDonna and I had to have the conversation nobody wants to have, but must have if they are facing a life-threatening situation. The potential of something unfortunate happening and my life ending on a surgical table was very real.

What would LaDonna do if the unthinkable happened? Where were all our important documents, life insurance policies, etc? Where would I want to be buried, and what would I want to have for a funeral service?

I needed to tell her; she needed to know. After a lot of tears we ended up going to the Lord in prayer, surrendering our uncertain future to Him, and entrusting our lives to the only One who has the power to give and to take life from us. Once again, He gave us His peace. The kind that Scripture says "passes all understanding."

It was settled. It was done. We were ready for what would come.

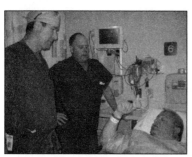

Discussing the surgery with Drs. Duhon (ortho) and Erickson (vascular).

Tuesday, March 8, 2011
3:32 p.m., MST
Dad's surgery to repair the heterotopic ossification that has encapsulated his hip, restricted movement, and prevented physical therapy improvements was performed today. To get right to the point, I am pleased to say he has made it safely through the procedure. He is alert and awake, and is already feeling improvements from what his surgeons did today!

According to Dr. Duhon, everything went well, and as far as he is concerned, it was a success! He said that prior to the surgery, Dad's hip was almost unmovable—possibly due to the pain during movement—so once Dad had been knocked out with the anesthetic, they tried to move his leg and his hip again to see if some of the restriction in movement was non-pain related. He said that Dad's leg was almost fused into his hip due to the bone growth, and they realized how serious that growth had become.

They were able to free up most of the bone growth and replaced the head of the femur (the ball of the hip) and the acetabulum (the lining of the socket of the hip) to give Dad a fresh start again.

They were able to free up his hip movement to 90 degrees of flexion (you need this to sit down correctly), and 20 degrees of internal rotation, and 45 degrees of external rotation (which you need to shimmy and shake yo' booty on the dance floor). On the side of the hip that is towards center of the body was where the important blood vessels run.

They were unable to get all of the bone growth cleared out of that area. They thought the risk of trying to get that part out and accidentally causing a massive loss of blood outweighed the benefit. Extra bone growth on that side of the hip wouldn't impede his movement too much anyway.

Now that they've cleared out the hip, there are a lot of open spaces in the soft tissue where the bone used to be. Soft tissue holds the bone in and usually stabilizes the hip, so they will monitor Dad closely as he starts to bear weight to make sure the hip doesn't dislocate easily. Dad will most likely have a limp from now on, but getting him walking is the important goal right now.

He is now awake and resting in his room, and smiling ear to ear. He says when the nurses were adjusting his legs and moving them, he can't feel any of the terrible pain he noticed before! He has already sprung out of bed and challenged the nursing staff to limbo contests since waking up and . . . er, no, maybe that's not true, but we're hoping he WILL make leaps and bounds in his recovery process as a result of this surgery.

The next step is for Dad to get radiation treatments (like the ones given in cancer treatment) to prevent the bone from growing back into those open spaces. This will take place tomorrow.

Good news, excellent results so far, and a happy Dad, and that's a good day of surgery.

Dallas

P.S. My wife Elizabeth and I are expecting a baby boy in July! We had a 22-week ultrasound today and he looks healthy and ready to make Dad a grandfather again! Sweet!

The pain and lack of mobility had peaked at its worst in the months leading up to this surgery. I could barely move my left leg, and when I did it was accompanied by excruciating pain. When I was in my wheelchair, the stiff leg would push up on my upper body and lean my torso off to the right so much that my body was hanging over the right side of the wheelchair. This ever-increasing misalignment of my spine was producing really bad back pain as well.

How thankful I was that God was pleased to answer our prayers by guiding Dr. Duhon and team through to a very successful surgery. The hindrances that were holding up my progress have been removed and now my rehab future looked more promising than ever. There was an immediate result; I felt that my quality of life had already improved dramatically.

Physical therapy came by that first evening and began to move my leg. My initial response was to tighten up and get ready to yell, but no yell was necessary! For the first time since the accident my leg moved without resistance and the pain so often accompanying me was left back in the operating room.

Thank you Lord!

Day two was a mix of celebration and some challenge as I began the healing process in earnest. The therapists came back in the morning and did more exercises with both legs. How wonderful it was to cooperate with them and be able to do so again without hindrance and pain. I sat at the edge of the bed for a half hour, looking normal at a ninety-degree angle.

I mused, "I'm kinda liking this new chapter in my life!"

One of the procedures scheduled was to undergo radiation treatment directed at the hip. I was wheeled over to another building and for an hour or so endured lying on that hard slab, which was still so difficult on my pelvis.

As I was undergoing the treatment I suddenly got hit with extreme light-headedness and nausea. It was a really awful feeling made worse by the bumpy ride back to my room.

My internist told me I was anemic due to some major blood loss during surgery. He contemplated giving me blood transfusions (they had already infused some of my own blood back into me through an interesting filtering system) but wanted to wait and see how I would do over the next few days.

Dr. Duhon thought it was a combination of blood loss and high dosages of pain medicines. One of the things he did was reduce my pain med intake, which I was happy with.

The downside of that decision was I began to feel more acutely the pain in the leg from the surgical procedure. Imagine hitting your shin on a sharp object and how that feels for a few hours—enough said!

The next two days in hospital were tough ones but my numbers started climbing back up. All I wanted to do was go home. On Saturday I was well enough to be discharged but still felt totally lethargic and weak.

One of the highlights of this season of surgeries has been my frequent office visits with Dr. Duhon. He's a wonderful surgeon and definitely knows the Lord. He shared how God was using us among the medical personnel who interacted with us. Those were encouraging words to LaDonna and me.

He asked me for permission to tell my story to his small group Bible study. God once again used our story for His glory!

That's all that matters! It's what Paul said in Philippians 1:12: "Now I want you to know, brothers, that what happened to me has really served to advance the gospel . . ."

There was a Native ministry conference going on in Phoenix around the time of this surgery. Many of the ministry colleagues we've been in the trenches with for decades were in town, and my desire was to see them. It would be such an encouragement to me just to renew old friendships. I was asked to speak at the conference as well.

I had a lot to say to these dear co-workers from my vantage point on the sidelines. I wanted to encourage them as they continue on in the front lines of the spiritual battles they were engaged in throughout the Western Hemisphere. These indigenous leaders were coming from North, Central, and South America.

Eight days after this major surgery they wheeled me into the conference center. Oh what a joy it was for me to be back among my friends and colleagues. My spirit was encouraged, my body was getting better, and it looked like my future dreams were closer than they had ever been.

Chapter 20

LET THESE HORSES RUN!

Friday, April 22, 2011 9:24 a.m., MST

Greetings from the bearer of some pretty good news! It looks like the long and painful chapter of pain and hindered recovery has finally come to an end.

It has been a little over six weeks since the surgery to revise my left hip. Yesterday afternoon I was back seeing Dr. Duhon for my six-week follow-up visit.

Since the surgery he has had me on weight bearing restrictions to allow the site to heal properly. Even though my hip was now freed up and the pain was gone, I still couldn't stand or attempt to walk until those restrictions were lifted. All my therapists could do was muscle-strengthening exercises to help me get ready for when I would be released from those restrictions.

Although my horses were ready to run, it took a lot of patience to keep them corralled.

My visit to Dr. Duhon started out with getting a set of X-rays that he could look over prior to coming in and visiting with us. In months past just getting onto an X-ray table was excruciating for me. The transferring from my specialty cushion on the wheelchair onto the hard slab was difficult, and the movement of my legs to get the right angles for the X-rays would make other patients wonder what forms of torture were going on behind those closed doors!

But this time it was different. My transfer was painless and involved only limited help from the technicians. Even laying on the slab was more tolerable to my very damaged backside, and there was no problem with me complying with the various poses needed to show off my healing body. I hadn't even seen the doctor yet and already I could tell great progress had been made.

The smile on Dr. Duhon's face when he entered the room was indicative of the good news he would share with us. "The X-rays indicate no reforming of the heterotopic bone," he said.

And then he gave me the news I've been looking forward to hearing for a long time: "I'm lifting the restrictions, and I'm moving you to *weight bearing as tolerated!*"

It's time to open the corral gate and let these horses run!

I'll be going in later today to the therapy gym and anxiously anticipating the moment when I stand and take those first few steps. My excitement is balanced with the reality that while the surgery did wonders for my hip, I still face real challenges with the effects of the nerve damage to my legs.

I still have numbness in parts of both legs, and while some nerves have awakened, most of my leg muscles still are not receiving the signal from the brain to kick in and participate with the others. Over half of my legs are still on vacation and haven't gotten the "return to work" memo sent out long ago.

Still to be determined is my ability to go from a sitting to a standing position, and how far I will be able to walk without having to stop and rest. At least now the hindrances that have held up my rehabilitation are a thing of the past. The next few months will determine, apart from further divine intervention, how much mobility I can expect to regain.

We continue to trust the Lord for His perfect will and plan to unfold for us. He has carried us through the deepest and most treacherous waters, and we continue to rest in His timeless truths that undergird all we do.

Many of you have walked with us throughout this whole ordeal, while others of you have joined with us somewhere along the way. We want you to know you all are greatly appreciated! I know you rejoice with us in this great news and will continue to be there with us as we start writing this new chapter.

Up on the right corner of the website it gives the number of times this website has been accessed by family, friends, and prayer warriors. I like the way it states the number of *visits* from family and friends.

Throughout this journey we've been blessed to have family and friends pay us encouraging visits in the hospitals, trauma centers, ICU units, rehab facilities, and visits at home. All these visits have been such an encouragement.

I'm equally amazed that through this website, almost 25,000 times our friends, family, and prayer warriors have paid us visits as well. You bring us such joy and encouragement as we share our journey with you. Your words of encouragement and intercessory prayer to the Father on our behalf have given us strength and courage to keep on going. The wonderful answers to prayer remind us every day there's no safer and better place to be than in the center of His will and covering.

It won't be long before we see the counter hit 25,000. I wonder who will be the one to put us over that amazing mark? Maybe we should have a contest and give a prize to contestant #25,000!

The Grand Prize will be all the leftover medical supplies we won't need once I'm up and walking! Any takers?

Until next time,

Craig and LaDonna

P.S. from LaDonna: Craig failed to tell you about the one restriction he still has. He still has to sport those cute ortho-pedic compression knee-hi stockings for a few more weeks. I should post a picture of him in his summer shorts and tees. He's too cute for words.

I began to settle back in again at the therapy gym. I was excited about what the future might look like, but cautious about my mind and heart not getting too far ahead of a still very beaten body. I decided to wait a few weeks before updating folks on how things were going. I didn't want to jump out of my chair on day one and give a false impression of major progress only to have to report on day two that the paramedics had to come to pick me up off the ground after doing a half-gainer!

I was reminded that the healing process is done best slowly and methodically. It's that kind of progress that gives you the best and most honest appraisal on how things really are shaping up.

Things were looking up for me, but it wasn't coming easy.

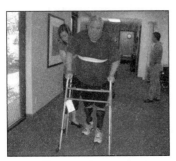

Finally starting to get my land legs back.

I spent about three weeks walking with the help of a walker and somewhat nervous therapists spotting me along the way. I began to see my stride returning, but my body was still feeling the effects of a very damaged pelvic region that let me know it's more happy in the comfort and safety of being in the sitting or semi-reclined position!

My excitement about my new mobility was tempered by the realization of still having to intentionally think about each step I take and having to will my legs into action.

Once I got rolling I hit an encouraging stride and began to see incremental lengthening of the distances I was able to go without tiring. The best walk came on a Monday when I felt strong enough to walk the length of the therapy gym and even do a lap around the parallel bars before stopping for a brief rest on one of the padded therapy tables. It was then back on my feet for a full-length march back to the starting point and a fairly painless dismount back into the wheelchair! It was the longest stretch I had taken in almost two years! It was such a great feeling to have gone that far and done so well.

The next day walking was much more difficult and my stamina was reduced. I walked about the same distance as the day before, but my body cried out most of the way to return to the locked and upright position of my nice comfortable wheelchair.

It's hard to describe how challenging walking is when for over fifty years it was something that came naturally and without any thought. Imagine having to think about each step and convincing a less-than-cooperative leg to lift and move forward. All the while I was doing that, I had to prepare the other leg to get ready to do the same.

I had to tell my body to straighten up enough to put the weight bearing on my legs and not on my quickly fatiguing arms. Those extremities needed attention; they were holding for dear life onto a highly movable and somewhat shaky old walker!

Believe me, it pays to be a good multi-tasker when you are forced to rehab your body this way!

What improved much more dramatically for me, in comparison to the walking, was my quality of life. We have a piece of equipment at home called a standing frame. I would need to utilize it everyday for one hour. Its purpose is to safely and securely bring someone like me, who can't do so on my own, to a standing position. It allows the legs and feet to bear weight again, which builds up the muscles, ligaments, bones, and tendons in people who have not been standing for a long time. The funny part about it, though, is it makes you feel like a bagel in a toaster.

Before my surgery, I couldn't even get in the frame due to the pain in my hip. LaDonna and others would have to struggle just to help me with the use of a slide board to get over to it. I would crank the lever to get to a standing position, the pain would be excruciating, both going up and coming down. Disembarking back onto the wheelchair was worse and we came to a point where we just couldn't do it anymore.

Now, I easily slid over without pain, lifting myself enough to put the padded leg braces in place without anyone's help. I was pain-free in the standing and sitting process!

A couple of times when LaDonna had been busy in the other room, I was able to slide myself back onto the wheelchair, put my wheelchair leg plates back into position and even smile with glee as a very surprised wife walked back in the room!

My progress enabled us to get out of the house more often. We began to enjoy those special times out including those extra special *stop for coffee moments* that we weren't able to do for months on end!

Encouraged by our progress, we decided another trip was doable.

Tuesday, May 31, 2011 9:15 p.m., MST

Nine months after the accident we flew to Chicago to speak at a weekend ministry conference at the Billy Graham Center at Wheaton College. After that we took about three weeks to go "home" to Minnesota for some much-needed rest and relaxation in July 2010.

The third trip took us to Kansas City to attend the 2011 General Council of The Christian and Missionary Alliance (our church denomination's biennial gathering). We just returned home.

While still difficult to travel, the struggles faded away in comparison to the joy in seeing many friends and ministry colleagues we've worked with for over four decades. We were moved to tears as warm hugs and embraces turned into long conversations about the goodness of God.

We sat under the incredible teaching of one of the world's greatest communicators, Dr. Ravi Zacharias. We heard the healing story of one of our dear friends, Pastor John Stumbo, whose own journey of pain and suffering mirrors ours.

I laughed when John told the stories of his hallucinations while in his coma, knowing all too well the crazy underworld we shared. I was brought to tears as he honored his dear wife who has stood by his side. I've seen the hand of God serving me through my amazing wife as well.

At the end of John's message, time was taken to anoint and pray for healing. Hundreds gathered around the broken and wounded, including me. This was the highlight of our trip.

Scripture says we are to "bear one another's burdens," and so many did on our behalf. This trip became an integral part of our healing. Not only are our bodies healing, our soul and spirit are "rehabbing" as well.

On the trip home I pondered the importance of the healing of the total person. One can't heal in body alone when deeply wounded. The inner man needs healing as well. The good news is that God is sufficient to do it all if we let Him.

"Jed and Granny" did well on the outbound portion of the trip, but returning home can only be described as a comedy of errors.

Our driver picked us up at the hotel at 4 p.m. to get us to our 6 p.m. flight. Our phones alerted us of a three-hour delay. That's when the fun began. Jets may be wide body, but aisles aren't.

The two-and-a-half-hour flight was tolerable thanks to those really cool and powerful "happy pills" LaDonna rarely has to give me.

We finally arrived in Phoenix about 10:30 p.m. After all the passengers deplaned, the wheelchair helpers came on board to get me. We made it as far as the passenger ramp and waited for my power chair. I was so happy to see it, knowing I could soon tilt back and lift the load off my achy-breaky tailbone.

Bad news—the electronics in the chair refused to cooperate and a very heavy chair and me needed a push up the passenger ramp. Two young helpers got a real workout getting me to the terminal. Then I realized where we were—at the very end of the longest concourse in Sky Harbor Airport!

Two US Airways gate agents, just finishing up their shift, joined these two young helpers. A very techie young man tried getting info from his smart phone about the chair after phone calls to sleepy chair reps proved unprofitable.

The only option now for these tired airport workers was to manually push and tug the chair and me the distance. We met up with our daughter, Nizhoni, at the security checkpoint. The helpers were so kind to keep pushing me all the way to the van. After a few more grunts, I was safely in and ready to go home. I was never so happy to tip a person! Dallas agreed to get up out of bed and meet us at the house and help off-load "cargo" Dad.

What a blessing to finally get home!

Traveling is still hard for me, but the joy of ministry exceeds the challenges. We're back to cruising speed to see how much further we can go in the next leg of the journey.

Though a bit weary, we are ready to press on! Thanks for being there with us along the way.

We are so grateful.

Craig

P.S. From LaDonna: We circled the airport for forty extra minutes before landing in Kansas City. Once we landed and got settled in our room, we were startled by a bullhorn announcement that nearly sent us through the roof. A tornado was approaching and we needed to take cover. Craig and I headed for the stairwell on the 8th floor, but not until he ran over my foot trying to get out of the bathroom! Whew!!! Ask him for the rest of the story when you see him sometime! (Why are handicap rooms on the eighth floor, anyway?)

Monday, July 11, 2011 9:59 a.m., MST

He's Here!!!

One of the great blessings of my extended life...Getting to be grandpa again!

What a thrill to announce this morning the arrival of our much-anticipated grandson, Colin Matthew Smith! Weighing in at a healthy 8 lbs., 15 oz., he joined our family last night at 7:52 p.m. Both Colin and his mom, Elizabeth, are doing well. What a proud moment for me to put my arms around my son last night as we thanked the Lord for this incredible blessing to their family.

Those who have been following all the challenges our family has faced in the past few years know that the arrival of this new life is cause for great rejoicing!

I'm so thankful LaDonna and I are alive to witness his arrival. It has put a new step into my not-so-good steps!

We believe that in 2011 we will continue to see the fulfillment of many of your prayers on our behalf. While the past few years have been years of great trial and tribulation, we are now enjoying a year of restoration, healing and hope.

To God be the glory!

Grandpa Craig

My time at Touchstone Rehabilitation was filled with intense therapy for sure, but we were having a great time doing it! Mr. Bonarati awkwardly greeted me most days wondering what surprises I'd have up my sleeve for him.

Practical jokes abound in these places, and Touchstone had their fair share of characters that covertly doubled as injured patients. Some of us were experts in the field and it was often our only way to get back at these therapists for the pain they inflicted on us as they pushed us to the limit. I'd often tell Dan that I just couldn't understand how I had to do all the work, and he got all the money!

Touchstone shared facilities with another therapy company called Swan. Combined, the number of patients on a given day varied, but it always seemed to be *sitting* room only (we're mostly in wheelchairs, OK?). Touchstone's focus was on spinal cord injuries; Swan's was on neurological needs, such as brain injuries, strokes, etc.

In our years of ministry, LaDonna and I found great joy and satisfaction as we invested our lives in the next generation. We loved mentoring and encouraging younger people in ministry and that love spilled over into our time in the PT world.

Part of Dan's business model was to provide supervised internships to new therapists who were almost finished with their schooling. PT students have to do a number of internships, all over the country. Most of Dan's students were there for eight-week stints—just long enough for us to build great friendships with them, and then they were off to their next assignment. It was both a joy and a trial, because I always hated seeing these "kids" leave.

The students usually had their hands full when they were assigned to me. The myriad of injuries I had offered them an 'all-you-can-eat' smorgasbord of therapy options on a daily basis. So many things needed their attention, and they could practice on injured parts not often present in your average run-of-the-mill patient.

One of the gals, Danika, became a great friend to LaDonna and me. She worked on me during some of the darkest and most painful days of my years at Touchstone when it seemed everything in my body was breaking down.

As she was finishing her time at Touchstone, she honored us with an invitation to her upcoming graduation from PT school. She would soon become Dr. Danika. We were thrilled with the invitation and made plans to be in the crowd that day.

As we arrived at the facility on graduation day we spotted her in the line-up of excited cap and gowned students ready to march down the aisle, turn their tassels, and set sail on their new careers. We went up and gave her a big hug and told her we were so excited for her. Just then we heard a yell from down the line-up!

"Craig and LaDonna!"

We turned, and there was another fellow student, Sara, who also spent time at Touchstone, running over to greet us. Then we heard another yell from another part of the room. Soon we were surrounded by five students who were among the graduating class. It was a privilege to join them for this important milestone in their lives.

I'm glad to know they are finally earning a paycheck instead of having to put out all those funds for tuition, travel and everything else associated with earning their degree. I told them that a part of my body has gone into that paper they will now hang proudly on the wall, so don't forget I helped you earn it!

l-r. Sara, Kristen, Lucy, LaDonna, Danika and me (not pictured... Tracy).

Right after the graduation ceremonies LaDonna and I returned home to Minnesota for another extended rest from a full year of surgeries and rehab. The first time we were able to be at the cabin was so refreshing for us, and we knew that another good dose of Minnesota nice and Minnesota accents would do our bodies good.

PT continued, but so did making memories. There's nothing like a good shore lunch cooked up by good friends at the cabin. Simple joys amidst the challenges were even more important to us now as well as a greater appreciation for our friends and loved ones. We just love the times when good friends come by for coffee and a good long visit at the lake.

It didn't take long, though, to find out our trip home would be nothing like we anticipated. I would turn from walleye-eating patient to walleye-eating prayer warrior.

Pastor/Fishing Guide, John Dainsberg fixing an amazing shore lunch.

We got a call late one night. My oldest brother, Russ, had been experiencing a medical condition that resulted in him being taken by ambulance to our Indian hospital in Cass Lake.

Russ has been one of those faithful followers of our journey through CaringBridge. Our hearts broke when we found out he had been suffering with this condition for a while. Further testing revealed a large tumor and he underwent surgery. The following week or so would tell the extent of the spread of this tumor.

So there I was one night, sitting by his hospital bed, thinking about the irony of me being so often the one in that bed in need of prayer and divine intervention. Now here was my brother, the one who was consistently on the receiving end of these updates, being the one who needed an army of prayer warriors to fight on his behalf. Our CaringBridge site expanded as we called on our many praying friends to include Russ in their prayers as well.

Thankfully, Russ pulled through this ordeal, but not without great challenge and effort on his part. Our time "up North" became a time where we were there for Russ, and everything else became secondary.

We love being back home, and every stay is always too short. So it was with this one. The days flew by and it was time to turn our bodies back to the Southwest in anticipation of my next surgery, which now had a date in Dr. Gottlieb's schedule book.

We didn't want to leave, though, without a time of thankfulness for how God had been working in our family.

Wednesday, September 14, 2011 8:15 a.m., MST
Thanksgiving in September
Dear friends,

Greetings once again from "Up North," where tonight the lows are expected to be in the upper 20s! Can you believe it? Fall is definitely in the air. We've been having a great time back home and enjoying a steady stream of friends, family, and good times, along with navigating through some stormy seas as mentioned last time. We've also been blessed to share the story of God's faithfulness in some of the area churches, many of which have been praying so diligently for us.

We've had many a great meal together out on the deck with family and friends, but tonight will be extra special as we gather for what we're calling our *Thanksgiving in September.* We have much to thank God for, including both the good and the "bad" experiences and challenges that our family has faced.

There definitely is some good news to celebrate pertaining to my brother Russ. After a successful surgery to remove a large tumor, we got word that the biopsy indicated he has a form of cancer called Seminoma. There were a few nervous days before he had his first visit with the radiation/chemo doctors who are working together to chart out his course of treatment. Two days ago his radiologist told him that the course of treatment he would undergo should take care of the cancer.

"This is treatable and curable, Russ," were his words.

It may take a few months of treatments, but we trust the Lord for full recovery for him. We're grateful for your intercession on his behalf and he thanks you as well!

I'm also thankful that we now have a date confirmed for my 19th surgery. I got a call recently that this abdominal reconstruction surgery will take place on October 11th in Scottsdale, Arizona. I've seen much progress in my walking since my 18th surgery last March, and I anticipate similar progress in my standing and balance abilities after this one. Dr. Gottlieb will be finishing the reattaching of my core muscles. I plan to graduate from a Weeble who wobbles and falls down to one who won't.

First Thessalonians 5:18 reminds us, "In everything give thanks for this is God's will for you in Christ Jesus."

We don't have to wait till November to stop and give thanks. It should be an attitude of the heart every day, regardless of the circumstances. Since we'll be in warmer country in November, what better time than just before we head south with the snowbirds to gather the family and friends and celebrate God's goodness with a thankful heart and feast.

So even though it'll only be 50 degrees outside, we're looking forward to cousin Steve's deep fried turkey, LaDonna's ham, potatoes, stuffing and gravy, Roberta's green bean casserole, Joel's mac salad, Aunt Barb's salad, those fresh baked buns, pumpkin and apple pies and everything else that will show up tonight; all as we celebrate the goodness of the Lord. Good luck, Dr. Gottlieb, in trying to attach those core abs after tonight's meal!

We're grateful for God's grace, and grateful for you, dear friend!

Craig and LaDonna

Well, that evening the temperatures dipped, and the cold rains pounded our uninsulated cabin. It was an unexpected storm that took even the weathermen by surprise. About twenty-five of our closest family and friends ended up being squeezed into our nine-by-fifteen-foot living room. People were literally crawling over each other to get to the food in the kitchen. It was a wild night, but oh, was it fun, and a night we will not soon forget!

Chapter 21

ANYBODY SEEN MY SIX-PACK ABS?

Sunday, October 9, 2011 9:07 a.m., MST

19th Surgery Two Days Away

Dear Friends,

Is it possible to say with a straight face that you are really looking forward to an upcoming five-hour surgery, especially when it's the 19th one in less than two-and-a-half years? Well, to be honest with you, I really am.

When the body has been so severely affected by trauma, and you live with decreased abilities, the hope that help will come through your body being once again traumatically invaded, I've found, is a real genuine emotion and thought.

The surgery really isn't the tough part. A couple of needles into your vein and then IV fluid starts to carry the powerful medications that will take you down into another submarine experience. As you are being wheeled up to the operating table you start corralling the thoughts of impending doom. Then you *willingly* help the attendants slide your body onto the table when you know full well what is about to happen to you.

You hear the anesthesiologist say, "You're going to go to sleep now and we'll see you in the recovery room."

Then its lights out and the next thing you know you're rolling down a hallway heading to your new home for the next four or five days. That's the easy part.

The hard part is what comes next. The road to recovery is difficult, often painful, but you continue to be motivated by the assurance that what was done to your body was not intended to hurt you, but to help you. Sometimes the results are immediate, like the evening of my 18th surgery when the therapists came into my room and actually moved my left leg far beyond what I could for almost two years. The months that followed that event have resulted in me regaining more mobility than I have had since the accident! The potential help of this surgery holds out similar hope for improvement as well.

After two and a half years of not having functioning core muscles, all the King's men will finally be putting this Humpty Dumpty back together again—at least as much as can be after being so broken.

Dr. Gottlieb, Dr. Duhon, and the other surgeons are the King's men, on my behalf, because so many of you have joined together in prayer to the King of kings. They have been Christ's hands of healing, and I'm so thankful for each and every one of them.

I've often heard that the core muscles are important for so many things, and I've sure missed their involvement in my attempts at regained mobility.

A year ago, Dr. Gottlieb did the first part of the reconstruction surgery, and my ability to hold myself up improved. Now as I'm walking more, I struggle greatly with balance issues because the core muscles are not fully attached. I'm anticipating that I will be able to stand for longer periods of time, balance much better, and improve my walking after I heal up from the procedure.

There's a lot on our plate between now and then. Tomorrow the leadership team that oversees our ministry will be assembling here in Phoenix for a full day of committee meetings. They will meet and interact with my therapists and the insurance folks that oversee our medical and rehab care.

It's an honor to serve with these godly men. I am so glad they will be with us in advance of the surgery to pray with us and for us.

God's presence is very real, and every challenge has been met and exceeded by His grace and mercy.

Our journey through trauma and trials has been great, but our God is greater.

"Near the cross, I'll watch and wait,
    Hoping, trusting, ever;
Till I reach that golden strand,
    Just beyond the river.
Near the cross, near the cross,
    Be my glory ever;
Till my ransomed soul shall find
    Rest beyond the river!"

If you're looking for me, you'll find me camped at the foot of His cross!

Looking forward to sharing God's goodness again with you the other side of the surgery.

Peace,

Craig

Friday, October 21, 2011 12:38 p.m., MST

Girdles and Kudos

It's been ten days since the surgery and four days since my release from Scottsdale Healthcare/Shea Hospital. More importantly, I've finally weaned myself away from those very potent *happy pills* enough to hopefully write a legible and understandable update.

A few days before surgery I got a call from a company to come in and be measured for a "compression binder," which I found out was a sneaky way of saying I'd be living with a girdle for a while after surgery.

Most folks probably don't like having their bellies measured for anything, including me, especially after two-and-a-half years of unattached core muscles. But there I sat, as a good patient should, while the tape measure made its way around my circumference. The technician took notes, stared a bit at his tape measure, cleared his throat and re-measured a second time!

"I'll put the order in and we'll bring it to the OR."

Sounds good to me.

I had a good pre-op check-in. Normally I'm awake as they roll me from there into the OR. This time, though, I don't even remember leaving the pre-op cubicle. All I remember was waking up in recovery over five hours later.

Seven hours after being checked in, I finally arrived at my room with a sumo wrestler-sized girdle on the table beside me. The staff didn't even have to wrestle with me as they put the girdle on. It was so big that it slid almost up to my earlobes!

I'm not sure what happened, but apparently the technician who measured me got confused somewhere between metric and standard measurements. A revisit and second measuring resulted in my first-ever form-fitted undergarment that I could call my own! Ladies, I feel your pain.

Recovery went well, and thankfully there were no complications during my week-long stay. This is the second time I've had surgery in this facility. The last time was in March, when Dr. Duhon did the hip revision.

In a previous update, you might recall I mentioned the joy I had then when the therapists came in the evening after that surgery and moved my leg farther than it ever had since the accident. Well, what a joy it was to see the same PT team who worked on me back then come into my room to help me this time around. One of them, Audrey, came in with a big smile. I told her, "I remember you from the last time!"

She replied, "I've been following your journey on CaringBridge ever since then!"

It really touched me to know that, even though they see and treat hundreds of patients

Scottsdale Shea Hospital PTer Audrey can't seem to get rid of me.

routinely, there is a level of interest, care, and concern that motivates them in the great work they do.

Needless to say, kudos to all the therapists who have and still are involved in our lives. You all have helped us on our long road to recovery!

The first time sitting up I was pleasantly surprised to not feel a lot of the pain I was anticipating. In fact, it felt great to sit up and for the first time in two-and-a-half years, my torso felt "complete." It was a happy moment for me. The second day I was able to stand for a while and again, there was a sense of togetherness in my abdomen that I hadn't felt since the accident. It makes me hopeful that this surgery will help me in my abilities to stand and balance much better than before.

I'll be back to see Dr. Gottlieb next Monday for my first follow-up visit where I hope the eighty or so staples will be removed from just under the girdle. That's always a milestone moment, knowing the outer layer has healed up enough to stand on its own, giving me faith to believe the inner layers are doing so as well.

Dr. Gottlieb feels that within a month I should be able to resume full rehab PT and start including abdominal exercises to the routine. I'm excited!

I'm also excited about another appointment I have next week. It's finally here—my *driving evaluation!* The experts will check me out as they evaluate what kind of driving tools I'll need to get back behind the wheel. It's looking like I'll be needing hand controls at the least. I'm really looking forward to relieving LaDonna of driving me whenever we venture out of the house. It will be another step towards the "new normal" we're anxious to live in as we move forward.

My healing continues, I'm feeling better every day, and hopefully the last major surgical procedure is now in my rear-view mirror (which I'll be able to look into once they let me drive again!).

I'm encouraged by the progress, and challenged by knowing there's still a long way to go. Your prayers, love, concern, and encouraging thoughts in the guestbook entries and personal e-mails are greatly appreciated!

Let me give you a quick update on two other fronts. First, the wheels are now in motion for LaDonna to revisit the doctors who have been treating her as we seek to find out why her symptoms have come back so intensely lately. Pray for wisdom and clarity for the specialists who will be seeing her in the weeks and months to come. The reality is as I continue to improve, LaDonna has begun to suffer more and more effects of the trauma to her head and neck and even pelvic region.

Much is happening, and we'll keep you posted once again soon!

Grateful for you all,

Craig

Early in my rehabilitation efforts a therapist told me something remarkable: if injured to a point they cannot exercise as normal, professional athletes in prime condition will turn into *mere mortals* in only two or three weeks of inactivity. In that short amount of time, they will literally lose most, if not all, the strength, conditioning and effectiveness that helped them reach the pinnacle of performance. It doesn't take long for inactive muscles to grow weak and ineffective in even the fittest among us.

And then there's me. After *two-and-a-half years*, inactive and unproductive abdominal core muscles were once again reattached in what seemed to be one of my never-ending surgeries. It was hard for me to accept the reality of not having such an important part of my muscle system in working order, and did I ever pay the price in my rehabilitation efforts.

I wasn't sure what to expect once I healed from the surgery. Everyone kept telling me that the core muscles are so important for so many things. My hope was I would see some major steps of improvement begin to come my way, and that they did.

Ever since I started the grueling rehab process, I could never stand alone without support. I tried it once not too many months prior with two therapists spotting me. After only about eight seconds I was ready to fall over and had to grab onto the walker lest I bite the dust. Now, I was able to stand in between the parallel bars long enough to throw the football back and forth with my buddy Dan.

He even did a good job mimicking my fellow brother-in-Christ, Tim Tebow, overthrowing me so I would have to reach up, over, sideways, etc. For the most part, I was able to stand up, unsupported, and catch those passes!

It was still very difficult for me to stand because of the weakness in my legs and the pain in my back from my misaligned pelvis. So, while I rejoiced in the advances in the core, I knew I had a long way to go in strengthening important muscles from the waist down, not just the waist up. Regardless, I'm thankful and thrilled for the progress I've had since that last surgery!

I began taking my driver's education again! I guess they considered me a clear and present danger to the traveling public, even though I've lived on the road for four decades, driving literally hundreds of thousands of safe miles.

In two back-to-back days, I received two letters from the Department of Motor Vehicles. The first stated that my driving privileges were being suspended. The second said my license was now revoked! All because my legs cannot function enough to work the gas and brake pedals.

In a huge role reversal, I'd been downgraded to the co-pilot's seat while my amazing wife now had to drive me everywhere I needed to go.

We've both come to realize that while I may be a hazard to the driving public in the driver's seat, I truly was a hazard to my wife on the passenger's side! I can't believe how much better I could see the long list of calamities coming at us from that side of the car. I rarely failed to let her know in a way that, let's just say, took a few years off her life every time I did so.

So I reverted back to my sixteenth birthday as I made my way through the residential streets of Tempe (at least it's not in the area of town we live in), learning to drive with adaptive hand controls. I even passed by LaDonna Drive, of all things. I wanted to get out and have my instructor take my picture in front of that sign because of the hidden meaning it had for me, but she'd have nothing to do with it.

So, on we went, two times a week, learning all over again something I've done without thought for so many years. The goal was to get independent enough to where I would once again be able to drive on my own.

The long months of rehab continued as we drew to the close of yet another year. 2011 was ending and 2012 offered us renewed hope that my progress would continue.

The carrot on the end of the therapy stick was moved out just a bit farther as the year closed. Dan began to feel I was now

Waaaa, waaa, waaa, I want my walker!!!

ready to leave the stable world of old people walkers and start the next challenge, walking with crutches. You know, the wobbly kind.

I began to understand more clearly that if this journey were a mile long, then I would have to be content with measuring my progress in inches.

Chapter 22

LORD, I'M COMING HOME

Wednesday, January 11, 2012 12:16 a.m., MST

One of the decisions we made just prior to leaving on the trip that changed our lives in 2009 was to put our house up for sale in Glendale, Arizona. We were planning to have LaDonna's mom come live with us when the Lord would take her Daddy, Herman, home to Heaven. We had to sell our two-story house and look for something on one level.

Little did we realize that when we left early in the morning on June 9, 2009, it would be the last time we'd be in that house. Two weeks after the accident, as I lay in a coma hovering near death, LaDonna gets word that an offer had been made on the house, and the rest is history.

Once back in Arizona we didn't have the strength or will to go house hunting. So much of our time and energy was spent in continued rehab, surgeries, and more doctor visits than anyone should have. About a year ago we began the process of looking for a home that would meet our needs. We had a better idea about how my mobility restrictions would impact the kind of house to buy. We began in earnest to look, look, look, and look some more.

We found some short sale homes that we put offers on. After months and months of waiting, they all fell through. We decided to go the auction route and found that to be not for the faint of heart.

After bidding on several homes to no avail, we were beginning to wonder if we'd ever find a home suitable to our needs. For two and a half years, all our belongings have been stored in the garage, waiting to be released from their solitary confinement as well. We'd often laugh when we'd race to put the garage door down if a car went by, thinking they might report this house to the TV show, *Hoarders.*

Well, after two and a half years of still not coming "home" from that trip, I'm thrilled to report that's about to change! Two days before Christmas we won the bidding on a wonderful home that will fit our needs perfectly and the Trustee's Deed Upon Sale is now in our hands! Now that's a real Christmas gift!

There will be enough room for us all, it meets our ministry office needs and will have even enough room for the exercise equipment I'll need to continue working those weakened muscles!

Finally, we'll be able to close the chapter of this long, long trip in one sense, and it's cause for great rejoicing for us. Nizhoni has blessed us so much with her willingness to share her home, but we know its time for her to have some sanity in her sanctuary. Thanks, hon, for all you have done and continue to do for us. You reflect the grace and goodness of the Lord in your life! Mom and Dad can't thank you enough!

Thanks again for your sustaining prayers as we've lived "tentatively" for so long. Little by little the pieces of the puzzle are falling into place, and a life that is close to "normal" is just over the horizon.

As we finally cross over the threshold and move into this new home, we will do so holding on to it loosely, knowing it's not ours, it's the Lord's. As wonderful as this home will be for us, it doesn't even compare to all that is in store for us when we finally make it to our real home, the one with that permanent, eternal address, somewhere on some golden street in heaven. I'll even be able to walk to the mailbox there!

Craig

One of the great joys of my life had been the game of golf—a game enjoyed for years by many in the Smith family. Golfing with my father, Ray, has given us some real quality father/son times together. That's why I was so happy that my son, Dallas, took up interest in the game as well. We've enjoyed numerous multi-generational golf outings over the years.

After the accident I didn't know if I could ever swing a club again. Until recently I didn't even want to think about it. I didn't want to face the disappointment of not being able to golf again if my circumstances and injuries would not allow it.

One day at PT, Dan told me about a special golf cart for handicapped folks called the SoloRider. The seat actually pivots and stands a person up, and they are supported by a seat belt.

"One day we'll try it," he told me.

In early February 2012 it happened!

Spotted by Dan and his intern, and LaDonna and Dad teeing 'em up for me, I put that old club back in my hand and gave it my best shot!

Now I've got both good news and bad news. The bad news is the SoloRider is non-submersible. The good news is my limited range of motion has corrected my slice so I can hopefully keep it out of the water!

Teeing it up for the first time in years.

What a joy it was for me to be strong enough to maneuver the SoloRider onto the driving range and swing the club again. It was great to share that special moment with my dad by my side. Maybe, just maybe, we'll be getting out once and a while again having those special father-son times just like we used to do before the accident!

There was a bit of a downside, though. As pumped and excited as I was, I woke up the next morning feeling like I had been hit by a Mack truck.

My slowly improving core and quad muscles got a huge workout and, oh, were they ever sore!

As good as life now seemed to be, it was about to change, once again, dramatically and painfully. The new home we had purchased weeks ago was in jeopardy. The previous owners contested the legal process used in the trustee auction sale. They threatened to sue the trustee company who sold the house at auction, the mortgage company who foreclosed on them, and us.

We knew we were on solid ground legally in the purchase of the home, but it was painful to have to endure what came to be a long, drawn-out legal process to settle these issues. We were anxious to get the house ready to move into, so this distraction was very disheartening to us.

Once again, the Lord chose to use a new, difficult challenge to teach us, mold us and continue to shape us into His image and likeness. The lesson we learned was to hold all things here on earth lightly, and find our joy in Him and Him alone, no matter the circumstances.

I ended up telling LaDonna in the midst of it all, "I guess we still haven't graduated from the school the Lord is teaching us in. He's just added a new class to learn from. It's up to us to pass or fail." The legal issues persisted for about six months until the judge threw out the suit because the previous owners chose not to pursue their claim.

Our dear friend, Lois Claus led the painting efforts.

We didn't wait that long, though, to get the house ready to move into. Once again we were supported by wonderful friends who helped us paint, fix up and pack us up in anticipation of finally coming home to our own home.

After almost three years without our own home, moving day finally arrived.

On March 10 the moving truck cleaned out Nizhoni's garage of stuff, stored for over

two years, and made its way to our new place in Phoenix's northwest corner of the Valley.

> Saturday, March 17, 2012 7:20 a.m., MST

Here We Go Again: Surgery #20

It has been a while since we last updated you on our
progress. It's not because of little to report on, for just the
opposite is true. It has been an incredibly busy time for us as
we continue to navigate down this long rehab road.

First let me share the good news. We've finally moved into
our new home!

What a joy it was to have family and friends from
Northwest Community Church (NCC) help us make this move.
In some ways it closes a long and painful chapter for us, as
we are finally able to come home from the accident. Many
of the same family and friends at NCC who helped move us
out three years ago returned to help us once again! Thanks
again to all those who helped on that crazy day of *semi-orga-
nized mayhem*!

It's kind of like Christmas in March, unpacking belongings that have baked at 350 degrees in the Arizona heat for
several years. Is rock solid three-year old toothpaste still
good, I wonder?

The other important update is also filled with new challenge for us. It has been a year since Dr. Duhon performed my
18th surgery that helped free up the left hip joint and give me
more mobility. While I have seen greater movement of that
joint and a huge reduction in the pain I had with even the
slightest movement of that leg, it's still not totally free. After

a year of intense stretching by the therapists, they are still not able to get me to even 90 degrees of bend. It still affects my ability to go from sitting to standing and limits my ability to be fully mobile. The bottom line is, there are still some bone obstructions that will need to be surgically removed.

A year and a half ago, in my 17th surgery, Dr. Gottlieb attempted to free up compressed nerves in my lumbar plexus region in a seven-hour surgery. He planned to work on both sides of me, but due to the huge amount of damage on my right side, all seven hours were devoted to just that side. He never did get to the left side but said he'd be willing to attempt the same surgery on the other half of me should I be up to another such painful and risky procedure in the future.

In the past month or so I've been involved in a number of appointments with both these surgeons. They ordered new tests, including MRI's and CT scans to help them determine if they could perform, in one surgery, both the hip revision and nerve decompression procedures.   In my visit with Dr. Duhon yesterday, he affirmed he is ready to do the revision procedure. In my visit with Dr. Gottlieb last week, he, too, said he'd be very open to tag teaming with Dr. Duhon. Maybe, just maybe, I'll be able to see some significant gain that could help me move even closer to walking again!

Knowing how long it takes to get these things scheduled, I won't be surprised if the surgery happens sometime in late April or in May. From there, I'd face another six weeks of recovery before being back to "normal"—whatever that now is for me! Possibly, by mid to late June I'd be kick-starting my rehab, hopefully with full range of motion and new muscles coming off their three-year sabbatical and getting back to work.

LaDonna and I have been discussing the challenges and risks involved, and feel ready to face another major surgical event, knowing the potential gain it may bring. This would be surgeries #20 and #21, if anyone besides me is still counting.

We would ask for prayer for these two surgeons as they plan their course of action. Pray that they would find the best route to go in, the safest way to do what they have to do, and find every piece of boney obstruction and damaged nerve that can successfully be repaired.

So, while this old ship is battered, beaten and worn, and has been tossed about on a great sea of adversity, the Captain keeps His steady hand on the wheel. I know He will continue to keep me safe in the storms and ultimately guide me safely home at His appointed time. Thank God for His indwelling and abiding presence. I don't know how I could make it through it all with out it!

First Peter 5:10 says, "And after you have suffered a little while, the God of all grace, who has called you to his eternal glory in Christ, will himself restore, confirm, strengthen, and establish you."

Amen and amen!

Craig and LaDonna

Chapter 23

MORE SCARS A COMING...

B y early April the schedulers had wrestled down these two very busy surgeons and coordinated their calendars to accommodate my return to the operating table at Scottsdale Healthcare Hospital on May 15, 2012. Dr. Duhon and Dr. Gottlieb would be in one corner as tag team partners, and in the other, wobbly old me would have to take them on all by myself.

I was excited and somewhat naive about just how challenging two major surgeries would be on my body. I was kind of looking for a two-for-one special, I guess. Since I'd already be asleep, why not just do the two procedures together? Cut twice, suffer once.

I was sure that the pain level and recovery phase would be similar to the ones I'd already endured. I was glad to know this could very well be my last major surgery in this incredibly long ordeal.

A couple more speaking trips before the surgery would help keep my mind off the return to the fish-cleaning table. We had been asked to speak at two conference events, one in Chicago and one in southern California. Both were incredibly encouraging events that God used for His glory and purposes.

The first conference was in Chicago at the historic Moody Church. We had the joy of joining Moody's pastor, Dr. Erwin Lutzer, and other missionary presenters for a conference titled *Many Nations, One Savior.* We were reunited with a number of cross-cultural workers there and enjoyed the wonderful hospitality of the staff at Moody.

From there we traveled to The Grove Church in Riverside, California for a regional gathering of church leaders and church planters in the South Pacific District of The C&MA. What a joy it was to once again share about this miracle at mile marker 313! It seemed that everywhere we were sharing our story God was using it to speak to many lives.

Ministry work is one of the most challenging and difficult fields of employment, we're told. Many of God's shepherds are dealing with discouragements and challenges of their own, all while they are trying to lead their congregations to greener pastures.

Every time I've been privileged to tell our story, many of God's servants share their deepest pains and discouragements with me after the services. There's a lot of hurt out there. I guess they are finding a listening ear from someone who has tasted his own share of pain.

I'm grateful for the work of God in me through this ordeal. He is also using it to help bring encouragement to many of my colleagues and co-laborers as they face tough times.

Besides, all the difficult travel and hobnobbing kept my mind off those sharp knives that were waiting in a hospital in Scottsdale, Arizona—the ones with my name on it!

May 12, 2012 12:54pm

The Bracelet Says It All

I'm now just three days away from my 20th and 21st major surgical procedure, scheduled for Tuesday, May 15th at 11:30 a.m., PST. It's been a long time coming, and I'm so glad it's almost here. I'm glad because it will, hopefully, bring me all the closer to the finishing line of surgeries, recoveries and rehabilitation that has consumed the past three years.

Getting ready for this one has been different, and to be honest, much more challenging, though it's hard to put a handle on why. Most of the pre-op is "same old, same old" stuff—you know, seeing my awesome primary care doctor, Dr. Joel Sellers, with the laundry list of lab tests, heart tests, X-ray orders and all other necessities of what the surgeons want me cleared on. All that's been done, including yesterday's visit to the hospital where the surgery will be done.

I went yesterday to Scottsdale Shea Hospital for my last pre-op registration and to have blood drawn for what they call "type and cross." They find out what kind of blood I have and order enough to keep me alive in the event something goes wrong in surgery. Sometimes it's enough to just have blood products "in the building" for quick access, but this time, the blood will be *in the room*, as clarified to me by Dr. Duhon's physician assistant, when we met last week.

I know what that meant—this procedure is a dangerous one. The bone that still is in the way is dangerously close to the femoral artery, vein, and nerve. There is genuine concern any time you cut close to major vessels. That will be my situation on Tuesday.

"Yah-tah-hey" [hello in Navajo], I said to the lab tech that drew my blood yesterday.

I remembered her from the last time I was there. She is a Navajo gal, and we shared some good old Indian humor once again. I think I told her that with the last blood draw I lost my tribal status as I no longer had enough Indian blood in me. Since I lost so much in the accident, most of the blood now in me is from someone else. "Maybe that's why I have such a new-found love for lutefisk and lefse," I said to her.

She just looked at me somewhat confused. Then she came back in and tagged me with the bracelet that would be my link to all the blood products that would be waiting me in the surgical suite next Tuesday.

Once again LaDonna and I had that serious conver- sation about what would happen if things did go wrong during surgery, and God's plans were different than ours.

It happened last night and was one of those special, intimate moments between a husband and wife where we laughed, cried, prayed, and talked over all the contingencies that needed to be talked about in advance of Tuesday and in light of the bracelet. It was the ending of a pretty long and tiring day that started out on quite a funny note.

John, my driver for the past two and a half years, came by to pick me up at 8:30 a.m. for three scheduled appointments. So here I was, getting ready to leave the house first to get a major shot in the behind, then go to two hours of working with the physical terrorists, then on to another needle in the arm. On the way out the door LaDonna gave me a big kiss and said, "Have a fun day, Hon!"

That was yesterday. Here we are today. I woke up totally drained of energy and the heaviness of the surgery on my mind. I want to be honest with you because it's important to do so. God has been faithful to us through it all, but there are definitely times when, storm clouds gather, the winds start to blow, and we feel the full fury of it all. Today, the storm feels like a hurricane, and the going is rough.

It's at times like these all we can do is hold onto the promises of God, and that's what we are choosing to do. I was reminded of this last Sunday, while in church. I don't normally recommend this, but as our pastor was camped in a text in Mark, I read further along and came to the story of Jesus calming the storm (Mark 4:35–41).

I left his preaching behind and the Spirit of God began to minister to my soul in a powerful and personal way. The storm was huge; enough to send waves crashing over the boat that Jesus was sleeping in. It was enough for me to know that while we can still be troubled by the big storms of our lives, they really don't bother Jesus all that much. He got up after being awakened by His very scared followers. His mighty voice He calmed the storms. It's interesting to note what happened to the disciples after this miracle.

They were still terrified—no longer at the storm, but now at the storm stopper! Verse 41 says, "they were terrified and asked each other, 'Who is this? Even the winds and waves obey Him!'"

I guess I keep learning over and over again the same lesson. Storms, suffering, difficulties, and uncertainty about what's to come all lead to the same question: "Who is Jesus?" No matter what we face, it all has a divine purpose, to reveal Jesus to our lives.

In my weakness, yes, I admit, I still get fearful, but thank God, Jesus never does. Through my trials, difficulties and uncertainties, I'm coming to know Jesus all the better.

As I look at the bracelet on my wrist, I'm reminded that Jesus knows all about it, and even if I do struggle at times with fear, He's in the boat with me, having a nice and peaceful nap.

It's time to lay down beside Him and trust Him just one more time!

Thanks for praying, thanks for sharing your love and concerns with us, and our family, through it all!

Craig

May 15, 2012 10:15pm

Update on Dad's surgery:

The first part of the surgery was successful. Dr. Duhon removed a palm-sized bone mass out of Dad's hip joint along with several bone spurs. They cleared out scar tissue up to 2cm from the femoral artery, and now Dad should have ninety-degree range of motion when everything is

Dr. Duhon showing family the extent of bone removed from my left hip.

done with! Thanks for prayers and support so far. He's still in surgery while the second surgeon is stepping in to do the second half of the surgery. So far so good, though...

A few hours later...

Dad is done with his second surgery! We're waiting to see him in the recovery area at the hospital. Dr. Gottlieb came out to tell us that while they were cleaning out the heterotopic ossification (bone spurs) from his hip, they checked out his lumbar plexus of nerves (bundle of nerves that comes out of his spinal cord). It all seems intact so even if there is nerve damage from the accident, there is still possibility of regaining some nerve function in the future! They were unable to clean some of the scar tissue off the nerve bundles since there is too much risk of rupturing important blood vessels. Overall it was successful and Dad should notice improved mobility and possible nerve improvement over the next few months. Thanks everyone for the prayers! Dad's gonna be hurting from this surgery for a while, so please keep him in your prayers in the coming days.

Dallas

It was finally over. I had undergone two major procedures in one surgical event—close to ten hours on the operating table. I was starting to recognize the hospital's ceiling tiles again so I knew I had survived. It was either that, or heaven's mansions were made of material found at your local Home Depot.

The first few days seemed uneventful, at least compared to the four other surgical recovery experiences I was alert enough to enjoy. My numbers were looking good and the pain was being managed fairly well. I was resting as best I could in a facility that didn't mind keeping you up all night with nursing activities.

Both my surgeons were encouraged by my recovery. After about three uneventful days they were starting to look at a potential discharge date on either Friday or Saturday. Wanting to get out of there, I pushed for as soon as possible.

Friday came, and I was so ready for home. It would be, hopefully, the last time in my life I'd ever have to call this hospital home. I called LaDonna to confirm that they were going to be discharging me around noon so she could come by late morning to help me pack up for my relocation home.

Somewhere around 9:30 a.m. I was visiting with a friend and ministry colleague, Nick Piantedosi, who came by to visit. The nursing staff had come and gone after their assessments and giving me the docs order for my oral medications.

As Nick and I were winding down our conversation, I started feeling somewhat nervous, anxious, and I had a hard time focusing. As he left, I suddenly was hit with a full-blown shortness of breath. It hit me hard and fast and panic overtook me. I couldn't breathe; I was literally ready to jump out of my bed because of the extreme anxiety that hit me like a ton of bricks.

I screamed at the top of my lungs for my nurse. Within moments, the room was full of medical folks scurrying around hooking me up to various machines, and calling for the "crash cart." That only added to my nervousness and breathing problems.

I got hooked up to monitors, oxygen, etc., and tried to relax with the help of some pretty good IV calming-down juice. Within a half an hour or so the worst of it was pretty much over. My internist arrived and canceled my discharge.

"You're not going anywhere today, Craig," was his words as he left the room after giving me a good thorough going-over.

It wasn't long before a cardiologist came in, joined in the parade of doctors, and ordered an ultrasound of the heart and a nuclear stress test. Wheels were put in motion quickly and I got the two-part process going right away.

I had to call LaDonna to let her know what had happened as she was already on her way, thinking she was coming to take me home. It was quite a surprise for her. She took the news as she has all the other times, concerned, but trusting in the good hand of our Lord.

I fell asleep that night without incident, but I did wake up often through the night, wondering what the tests would show. I woke up early the next day and had a wonderful time with the Lord, praying, reaffirming my willingness to conform my will to His.

LaDonna arrived early and I shared with her how things were going. Finally the nuclear medicine folks came and administered the tougher, second part of the test where they put the full stress on the heart itself. From there I would go downstairs to a room for another twenty-minute picture taking of the heart.

It all went well, and I returned to my room mid-afternoon. My nurse got the call that afternoon from the cardiologist, and he said there was no damage to the heart! Oh how we gave praise to the Lord! Whatever happened didn't lead to a heart attack, and for that, we were extremely grateful.

Once the doctors were assured no damage happened to my heart from the incident, they began the process of getting me ready for discharge.

While the doctors couldn't pinpoint why it happened, the best guess was my body could have reacted to a large amount of very potent pain medications that were being delivered during recovery. I remember just before the incident being given a cup full of oral meds, including very strong painkillers. It was shortly after that when things went haywire.

We discussed this with the internist and I told them I wanted to pull back on the amount of medications they were giving me. I would much rather deal with the pain and discomfort of the surgical sites than with another episode like the one I just had. They agreed and returned me to what I was taking routinely in the months leading up to my surgery.

Being cleared by internist, they had no reason to keep me in the hospital so they discharged me that Sunday, two days after this horrible experience.

To be honest, I was still feeling too sick and actually somewhat concerned now about going home. Mr. "I wanna get out of here!" quickly turned into Mr. "Can't I just stay a while longer?"

Regardless, they couldn't justify keeping me there.

I went home and got settled in by that evening, wondering how the next few days would go. In one sense, it was great to be home, but in another, I still felt really rough. By Monday things were a little better and I had my first visit with the home health crew that would be involved in both nursing evaluations and physical therapy for the next few weeks.

Unknowingly, I was right in the middle of what would become one of my most dangerous and difficult experiences since the miracle at mile marker 313.

Tuesday came and went, my strength level increased and I started feeling better. I looked forward to Wednesday post op visit to see Dr. Gottlieb.

Tuesday night I told LaDonna I wanted to roll over on my side to get into another position. It's no fun being confined to just being on your back for days on end. I rolled onto the left side, the side where two huge incisions now decorated my body.

As LaDonna rolled me back, we were shocked to see the waterproof pad totally soaked in blood and fluid. She rolled me to the other side and cleaned and rebandaged the wound. For sure Dr. Gottlieb would need to know about that.

We met the next day and he looked over the wound sites. While pleased with most of what he saw, he was certainly concerned about the hip wound where it was continuing to drain. But that was Dr. Duhon's incision and he was the one who really needed to evaluate it.

Dr. Gottlieb said it was quite possible that they would have to go in again and surgically address this drainage issue. It was tough to hear I may need to go back into surgery, but we would need to do whatever was necessary to get this wound healing up correctly. After Dr. Duhon looked it over, they would discuss together what the course of action would be.

A large amount of bone and some tissue was taken out of my hip that left voids that became repositories of fluid and blood. If these voids did not drain well the wound would not heal. Infection could set in and become a very serious issue. Both doctors agreed that ongoing drainage this far out from surgery was concerning to them.

It was something that could not be left alone for long due to the risk of infection. He determined to give it a few days to see if the drainage would decrease. He wanted us to keep a close eye on the site over the weekend, as we all prayed for the discharge to subside.

I asked Dr. Duhon what they would do in another surgery if it came to that. He said in the best-case scenario, they would clean out the site, remove the affected tissue and hope that would be sufficient. The worst-case scenario would be if infection got into the prosthesis. Then they would have to remove the implant and replace it with a new one.

The challenge was I'd already had two major radiation treatments to that site to inhibit further bone growth. The danger in removing the prosthetic device was the potential of a new one not adhering to the bone. If it came to that, no metal implants would hold, there would be no stable hip joint, and the whole leg would have to be removed. It was that serious.

This recovery was getting more and more difficult by the day and wearing us out in body, soul, and spirit.

May 30, 2012 5:50pm

Growing up, I never was the roller coaster type. The few times I've been on one I couldn't wait for the ride to end. I guess you could say I'm more like the old comedian, George Carlin, who used to say he liked baseball so much, because the main idea behind the game was just to *go home and be safe.*

These past few weeks have seemed like an endless roller-coaster ride, filled with emotional ups and downs and severe testing of our faith for both LaDonna and me. We were wondering if we'd ever be able to unbuckle the harness, step off, and catch our breath.

The weekend went fairly well, although I continued to drain from the long incision on the outside of my left leg. We were hopeful Memorial Day Monday would truly be memorable for us by the leakage just going away.

That morning, as LaDonna was redressing the wounds, she peeled back the big ABD dressing and much to our joy, the drainage was down to just a small spot, and boy did we jump (at least she did) for joy and thanked the Lord the worst seemed to be coming to an end.

After redressing the wound, she helped me get dressed, so I could join the family and friends gathering for the cookout. As she rolled me onto my left side (the wound side), much to our surprise and dismay, a gusher of fluid shot out all over the bed. Our hearts sank as some of those greatest concerns and fears that just moments before had been stored away, came back with a vengeance.

"Craig, this is really weird," she told me. This isn't coming out of the hip wound, it's coming out of the other incision site! How can this be? There hasn't been any leakage from that incision since the surgery! What's happening?"

Once I got cleaned and patched up again, I put my best hurting face on and made my way out to the festivities.

We got through the cookout and visit with the tribe. By late afternoon we called Dr. Duhon's answering service. Not long afterwards I was explaining what happened to the doctor on call. He thought it plausible that, while the hip incision was healing up, the residue fluid was looking for another place to go, and perhaps found a tunnel from the one incision site to the other. He told us to monitor it, keep redressing it as needed, and keep my appointments with both Dr. Duhon and Dr. Gottlieb later in the week.

The next few days were tough ones for us as the drainage continued unabated. Sometimes LaDonna had to change the big absorbent pads several times a day. I was never so glad to finally get in this morning to see Dr. Gottlieb. He's the wound care guru, and I've come to really trust his judgment and experience in dealing with such issues.

Dr. Gottlieb came in and pulled back the thoroughly soaked ABD pad and without saying a word, he and his nurse gloved up and got right to work. I really wasn't ready for what would come next.

He just smiled at me, made a fist and started from one end of the incision, rolling his fist along those fifty some staples. He did it just like Grandma Irene used to do with a rolling pin as she rolled out the dough for her amazing sweet rolls. Can you imagine someone pushing down hard and rolling up and down a foot and a half incision site? He's all about results, and results are what he got as a whole lot of fluid was squeezed out of that wound.

He let me come up for air a few times and then gave me the best news ever.

He said there is no way the drainage is coming from the hip area and tunneling its way over to this surgical site. The drainage coming out is isolated from the area of biggest concern. The fact that the hip wound dressing has been dry for two days was the best news of the day! This is not a problem, he said, and we can take care of it with a simple procedure.

I go back tomorrow to Dr. Duhon to show off a completely dry dressing on his wound site so talk of further surgery will not have to be a part of the visit. From there, I'm going back to Scottsdale Shea Hospital, and actually back to the operating room, for Dr. Gottlieb to do the simple procedure he told me will help take care of the drainage in his wound site.

He's going to take a few staples out, numb the area, and insert a tube into that draining wound that will be connected to a spring loaded vacuum pump that will keep draining the fluid out until this wound finally heals. I won't have to go under anesthesia to do this, and the OR is being used simply because they want to monitor me due to the cardiac episode I had in the hospital a few days after the surgery.

Tomorrow should be a really good day for us. My prayer is Dr. Duhon will be happy with his incision site and the danger is finally over for that issue. Then Dr. Gottlieb will be able to get this drain successfully put in so that his incision will finally heal. We'll finally be done with this incredibly tough roller coaster ride.

I'll be happy to just go home and be safe! We will keep you posted as to how things go in the next day or so. Thank you for caring, thank you for sharing, and thank you for praying.

Gratefully,

Craig and LaDonna

Three weeks out from the surgery, it was looking like we were turning the corner on all the challenges facing us. I went back to Scottsdale Shea for the drain insertion procedure. This time I would be a *conscious observer* although as we went through the process I almost ended up becoming a *conscientious objector!*

I was wheeled back into the operating room and slid over to the OR table. It was flashback time as I looked up to bright lights and a room full of instruments, tubes, etc. Usually this would be the time they would turn the lights out on me. This time the lights stayed on, and I was able to look up and see the surgeons do what they do.

They laid my arms out on arm boards protruding from the side of the table and locked my arms down to the board with Velcro bands. I guess they didn't want conscious patients taking swings at the doctor when things don't go right. I guess upstanding ministers were no exception to that rule!

It was a weird sensation as Dr. Gottlieb stood over me, along with his intern surgeon helper. After twenty-one surgeries, I finally got to see how it all goes down!

He numbed my side and began taking out some of the fifty-plus staples holding the incision together. They then began inserting a tube that would be connected to the vacuum pump that would, over the next week or two, keep draining the fluids.

Dr. Gottlieb ended up putting two drains into the wound, and the staple gun went back to work closing up the opening they had made an hour earlier. Finally it was done, and I was sent home with those two pancakes, reminiscent of days of old.

Over the next week those drains did their thing, although it was quite painful at the insertion site. One of the stitches, I think, was put in too tightly and it stretched and pulled on my side constantly. The slightest turn of my body felt like a hornet having a heyday so I did a lot of staying still over that week.

When I went back to see Dr. Gottlieb, he concluded that the drains did enough work to warrant their retreat from my insides! I was really thankful that they finally came out, along with all those staples that had been in me since the surgery. It was a major step forward in my getting through what had turned into the most difficult and incredibly challenging recovery since emerging from the coma.

I told Dr. Gottlieb that he really needed to get those drains out because I was running out of space on my body for any other medical attachments!

I left his office to go to my new cardiologist who treated me during the episode I had in the hospital a few days after the surgery. He wanted me to wear a cardiac monitor for 10 days.

That day I lost two drains and gained one telemetry unit! I sure was more comfortable with the electronics hanging on me than the vacuum tubes! I kept telling myself, *this, too, shall pass!*

Then it was back to Dr. Duhon's office. His first words to me as he came in the room was, "Brother, I want you to know I've been so concerned for you and have been praying a lot for you during these tough days."

There were no better words that I could hear from him that day. He is not just my amazing orthopedic surgeon. He has become a wonderful brother in the Lord, and a man of God who approaches the medical world from not only a physical but spiritual perspective.

He was pleased with the healing of the hip incision site, so he went ahead and had the thirty-plus staples pulled out. So there I was, with all the staples and drains out, the wounds continuing to heal, and the cardiac monitor in place for the next few days.

Dr. Duhon cleared me to return back to my outpatient physical therapy to see what progress I could now start making.

That day marked an important milestone for us. All that surgeons and surgeries could do had now been done. I was excited to move forward to see what the Lord would give me mobility-wise, now that all the reconstructive work of men had been done.

I felt like I was only now beginning my physical therapy in earnest. The past two and a half years of therapy was always hindered because of the continuing problems that needed surgical repairs. Now I could see what this old body was capable of. It was time to finally finish two and a half years of PT practice, and suit up for the real home opener.

I'd have only about a month to try out my new legs before we would take another much-needed break back home, "Up North."

The few weeks back at therapy were encouraging ones. As I healed from the effects of the surgeries I began to move my body in ways it hadn't been able to in such a long time. I couldn't quite pinpoint the difference, but my left leg seemed stronger than before. Some nerves must have started flowing again through Dr. Gottlieb's efforts. My stamina still suffered, but increased cardio workouts started slowly showing positive improvement in my endurance levels as well.

While making plans for our trip to Minnesota we contacted the Cass Lake Indian Hospital to inquire about continuing physical therapy while we were there. They set up my initial appointment with their PT department, so there wouldn't be a gap in my much-needed therapy sessions.

Now, all we had to do was to pack and get ready for another much-needed visit to the lake. We would celebrate the progress made, and hopefully, no new challenges would arise like they did last year with my brother, Russ.

Cass Lake, here we come!

Chapter 24

ME AND HER IN THE MEN'S ROOMS

Packing up to leave Arizona for a trip back home was always the best time. The thought of another wonderful summer experience at the lake always brought great joy to us. Contrary to most real-life experiences, actually being there was always better than dreaming about it.

We never used to have to do this before, but since the accident we found ourselves having to print out a packing list of all we needed to take, lest we'd forget something.

LaDonna's memory loss and my inattentiveness to details made the possibility of forgetting something much more plausible. You can blame it on our age; we choose to blame it on the accident.

One of the main items on that checklist was to make sure we packed all the supplies needed for my trusty ole colostomy backpack. Those supplies were high on my list of must-have items. The last thing we wanted was needing supplies at 35,000 feet somewhere over Kansas only to find out it was left at home in the storage cabinet.

As we were collecting the supplies, we started laughing as we thought about the unique experiences we had living with this attachment that now graced my scarred up tummy.

It all started as I remembered waking up from the coma and looking down to see, for the first time, this "thing" hanging off my abdomen. UNM actually had a full-time nurse whose main job was colostomy care. I remember thinking to myself, "Now that's a dream job, for sure!"

She spent a good amount of time teaching LaDonna all the ins and outs of caring for this apparatus. She told her to be ready to go where most women dare not, because her future would likely now include spending some quality time with her husband in the men's room.

I remember going to PT—one April Fool's Day morning in particular!

Dan used to tease me that he was going to put a new sign over the bathroom door titled, "Craig Smith's Office"! I guess he thought I spent way too much time there. So there we were, back in my "office" once again, taking care of business.

That's when LaDonna commented, "Craig, isn't today April Fool's Day?"

We looked at each other somewhat sheepishly and, in unison, muttered, "Let's get him!"

We put our plan in place and got ready for our excellent adventure.

By then the gym was packed with patients and Dan happened to be, momentarily, in his office, away from center stage. We cracked open the door and saw one of the PT students happening by.

"Hey Jen, come here," we whispered. "We have this plan to get Dan today. When he comes back out of the office tell him, in a panicky kind of way, that Craig's colostomy bag just broke, and it's a total mess in the bathroom. Tell him it's everywhere!"

Anticipation built until Mr. Bonarati finally emerged from filing his paperwork. Little did he know more paperwork awaited him!

"Dan," Jen told him as instructed, "Craig just told me his bag broke in the bathroom, and there's a real bad mess everywhere!"

"What? Oh, no!" he cried. And then he jumped into his best community organizer mode and started barking out commands.

"Jen, go get some paper towels," as he gloved up and tried to figure out how he was going to handle this disaster. "Carlos, go get the mop!"

We then heard all this scurrying around as LaDonna and I were busting a gut inside the "pristine" bathroom. Then there was a knock on the door.

I cracked it open with a total look of disgust on my face. There my dear friend Dan stood, all gloved up, looking like a high-class waiter at New York's Plaza Hotel with one of those towels draped over his forearm.

He stuck his head in and said, "I don't see anything. Where is it?"

"Oh man, Dan, it's all over the floor."

"I don't see anything!"

"Hey, Dan, April Fool's!"

As he turned and walked away with a disgusting look of relief on his face, he was met with an ovation from the patients that had a front row seat to his Academy Award performance.

It wasn't the first, nor was it to be the last time LaDonna and I would share good laughs over very awkward moments.

On the trip back to Minnesota in 2010 we stopped in Albuquerque to visit our friends the Kinney's. Since we were there on the weekend we went with them to their home church for the Sunday morning service.

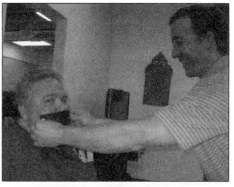

I promise...never again, Dan!

We finally got situated, and the praise and worship began. That's when something else began as well. My colostomy bag rapidly filled to the max. I looked over at LaDonna and had to let her know. She would have to continue the praise and worship in the restroom. It's at times like this that praise would have to be an act of the will.

"Hon, we gotta get to the bathroom or we'll have trouble on our hands," I emphatically whispered to her.

We high-tailed it out of the sanctuary and found the men's room. LaDonna opened the door for me and she shouted, "Anybody in here?"

At least we had the courtesy to let some unaware grandpa with prostate problems know there would be a woman coming in to invade the space. The coast was clear, so we proceeded with due diligence and caution.

Just as we got into the room the door swung open behind us, and a young boy came rushing in. He didn't even flinch as he saw LaDonna standing there with me.

As if we were invisible, he hurried to the urinal for relief. This young man was not going to be denied nor was he going to be delayed. As fast as he flew in, he flew back out. Basically we were left there, somewhat speechless, just looking at each other.

Snapping out of our shock, I told my bewildered wife, "Let's get this over with before someone else comes in."

A few days later we were heading east on I-80 somewhere in a desolate corner of Nebraska. The old bag started filling up and I was so concerned, as it was quickly reaching the way-too-full mark.

"Hon, we need to pull off and take care of this," I said with some urgency in my voice.

Exits, however, were few and far between. She kept driving and I kept looking, while I sat there supporting the goods, lest the buildup be too much and disaster strike.

Finally an exit was on the horizon—no restrooms, but we were in such an isolated place, all we'd need to do was pull off, park on the side of the road, and deal with it right there in the car. Nobody would see us, right?

We exited the freeway onto a small country road that seemed to lead nowhere and came to a railroad crossing that looked like it hadn't been used in years. We stopped just short of the tracks and proceeded to get out the canister we used for such an occasion. At least we were all alone. Or so we thought.

Just as I pulled up my shirt and LaDonna started fulfilling her duties in her recently amended marital job description, the red lights and drop-down arm of the railroad crossing came to life. Pulling up right beside us was a souped-up F-350 Ford Crew Cab pick up truck, loaded down with cowboys heading for who knows where.

As all good cowboys are taught to do, the boys leaned over, took a good look, a second good look, smiled at us, and tipped their hats. They had a front row seat as the mile-long train made its way leisurely across that isolated road that nobody probably ever traveled on, except for this inopportune moment.

As if the cowboys weren't enough, it happened to be an Amtrak train that was passing by in front us. It was loaded down with way too many passengers, all gazing out of what seemed to be endless windows at the amazing scenery afforded them by some of Nebraska's finest cornfields—and of course, us.

I wondered what all the journal entries read that night as these folks tried to articulate what they had just seen, on what turned our to be a very interesting day in their summer vacation.

Our funniest and scariest incident happened on a visit to our neighborhood Costco one hot Phoenix summer day. The outside wall was lined with about twenty handicapped-accessible parking slots. Only about three slots were being used, because most of the mobility challenged snowbirds had already flown north.

I had just become mobile enough that I wanted to try one of their motorized shopping carts. LaDonna found one and brought it out to the car. I shuffled along the open car door to the cart. I got my leg over it and began settling down into the seat. Unfortunately, the handle bar caught the lid underside of my somewhat full colostomy and, oh, what a mess we had on our hands!

"Oh no!" I shouted to LaDonna. "What are we going to do?"

LaDonna had much more of the grace of God on her that day than I did. Without an ounce of panic, she started organizing the response.

"I'm going to go in and buy a new shirt for you. You can start getting the supplies ready to change out the bag. When I get back we'll change it, put the new shirt on, and we'll just keep on going."

So, there I was, so wanting to just go home. But that wasn't an option, at least in this condition. I looked along the 17 open handicap slots and thought the best thing would be to go way down to the end, where no one was, and start the cleanup next to aisle twenty. At least it offered me the best chance at privacy in a very open parking lot.

As I baked in the 110-degree sun, I started cleaning up the mess as best I could. About that time a 90's something grandma and grandpa pulled into the very last slot, right in front of me, bypassing sixteen other open ones closer to the entrance door! There they sat, trying to figure out how to get out of their car, I guess, as they gave me the once-over in elderly slow motion. Their doors slowly opened, and after about five minutes of trying to get their legs out, they finally exited the vehicle. There I sat holding my mess I was trying to hide.

LaDonna finally returned after I was about medium well, and I told her what had just happened. She said, "Let's go around the corner of the building and finish changing this out by the loading dock. It looks like a more private place."

Embarrassed, I took my shirt off. She finished cleaning me up and then replaced the new crazy apparatus. I happened to look up and notice security cameras trained on us. It wasn't long before several Costco employees, with walkie-talkies in hand, just happened by us, paying us a questionable glance, and then communicated something to security.

All I can say is I'm sure we ended up on Costco's Funniest Home Videos at their annual Christmas party. What a joy it was to be so helpful to them!

My doctors continue to hold out hope that someday this apparatus can be removed and my plumbing reattached. This is one surgery I would gladly look forward to.

Lastly, another surgery was behind me, and I was back home on my specialized bed and a heavy dose of pain meds. Near daybreak I started coming back to consciousness. My sleepy eyes opened and began to focus on my left hand that was raised in the air holding something-my colostomy bag!

I yelled for LaDonna at the top of my lungs and woke her up. Stumbling into the room, she turned on the light, took one look at me and said, "What in the world are you doing?"

"I don't know! I woke up holding this crazy thing in my hand! HELP!"

I've come to learn to live with this situation, and while it provides us new and sometimes comical relief, I don't want this bag to be with me for the rest of my life. With the progress I've already made, I have hope that I can be free of it someday. Until then I'm sure there will be a few more stories to tell.

Chapter 25

IT HAPPENED AGAIN
AND AGAIN

W e were anxious for a less stressful experience "Up North" this time around as we made our final preparations for the trip. All the colostomy supplies were present and accounted for, so we were confident that we were ready for the flight back home.

Just before we were scheduled to go we got a call from my dad, Ray "Jeep" Smith. He was in Wisconsin where he and my stepmom, Barb, spent the summers at her home in Marinette.

Dad had noticed a growth in his left leg, and it was causing him some discomfort. A recent doctor visit resulted in a biopsy, and he had just received the results. "Craig, the doctors told me I have a cancerous tumor called *sarcoma* in my leg. They say I need radiation treatment and then surgery."

We couldn't believe we were once again facing another extended family challenge to go along with our time at the cabin. Maybe it was time to rethink our summer routine.

My father and I have been very close all my life. We've spent years together on the road, singing and preaching the gospel. He was there with LaDonna and me in the painful days following the accident and was there for Russ as he faced his battle last year. This time, Dad was the one standing in the need of prayer.

We mobilized our CaringBridge family to include Jeep in their prayers and committed to keeping them updated on both Dad and our situations. Once again, our time "Up North" would be tempered by the burdens and challenges of one we loved so deeply.

Encouraging Progress Gives Us Reason to Sing!

August 16, 2012 7:29 p.m.

What a joy it is to come to you with an update on our continuing progress on the long road to healing and restoration. It has been three years and two months now since the accident. So much has happened since those four seconds that changed our lives.

As I've noticed in re-reading some of the early postings shortly after the accident, many of our reports were filled with much anguish and concern. Now, it's encouraging to see new levels of mobility and healing.

We are back on our home reservation in northern Minnesota for an extended break from Arizona and its summer heat. It has been quite chilly the past few days, and that's been a welcome sight for our scorched bodies.

One of my goals for our time "Up North" was hopefully to leave the wheelchair in the car and walk into and out of the cabin with just my crutches. I navigate up and down the ramp pretty well now. Once I get inside the cabin I walk from my lift chair to my adjustable bed without falling, at least so far!

LaDonna bought me a swivel barstool with a back support from Wal-Mart (aka the Ojibwe Happy Hunting Grounds), and that's what I use at the dining table and when I head to the bathroom for my grooming!

I'm thrilled to report after two weeks here, the wheelchair has not come out of the car yet!

The tribal hospital I was born in so long ago now has two full-time physical therapists, and they have picked right up where my buddy Dan and the team at Touchstone Rehab in Phoenix left off. I continue to be stretched beyond my comfort zone on a regular basis.

We also are excited to report that my father, Ray Smith, is halfway through his five-week radiation therapy in northeastern Wisconsin. In my last conversation with him he said he's feeling well and tolerating the treatments without problem. Often there can be irritation and damage from the radiation to the skin around the growth, but he's not having any symptoms of that so that's something to sing about!

Dad and my step-mom, Barb, came over to see us the first weekend we were here. They joined us for a great time singing and sharing at the Lake Itasca Family Music Festival and with our friends at Faith Baptist Church in Park Rapids, MN. It was a wonderful Sunday to "tell of His might, and sing of His grace" to a lot of people that weekend.

The Smith Family Trio: Together again!

The Lord has done a great work in our bodies, and we are full of thanksgiving to

Him! It definitely puts a song in our hearts, and we just gotta get it out!

Craig and LaDonna

Standing on the Promises

Sept. 8, 2012 5:08pm

Dear Friends and Family;

Greetings from a chilly "Up North" evening in northern Minnesota! We have been having a wonderful time back home with family and friends at the cabin. The rest has been refreshing; the get-togethers with many friends and family members have been a real treat and a contributor to our getting better!

My father, Ray Smith, and stepmom Barb, have been here for over a week as Dad rests after his twenty-five rounds of radiation treatment to the sarcoma in his leg. He will be returning to Wisconsin on September 10 to meet with his doctors and determine when the surgery will be performed to remove the growth from his leg.

Labor Day Sunday we were back at our home church, the Cass Lake Alliance, to worship together with our home folks.

First time standing up to sing in over three years.

I had the joy of sharing from God's Word and the trio did an old classic gospel song, "More About Jesus."

As you can see from the picture, this was the first time I was able to stand on my feet and sing a song since the accident!

321

God gave me the strength, the crutches gave me the balance, and these rusty old voices did it just one more time!

Afterwards we were treated to another one of those great Cass Lake Alliance potluck dinners. Nobody does it better, especially with those good old Minnesota hot dishes that filled the serving table! Thanks again to our entire home church family for your prayers and encouragement through it all!

It has not bee all rest and relaxation. We've had regular visits with the therapists at the local Indian hospital. It's so important for me to keep my joints moving. My new most favorite therapist, Paul, has been practicing some new moves on me! I think before this job he might have worked in a pretzel factory since that seems to be what he's trying to make out of me.

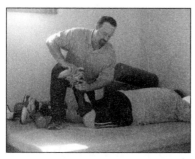

Paul, my therapist in Cass Lake, doing his thing.

He's also doing some very helpful work on LaDonna. Our doctor felt it important for her to get some treatments on her neck, and she is feeling relief.

It won't be long and we'll be making our way home to Arizona where sometime in the near future we'll begin having discussions with the insurance folks and my main doctor about my reaching the end of the long road to recovery.

Most, if not all, of the surgeries have been done that can be done, so it's time to start taking a good hard look at whether or not the recovery I have had is enough to enable me to return to full-time work once again. There's still so much to be worked out, but I'm thankful that we've come so far in these three-plus years of recovery.

I've got a new name for all of you who have stood with us through this storm. I like to think of you as our *Team 314*. The accident happened at mile marker 313. With your help, you've encouraged us to move to mile marker 314 and beyond. Thank you for being such an integral part of our healing and restoration. You all have prayed. I've recovered enough to get back on my feet, at least for one more song. There are many more to come, and we're excited about keeping on keeping on!

Craig and LaDonna

One of the issues raised just before this trip was a concerning CT scan that was done on my lungs. The cardiac challenges and the history of my collapsed lung meant I needed to watch myself carefully. The CT scan had uncovered some abnormalities in the lung that was concerning to the radiologist.

The radiologist's report indicated that they still could see the effects of the trauma. This meant I was susceptible to pulmonary problems, and I shouldn't take any sicknesses lightly.

Toward the end of our time at the cabin the weather turned unusually chilly and with it came seasonal illnesses. I hadn't been hit this hard by a cold in many years. My throat ached and my lungs started to rattle, leaving us somewhat concerned.

The day after we flew home to Arizona, I got into bed and began to have some difficulty breathing. Over the next few minutes it became more and more alarming. I was flashing back to that day in recovery from the last surgery when everything went haywire and I couldn't breathe.

I sat up on the edge of the bed and started coughing violently. The tissue I was coughing into filled with blood, so I knew something needed to be done right away.

I called for LaDonna, showed her the gunk, and told her I couldn't catch my breath. We chose to drive to the hospital rather than call an ambulance. So here we were, once again, visiting another ER late in the evening. My symptoms put me at the top of the waiting list, and it wasn't long before they had me back in a room on oxygen and IVs for precautionary measures.

A portable X-ray was taken and soon the physician on duty came in to visit with me. "Craig, your X-ray shows you have double pneumonia and your EKG shows some abnormalities in your heartbeat. We're going to admit you to the cardiac unit and run more tests to see what's going on. For sure we're going to start you on some big doses of antibiotics to deal with the lung issues. So settle in, your going to be here a while."

It was pretty disheartening to once again be in a situation that came about because I was more susceptible to these kinds of issues. No one wants to be in the hospital, and after three and a half years of having that be my world, this was the last place I wanted to be, especially when my dad's surgery was coming up in only a few short days.

I ended up being hospitalized for three days. No more cardiac issues arose, and once the antibiotics started doing their thing, my breathing improved dramatically. I returned home the first part of October 2012, ready to pick up my therapy where I had left off.

Scripture says in Romans 5:3, "Not only so, but we also glory in our sufferings, because we know that suffering produces perseverance." My school of suffering had been a long one. I guess it is taking a long time for perseverance to be perfected in my life, and maybe there were more lessons to be learned.

As painful as it had been to this point, we continued to live in the inexplicable peace of God. It was tough, but it was all right. We were weary, but we were well cared for. We were loved, and that unconditional love covered a multitude of our troubles and trials.

Healing in Wisconsin, Weightless in Phoenix

January 3, 2013, 6:51 p.m.

First, let me say that LaDonna and I wish you all a wonderful New Year. We are hitting the ground running as we begin 2013.

The healing continues, and that's the best news for sure! Healing not only for me but also for my father, Ray, in Wisconsin.

Dad had a very serious setback shortly before Christmas. As you know and have been praying much about, he has had a difficult time with his surgical wound healing thoroughly. He ended up having the wound packed and was given a "wound vac" unit to draw the drainage out of the site so it could heal. One morning as he got up the wound began to bleed, bleed, and bleed some more.

Barb couldn't get the towels to him fast enough. She called 911 and the paramedics came, put hand pressure on the wound and rushed him to the ER. Thankfully they saved his life and stopped the bleeding. He ended up getting two units of blood, and he recovered enough to be discharged a few days later. The right decision was made to bring in EMS, because they said he would not have made it. The healing process is moving forward for Dad.

I continue to keep my nose (and pelvis) to the grindstone, working hard at PT three times a week. Along with that routine, I've been having very important appointments with my surgeons. They are ready to "sign off" on me, now that six months have past since my last and hopefully final major surgery.

I will meet with my primary rehab doctor who oversees the whole process, and he will then determine if I've reached "maximum medical improvement." If so, I'll close this long three-and-a-half-year chapter of surgeries, rehab, and recovery. I would then move to what they call *supportive care*. It will be an important milestone for me and one I'm looking forward to crossing soon!

On the amazing Alter-G anti-gravity treadmill.

My therapy group just got a brand new expensive treadmill called the Alter-G, an amazing machine designed by NASA. It has a sealed air chamber I stand in which inflates to offset by percentages my body weight. This aids in treadmill walking for people with limited use of their legs.

When I've tried walking on a normal treadmill, I could only do it for a few minutes at a slow pace. My stamina gives out, and my back starts to hurt too much. After five sessions

I am now walking at a fast pace for well over twenty minutes! There are cameras on both sides and at the front and back of the machine. I can see my legs going to town in high definition on the big screen in front of me. It literally brought me to tears to see my legs move the way they used to before the accident!

Dan, my therapist, told me the other day, "Craig, I think this could be a game changer for you!"

Already my cardio workout has greatly increased, and my weak legs are getting a full stride workout in a way I could only dream of without this amazing machine. I can't wait to see what a few months on this machine will do for me.

It should be an exciting year!

Craig and LaDonna

Chapter 26

REACHING THE HOME STRETCH

January 18, 2013, 1:55 p.m.

A s I write this, LaDonna, is ready to enter an MRI tube for a difficult scan on her neck. She has been experiencing ongoing neck and shoulder pain that has been radiating throughout her body for some time now. She's tolerated it as best she can while focusing on caring for her mom and my needs. We've tried to encourage her to get checked out, but it's easier said than done. What moved it up the scale of urgency happened two days ago.

The wear and tear of her constant caregiving for us has taken its toll on her body. It's been harder and harder for her to get my manual wheelchair out of the car. The emotional strain of seeing her aging, recently widowed mom go through medical issues has been taking its toll on her as well.

Two days ago she took her mom to a doctor appointment and ran a few errands. She got home and lifted some stuff onto the kitchen counter and something popped in her lower back. She could barely move and has been primarily bedridden since.

We took her in to the doctor yesterday and he ordered an MRI on her neck. He said that the injury to her back is too recent to do an MRI there. They wouldn't get a good read on it until the injury had time to calm down a bit.

She continues to be in much pain, even as she headed out the door with our dear friend Kathy, who is helping her get to this scan today. I let our case manager know, and they are trying to expedite some in-home health and home aid while LaDonna heals, possibly for the next few weeks.

The doctor thinks she strained the muscles in her back, and that will heal with time. The more significant concern has been the reoccurring neck pain and memory loss.

We haven't said much regarding LaDonna's condition over the months we've been posting, primarily because she'd prefer the focus be on others. But our hearts are concerned for her and pray that, ultimately, the Lord will do a healing work in her body.

It saddened me yesterday when she shared through her tears, "Craig, you're getting much better, but it seems like I'm going backwards."

I come to you today thankful again for your prayers, support, and encouragement. So much of it has been directed towards my condition. I'm asking that you once again pray earnestly on our behalf, especially for my beloved wife, LaDonna. She is standing in the need of prayer.

Craig

I've been concerned for LaDonna ever since the accident. She has always aimed the focus on others. She has suffered greatly and mostly privately.

Traumatic events wear on not only the patient, but the spouse and family as well. I grieve for what my children and other family members have gone through, especially in the early days of this journey.

LaDonna is not just the spouse of a seriously injured person. She, too, was seriously injured and had to work through the recovery of her own, all while carrying the burden of caregiving and advocating for my ongoing needs and issues.

She's not the only loving spouse who stands by her husband day by day. The therapy gym is filled with them. How often we see the stress in their eyes and on their faces. For some, the burden has become too hard to bear, and they have chosen to let their loved one go it alone. Those were the cases that broke our hearts the most.

The reality is this. It is what it is, and there's no jumping off this moving train, at least without inflicting more pain on yourself and your spouse.

LaDonna would never jump off that train. I've been comforted to not even have to entertain that thought for a moment, but seeing her suffer has been one of the hardest things I have had to experience throughout this whole ordeal.

The doctor said that the MRI showed no "acute disease" showing up, which was good news. He believes that the pain in her neck is the cumulative effect of the neck injury and her ongoing, very active life as caregiver. She needed to rest more and find ways to off-load the stressful burdens she carries. As we all know, that's easier said than done.

Thankfully, her back injury was healing up well. Our doctor confirmed his suspicion that she strained the muscles around the lower back and good old bed rest was about the best medicine she could take.

It sure turned her old beat-up hubby into the caregiver for a few days. Thankfully, I didn't burn anything on the stove (the meals came out actually quite well), and I did a fairly good job at caring for the needs of all three of us.

It is a real challenge when you can't bend over enough to put on clothes, shoes, etc. I was reminded about how truly dependent I am on her help.

A month before all this happened I knew she was in desperate need of a break. She not only had been bearing the challenges of being my caregiver, but has been caring for her mother as well. Gramma Fern has been in deteriorating health for the past year or so. A fall in our garage in late 2012 eventually caused multiple breaks in her lumbar spine. Compounded by advanced osteoporosis, she has been bedridden most of the time. She also has been battling chronic lymphocytic leukemia after being diagnosed shortly after Herman passed away. Our home had become somewhat of a nursing facility, with LaDonna being the lead administrator, charge nurse, nursing assistant, dietitian, chef, maintenance worker, and chauffeur of the aged and infirmed to all our doctor appointments, etc. We knew LaDonna loved us; there's only so much she could do when facing the cumulative effects of all these pressures. It was truly taking a toll on her.

In light of these realities, I made the decision to surprise her with the trip of a lifetime. She always wanted to go to the Holy Land and walk where Jesus walked. No matter what it would take or cost, it was something she needed and something I wanted to give her.

Dr. Erwin Lutzer of Moody Church was hosting a trip there in March 2013. I covertly booked her for the trip and asked her best friend, Bertha (Aunt Bert to my kids and grandkids), to go with her in my place.

It was one of the most difficult things I've ever done to keep the trip secret until Christmas. I was getting tired of doing so many 'unholy' things to hide her Holy Land trip, so Bertha and I decided to surprise her with the gift while LaDonna and I were on a dinner date a week or so before Christmas. We arranged it so Bert would conveniently crash the party and confirm she was going to be her travel partner. It all worked according to plan, and the two began preparations for one of the greatest trips ever for these long time pals. We prayed that she would heal quickly and that this wouldn't hinder her from going. Thankfully, the Lord restored her back. She began to experience relief in her neck and things were looking up for her as she eagerly waited her departure date on March 9, 2013.

A request I gave to the family was that if anything happened to me during her trip, she was not going to know about it until after she returned. Even if it was death, we could surely wait to make plans for my funeral after she got home. Nothing was going to ruin this much needed get-a-way!

What an incredible trip it was for her. She came home spiritually renewed, though physically tired. She told me, "We were usually up by 5:30 a.m. and didn't fall into bed until 11 at night."

Thankfully, the insurance provided me some in-home health care. Everything went well, except for one minor issue. It wasn't a "big" thing, so I thought I'd wait until LaDonna got home to tell her what happened.

Bert and LaDonna experiencing the Holy Land.

A few days into her time away I was attempting some in-home stretching exercises, the same stuff I do at therapy. The only difference was that it was not on the firm therapy mat at Dan's place.

As I turned and stretched my trunk down and to the left, I heard a popping noise come from my recently repaired left hip. I stood up and knew something wasn't right, because I couldn't put any weight on that leg.

"I think I just dislocated my hip," I told my new caregiver.

She helped me back into bed, and I called Dr. Duhon right away. He told me to go to the office closest to me for an X-ray. He would then be able to read it remotely at the other location.

I called my driver, John, to see if he could come get me. He had several patients already scheduled, but said he'd get there as soon as he could. The incident happened at about 9:30 a.m. He arrived by 1 p.m. to transport me.

As I lay on the table, Dr. Duhon viewed the X-ray from the other side of town. The X-ray tech informed me I had dislocated my hip and off to the ER I went. Thankfully,, we were conveniently situated next to Arrowhead Hospital.

Like I said, it wasn't a "big" thing. Just a minor dislocation!

Thankfully, Dr. Duhon's staff sent me over with a CD of the

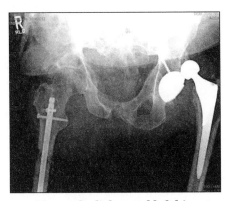

My newly dislocated left hip.

X-ray they had just taken. I wasn't about to get back on another X-ray table for more painful pictures. Or was I?

I got checked into the ER around 3:30 and was seen rather quickly by one of the attending physician assistants.

"We'll get an X-ray of your hip and then look to see what you've done, Mr. Smith," she confidently said to me.

"I've already got some pictures for you to see. Here's the CD that will tell you what's going on."

"No, sorry, but our system can't read those images. We're going to have to get our own films, sir!"

Maybe this is how hospitals fund their X-ray departments. So they came to get me, rolled me onto yet another rock-hard surface, enabling their billing department to keep busy. I almost wanted to lay the CD, which was still in my grasp, on top of the joint, hoping in some way to block the view. As I lay there in pain I wondered what planet their computer system was mail-ordered from to be incompatible with a CD that could be read anywhere else on earth?

Then it was back onto the thin mattress of the ER gurney and back to the room to wait for the next steps in this unexpected experience.

Around 5:30 they finally got me to the room to start an IV with medication to relax me.

"You won't even remember any of this, Mr. Smith," they told me.

"This ain't my first rodeo," I cynically thought as I attempted my best *Duck Dynasty* impersonation.

I came to as the techs were leaving the room.

I asked my caregiver, "So what did they do?"

"Well, you went to sleep and one of them pulled your leg out sideways while the other one pulled your foot downward and then it just popped back in," she said.

"So how did I do while all this was happening," I asked?

"You just did a quick moan, and that was it."

Thirty minutes later, I was back home and tucked in bed.

I promised her I would tell LaDonna as soon as she got home, but no sooner!

Dear friends,   March 27, 2013, 8:07 a.m.

LaDonna just got home from her trip to Israel. I asked her what the highlight was, and of course she said it all was a highlight, and then she broke down. She said the most meaningful part of the trip was when they went to the Pools of Bethesda where Jesus healed a paralytic man who couldn't move to the healing waters in time to be healed, as was the custom of that day. She said, "I could only think of you, Craig, and cry out to the Lord for your healing!"

I was speechless and moved by her words. There she was, thousands of miles away, and her thoughts were still focused on me. What a tremendous wife I have! I love her and thank the Lord that He did a great work of encouragement, rest, and renewal for my beloved LaDonna! She's now home, invigorated and back in the saddle. Continue to pray for her as we keep moving forward.

As for me, I'm very close to the moment when my doctor will officially make the call that I've reached "maximum medical improvement." That is both a medical and a legal determination. The insurance folks will finally be able to close my case and move me from *active* to *supportive care.*

I'm doing well and therapy continues to reap incremental rewards in this old body. Please pray for us as we consider how the ministry will move forward from here.

For the whole Smith family;

Craig

As we consider how we will move forward from here, we have been greatly encouraged by the many friends, family, and medical professionals who have heavily invested in our the healing process.

In the spring of 2013, my PT buddy Dan nominated me for consideration for Arizona's 2013 Rehabilitant of the Year award. My name was one of thirteen nominees from across the state. An award banquet was held in Phoenix on May 14, 2013, attended by medical, insurance professionals, and amazing survivors of horrific accidents and injuries.

I was honored and surprised to hear my name announced as the first-place winner of this award. All the nominees had incredible stories of survival and rehabilitation and would have been worthy of this honor. LaDonna and I were so touched to have this affirmation by these medical and insurance professionals.

After almost four years of trauma and trials, we've held on to the timeless truth of God's Word that has sustained us time and time again. Our faith has given us the greatest award ever–the smile and favor of our God, and His peace in the midst of our own "perfect storm".

Some of the other nominees for the 2013 Arizona Rehabilitant of the Year Award.

Chapter 27

LESSONS LEARNED

Along the way there have been many lessons the Lord has taught us in our "school of suffering." We've reflected on some of them throughout this book. Our hope is that God will use our story to encourage others, including you.

The gospel is all about hope, especially for those who face life's greatest challenges. You may not think you need these truths today, but some day you will. I pray that the lessons we've learned will help you find faith and confidence in the One who is the giver and sustainer of life.

None of us are guaranteed another day. None of us are guaranteed smooth sailing throughout life. Most of us experience some form of painful disappointments as we live out the hyphen between the dates on our tombstones.

What I share is from a Christian perspective. If you do not have a personal relationship with Jesus Christ, this will, no doubt, be strange speak to you. It won't make sense. What I refer to is described in Scripture as a *mystery*. Colossians 1:26–27 says, . . . "the mystery that has been kept hidden for ages and generations, but is now disclosed to the Lord's people. To them, God has chosen to make known among the Gentiles the glorious riches of this mystery, which is Christ in you, the hope of glory."

In one of our daily devotional readings, Dr. A.B. Simpson noted that, when you boil it all down, Scripture basically holds out two great and precious promises regarding Jesus Christ. First, *He will come to us;* secondly, *He will come into us.* These are great truths worthy of our consideration.

The first promise was about His *Incarnation.* The Bible teaches that God, the Creator of heaven and of earth, put on human flesh and came to live among His creation. For thousands of years the world awaited the fulfillment of that promise. Two thousand years ago that promise was fulfilled when Jesus Christ was born in Bethlehem of Judea. *He came to us.*

There's more to the story. Not only did He come to us. He promised us something even more amazing. *He would come into us.* We preachers call that the *Indwelling.*

I personally believe what the Word of God has to say on these matters. Jesus, God's only begotten Son, came to earth to pay the ultimate penalty for all our sin. To those who receive Him, He gives the power and the right to be called sons and daughters of God.

Those who place their faith and trust in Jesus Christ, and in Him alone, have a unique privilege that the rest of the world does not enjoy. That privilege is to participate in the divine nature of God (2 Peter 1:4). That doesn't mean we become God. What it means, is God comes to take up his dwelling place inside us. He comes to live within His people. That's the mystery I'm talking about.

World religions cannot offer this. It's nowhere to be found in secular humanism. The traditional animism of my people cannot provide its followers the personal indwelling of God Himself. Nowhere else can this truth be found. It is found exclusively in the pages of God's Word, reserved only for those who place their faith and trust in the finished work of Jesus Christ. This gospel, this good news, is available to you, too, my friend! You can experience God's amazing grace by surrendering your life to Him.

We were all created by God to be in a relationship with Him. Sin separates us from God and there is only one remedy — His remedy! The simplest explanation of our sin predicament is to see that we have hijacked our lives. Many people say they believe in a God and may even acknowledge that God is capable of taking care of the universe. We expect Him to and He does a pretty good job at it. "Just don't meddle in my life, God. I'll take care of myself." That's the hijacking I'm talking about. As you and I know well, hijacking carries a severe and lethal penalty.

Colossians 1:16 says, "All things were made by him (Jesus Christ) and for him." Salvation begins by acknowledging that my sin separates me from God and from His purposes. Repentance means I'm broken and sorry for my sin and acknowledges that there's only one way to remedy my condition. It means believing the very words of Jesus as recorded in John 14:6, "I am the way, the truth and the life. No one comes to the Father except through me." It involves total trust in the finished work of Jesus Christ, which he accomplished on the cross two thousand years ago, as the once for all penalty for my sin. It includes asking Jesus Christ to forgive me, save me! He saves me, and then He indwells me as I begin serving Him and His purposes for the rest of my earthly life. A person who truly repents, believes, and is converted will live differently from that moment on. The transformation will be evident to others as godly living replaces selfish living. That's God's grace, my friend! It truly is so amazing!

I began to understand in a much deeper way the mystery of the indwelling Christ in my own journey through these deep dark waters. It's hard to explain it, but I know my Lord so much more intimately now. He was there through it all. We wouldn't be here if it had not been for His supernatural interventions when the battle was on for our lives. He is not far from His children. All that He did for me personally, He did from the frontline position of my inner man.

So what were the lessons learned?

Lesson One: God is In the Disasters

A few days after arriving at HealthSouth in Glendale, Arizona, Tom and Alfreda Claus came by for a visit. I've known this dear couple most of my life. They are like second parents to me. It was through Tom's preaching the gospel message back in 1971 that I surrendered my life to Jesus Christ at an Indian Christian Camp on the Assiniboine River near Winnipeg, Manitoba.

Tom and Alfreda pulled chairs next to my bed that morning. Tom said that they wanted to sing a couple Indian hymns for me. Their beautiful voices blended so smoothly, even then in their advanced years, and the harmony filled the room and beyond. The Kiowa and Mohawk hymns were moving and so reverently sung. People out in the hallway stopped to listen. Many commented later that they had never heard anything so beautiful.

Then Tom pulled out his Bible and said, "Craigy boy, I've got a portion of Scripture that I want to read to you. These verses are for you. Take them as your own."

He opened to Psalms 57:1–2. It read, "Have mercy on me, my God, have mercy on me, for in you I take refuge. I will take refuge in the shadow of your wings until the disaster has passed. I cry out to God Most High, to God, who fulfills his purpose for me."

"You think on these verses, Craig, and let the Lord speak to you in your time of need."

They stayed a while longer, prayed for me, and then left. The words of that passage rang over and over again in my ears. I meditated on those truths for hours on end. It brought so much comfort to my heart and helped clarify my response to God in light of his Holy Word.

I found out that God is in the disasters of life. Our natural desire is to escape life's tragedies, and that's how we often pray. None of us want to face pain, discomfort, or harm. That goes against all human nature. We prayed a prayer the morning of the accident that God would keep us safe and in His protecting hand. A rollover at mile marker 313 wasn't in our plans for that day. God, in His foreknowledge, knew all about it, though, and determined to answer our prayer in a way we never dreamed He would!

God not only keeps us from disasters, but also, at times, allows them to come our way. When He does allow a disaster, He wonderfully carves out a hiding place underneath the shadow of His wings where we can rest and hide, *until the disaster has passed.*

It's interesting that the psalmist, David, trusted God enough to take refuge in Him when facing deep trouble. David was running for his life as he was being pursued like a trophy animal fleeing a well-organized and well-armed hunting party.

If David was to take refuge in God, he first had to understand the goodness of God, regardless of the circumstances He allowed in his life. It's all about trust. David would have to trust the very One who, if He had chosen to, could have allowed the disaster to not happen. David did so, and now we were being called upon to do the same.

It puts us as God's kids in a rather vulnerable place. We have to settle the issue of the Sovereignty of God when deep trials come, whether it be related to what we would term "an accident," or even if it involved intentional evil done to us at the hands of perpetrators. Surrendering to His Sovereignty in our lives can only happen if one has a deep abiding love for Him.

Is He, or is He not, in control of all things? If He is, then whatever happens in our lives, be it good or bad, comes with the stamp of His permission. It may be unpleasant or difficult, but for God's children, all disasters are God's disasters, because He has an ultimate purpose in it all – His glory. Subordinate to that is the deeper work He does in us, which builds faith and trust. He shows us the power of forgiveness when we also forgive those who have done us wrong. These are great truths that accelerate us down the healing road in body, soul and spirit.

After hearing those verses, doubts or questions still lingering around me, were completely surrendered over to the Lord. I affirmed that day His Sovereignty over my life.

I came to embrace the reality that the rollover accident at mile marker 313 was God's rollover accident—not *caused* by God, but at the least *allowed* by His Sovereign hand. It helped to give purpose to all the pain and anguish we were suffering.

I learned another lesson that day, the lesson of *purpose.* In verse 2 David said, "I cry out to God Most High, to God, who fulfills his purpose for me."

The good news about disasters is they never stop God from fulfilling His purposes in our lives.

Not only was this disaster God's disaster, but His plan all along for my life was to include a season of deep trauma and trials, all for the purpose of fulfilling why He placed me on planet earth.

You may be thinking, *That's horrible! God made you so He could put you through all this? What kind of God is that?*

Well, my friend, I have to say that the more I serve God, the more I don't understand His ways, but the more I love and trust Him. God's Word tells me that in this life we see things as if looking through a clouded glass, but someday He will explain it all to me personally, and it will all make sense. I don't have to wait until then to experience "the peace that passes all understanding." That abiding peace is my present reality.

Scripture tells me that His thoughts are much higher than mine. His ways are past finding out. But the key is this: I love Him enough to trust Him. I love Him enough to take shelter under the shadow of His wings until this disaster, that He has permitted for me, passes. That's good enough for me!

We are just now beginning to see God's purposes being fulfilled through this traumatic experience. As I've had opportunity to share with people about our journey, I am amazed at how God is using this to encourage and help many who are also facing deep waters.

Whether in a hospital room with a new-found roommate, at the therapy gym, or on the stage of a gathering like the one I spoke at on June 2013 at the Tampa Bay Convention Center in Tampa, Florida, the deeper life lessons He has taught me is being used by God in some powerful ways.

Craig, Zane, and LaDonna together on stage at the Tampa Bay Convention Center, June 2013.

Sharing the miracle at a First Responder Appreciation Night Out, Little Falls, MN.

Sharing the lessons learned at Constance Evangelical Free Church, Andover, MN.

345

God has a purpose for every life, including yours. He was intimately involved in forming you in your mother's womb and has given you not only life, but also a life story. Everything that happens, especially in the life of the Christian, has an ultimate purpose. Our experience affirms what Romans 8:28 says, "And we know that in all things God works for the good of those who love him, who have been called according to his purpose."

Lesson Two: It's All About His Glory!

The ultimate purpose in this tragedy, as in everything in our life, is God's glory. The fact that God has chosen to allow this gives great purpose for me.

I don't know how many times I have either preached or sung truth of the gospel through a phrase like, "He is Lord." Well, is He truly the Lord of my life? In order to have a Lord, you've got to have servants. Who am I? I am a servant of the Most High God! That's my title, my job description, and it's my honor.

When Paul wrote to the Romans he said something very interesting in his opening words as recorded in Romans 1:1: "Paul, a servant of Christ Jesus, called to be an apostle and set apart for the gospel of God."

When he used the word, "servant," it had great significance.

In New Testament times it was estimated that two thirds of the Roman Empire's population were slaves who came from every social and economic background. They were the educated, the uneducated, the rich, the poor, and the foreigner, as well. It was a statement and condition that the Roman Christians knew well, too. Before Paul was a Christian, he hated Christ and his followers. In fact, he was a persecutor of them. He rounded them up, threw them in prisons, and even had them executed.

For Paul to now call himself a servant of Christ Jesus was huge. In fact, he used the word that described the lowest form of a slave that there was—a slave who, in a very real sense, had no personal identity. Their identity and significance was wrapped up in their master. Even names weren't important; they were known only as 'the servants of' their owner. They owned nothing, were nothing, and did whatever their master ordered.

A servant back then could not dictate to the master what he or she was willing to do and not do. They didn't have that prerogative. Neither do I.

If Jesus Christ is truly my master, then I am His servant. I am nothing more, and I am nothing less. My identity and significance is tied up completely in Him and Him alone. A follower of Jesus Christ needs to embrace the biblical reality that we are either a slave to sin or a slave to Christ. One leads to death, the other to eternal life!

Romans 6:19-23 says, "I am using an example from everyday life because of your human limitations. Just as you used to offer yourselves as slaves to impurity and to ever-increasing wickedness, so now offer yourselves as slaves to righteousness leading to holiness. When you were slaves to sin, you were free from the control of righteousness. What benefit did you reap at that time from the things you are now ashamed of? Those things result in death! But now that you have been set free from sin and have become slaves of God, the benefit you reap leads to holiness, and the result is eternal life. For the wages of sin is death, but the gift of God is eternal life in Christ Jesus our Lord..."

Being a slave to sin brings bondage, brokenness and ultimately, eternal separation from God. God's grace pulls us out of the pit of sin and places us into His eternal family. Being a slave to Christ is a great honor. The slave to Christ becomes a joint-heir with Christ of all things eternal. The slave to Christ escapes eternal punishment in what the Bible calls "utter darkness" and enjoys not only His indwelling Presence now but also the assurance of eternity with Christ, who is the only Hope of all mankind! What an amazing exchange that is!

Sometimes servant duties are not too difficult. Sometimes, though, they can be incredibly challenging. If my Lord so orders, my responsibility is to do it, all for His good purposes.

LaDonna sharing about God's goodness and grace in her life.

Orders given from my Lord meant I would be called upon to endure hardship and suffering. My response will dictate how well He evaluates the life He gave me.

When tempted to complain about what I have been through, I only have to look heavenward to see His nail scarred hands and feet. I am reminded of the brutal beating He took for my sin, and it takes away all desire to complain about mine.

You see, my Master is a good Master. He never calls me to do anything that He, Himself, has not already done. If He calls me to suffer, He knows quite well what it is He is calling me to do. It brought me to a place where I could rejoice in my sufferings and present it to Him as a sacrifice of praise. Every broken bone in my body, every surgical scar imposed upon my flesh, and every part of me that was now missing, has become my offering to Him.

My experience in Him goes against the all-too-familiar false teaching of today's easy believe-ism. Christian television is filled with health and wealth preachers, promising an easy life if you'll only plant your seed faith gift today.

That's not the gospel of the Bible, nor is it the experience of my life. A person who is being drawn to Christ needs to count the cost of becoming a follower of Him. All of us will go through varying levels of suffering in our lives, some more than others.

When Jesus was baptized in the Jordan River, the Spirit of God descended upon Him and His Father spoke from heaven, "This is my Son, in whom I am well pleased." The very next verse, Matthew 4:1, says, "Then was Jesus led of the Spirit into the wilderness to be tempted by the devil."

Jesus modeled obedience for us. He modeled the importance of being filled with the Holy Spirit, though He is God Himself. He did it as an example for us. So what was the evidence of Jesus being filled? It wasn't tongues, it wasn't extravagance—it was *trouble*!

If God spoke from heaven, endorsing the obedience of His Son and filling Him with the Holy Spirit, why then was He immediately met with the onslaught of Satan's fury, temptations, and wrath?

Trouble is lurking at every person's door, regardless of his or her faith or religion. The question is will you have what it takes to make it through those deep waters? When you have Christ's indwelling, there is power to face it all. When you allow the indwelling Christ to take over the control of the unexpected and unwelcome experiences, He gives you the power to endure and overcome. The end result is the glory of God!

Lesson Three: The Believer's Big Test—Is Jesus Enough?

Emerging out of the coma, unable to move a muscle in my body, I was met with the reality that my life would never be the same again. I didn't know if I'd ever walk, sing, preach, or have any kind of normal life. I began to face a very real challenge, one that is especially significant for those of us called to full-time ministry.

It's quite possible that we can go through our whole life missing so much *of Him,* all while we are so busy doing so much *for Him.*

The question I was facing was simple: If everything I had was taken from me, and all I had was Jesus, would He be enough? That is the believer's big test. Corrie ten Boom once noted, "You'll never know that Jesus is all you need until Jesus is all you have." How right that dear old saint was!

At the point of my deepest need, the indwelling Christ met me in a powerful way. Though my body was racked with pain and an uncertain future lay ahead, Christ was doing an amazing work deep inside me.

I began to find deep peace and joy, while others around me were mobile and in good health. The deeper my challenges, the deeper the sustaining presence of the indwelling Christ went as well.

I came to the point when I could truly say that if I never could speak, or sing again, I had all satisfaction in my relationship with Christ. If I never could walk again, the truths of a new resurrected body assured me by God's Word meant I'd be back on my feet someday.

I realize now that with my age and the effects of the trauma, there are many more days behind me now than ahead of me. If the remainder of my life was to be spent confined to a bed or wheelchair, then that was going to be OK. The assurance of a new body is awaiting me on the other side of the grave.

The Apostle Paul noted, "If we endure, we will also reign with him" (2 Timothy 2:12). In God's eternal order, those who suffer for Christ in this life will someday reign with Him in the next. I don't know what that all means, nor do I need to. It is a promise, though, that I'm looking forward to seeing fulfilled for me. My goal in life is to endure suffering as a good soldier of Christ. How He chooses to honor that service is up to Him. All I know is this temporary situation will one day give way to THE most incredible life complete with the smile of my Master, and it will last an eternity.

It's what led the psalmist to declare in Psalm 73:25, "Whom have I in heaven but you? And earth has nothing I desire besides you."

Was Jesus enough for me in my condition? The answer came over time, and it was a resounding yes! He was, and still is, all I need in this life. Everything else He gives me is added blessing and an added benefit.

Lesson Four: He Fights My Battles for Me, Especially When I Can't

As those spiritual battles raged at the UNM Trauma/ICU Unit, I found myself physically unable to rise up and fight. It was all on LaDonna's shoulders as she faced the manifestations from the spirit world that affirmed there was a huge battle going on for my life.

I learned a valuable lesson during those days. One of the great blessings of the indwelling Christ is that He fights my battles for me when I am unable to do so. Of greater value was the knowledge that He wasn't doing so from a distance, but was right there with me.

God spoke to Moses when he and the Children of Israel were sandwiched between the Red Sea and the fast approaching Egyptian army. They were going to recapture them and bring them back into bondage and slavery. God's assurance to Moses was the same assurance He gave us, as recorded in Exodus 14:14: "The Lord will fight for you; you need only to be still."

Sometimes being still takes an act of the will. Sometimes, though, it can be imposed on you, as it was on me in my comatose condition. It was encouraging to know that the indwelling Christ was not only allowing the storm, He was the great storm-stopper, allowing it to progress only as far as His Sovereignty would allow.

I've often been asked the question, "Did Satan cause your accident?" or, "Where was God and why didn't He prevent it from happening? You were on a ministry trip serving Him, so why would He do that to you?"

These are difficult, yet valid questions to ask. I can only respond by sharing with you what I have come to embrace as biblical truth regarding these issues.

It has become clear to me that the Bible offers up what I would call *co-existing biblical realities*, that at first glance seem to be contradictory, but are not. In fact, I've come to view these realities as *life's bookends*, in between which we live out our lives in our earthly journey.

I've already talked about the first bookend, the Sovereignty of God. The other is what the Bible has to say about Satan. Scripture calls him a thief. In John 10:10 it says, "The thief comes only to steal and kill and destroy; I have come that they may have life, and have it to the full."

Every person on planet earth has the same mortal enemy: the devil, Satan. The Bible says his only job is to steal, kill, and destroy. He wants us dead. He seeks to prevent us from coming to Christ, and for those who have come to Christ, he wants to cut our life short.

As a follower of Jesus Christ, I have a huge target on my back. This thief is constantly trying to find ways to bring harm to me. That's the other bookend.

The wonderful truth is that no matter what Satan wants to do to me, he can go only as far as my Sovereign Lord allows him to. Just read the book of Job in the Bible and you will see, in that one man's life, the battle that goes on for each and every one of us.

So was Satan the cause of our accident? I'd have to say, yes, he was there trying to take not only my life, but also that of my beloved wife, LaDonna, and my brother-in-law, Zane. That's his job.

What sends shivers down my very broken spine, though, is the reality that while Satan was there in full force, my Sovereign Lord was right there in the vehicle with us. He allowed what He allowed, but no more. As my wife's C-1 vertebrae fractured *through and through*, Sovereign God said, "This far and no more."

He allowed the bone to fracture, but left the spinal cord intact and complete.

He was there with me as I coded on the emergency room gurney, and He moved the hands of a team of doctors, nurses, and technicians to help bring me back to life. It truly is God's miracle, and He chose to employ human hands in the process.

God could have said to Satan, "I give you permission to take them all the way," and those injuries would have led to the end of our lives here on earth. That would have been an incredible outcome as well, because while death is called, in the Bible, "the last enemy," God still uses it to accomplish His eternal purpose. I would have ended up not just putting my foot into heaven's gate, but staying there where there's no more tears or pain. It all ends up well for the child of God, no matter the outcome.

It never was more clearly illustrated for me than one day when we were back in Minnesota the second year after our accident. You remember the story shared about my pastor friend, Randy, and the tragedy suffered in Grand Rapids with the drowning of the two men?

Well, on one of the Sundays back home I was going to speak at Randy's church. It was a beautiful August morning. It was so good to be back with my brother and to minister again at their fellowship.

As we went over the order of service, Randy mentioned that before I would speak, one of their teens would be sharing about a recent short-term summer missions trip she and others had taken to serve at a Bible camp.

She gave a brief update, and then she talked about their trip back home. The van was loaded with young people and pulling a trailer loaded down with ministry equipment and supplies for

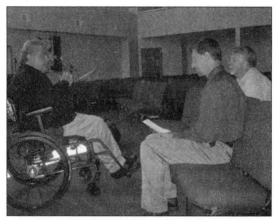

***Visiting with Pastor Randy and Dave Toth of
Big Sandy Bible Camp prior to the service.***

the summer-long trip. Somewhere on the interstate highway the trailer started fishtailing, and the driver lost control. The vehicle ended up heading toward the ditch as the teens screamed out to Jesus for His help.

She summarized the experience by saying, "I'm so thankful Jesus was there with us and He kept the van from rolling. None of us got hurt. We arrived home safely! Thank you Jesus for keeping us from harm!"

My initial thoughts were, "Wait a minute! She's stealing my thunder!"

I'm getting ready to talk about another trailer that was fishtailing and then heading for the ditch, but ours had a very different outcome.

Then I looked over at my brother, Randy, and was taken back to the tragedy they had faced in the loss of their son. I sat there somewhat overcome by these three different scenarios playing out in front of me.

I thought about our story. The obvious question was, "If Jesus was there with those teens and He kept them from rolling, then where was Jesus when we were heading to the ditch? Where was Jesus when Randy's son, Nathan, and the other man drowned?"

It was almost too overwhelming for me as Pastor Randy got up to introduce me. It was then that the truth of these bookends came alive in my soul. It gave back my composure, and I was able to get up, preach and affirm the answer to not only myself, but to the congregation assembled that day.

So where was Jesus at mile marker 313? He was right there, going for a roll with us as we tumbled across the northbound lanes.

I could also say, "Thank you, Jesus, for being there with the teens and right there with those rescuers who lost their lives saving others!"

Lesson Five: At Death's Door, He's All I Need!

The reason I can say this is because of what I experienced in the emergency room of St. Vincent Hospital in Santa Fe. It was there I, too, passed through death's door.

I've often sung songs and preached messages about going home to be with Jesus. That is a biblically accurate and theologically sound statement. The Bible tells us that when Jesus completed His time on earth, he ascended back to heaven where He sits at the right hand of the Father.

Another biblical reality affirms the Omnipresence of the Lord. While He is there in heaven, He is also present here in this world. How could He not be if He has promised His indwelling presence within us?

I tell people that I am now a card-carrying member of the *Lazarus Club!*

"What's it like to die?" is a question I now get asked quite often. "Did you see heaven? Are there really pearly gates and streets of gold?"

Many people have written about the death experience.

The problem is you can find all kinds of experiences that people say they've had, but how can you confirm the veracity of the claims? Some of the experiences line up with biblical teaching. Some are the farthest thing from the truths that are revealed in God's Holy Word.

The bottom line is, we cannot depend on the personal experiences of others to provide an understanding of God and His ways. What anybody says experientially ultimately needs to be examined in the light of biblical truth. Anything otherwise is not truth, and is not to be believed as such.

I want to be very careful in explaining this, both because of the seriousness of this issue, as well as the special treasure the death experience has afforded my life. It was a very holy experience for sure and one that is hard to put into words.

My death experience is simple, yet profound: what I have preached, sung, and lived for since coming to Christ at age thirteen is real! The Bible is true! There definitely is a place called heaven, and its beauty defies description. Even more significant for me was something that far outshone the destination.

For the first time in my life, as I passed through death's door, I became overwhelmed by the profoundness and completeness of the very presence of Christ! The Lamb of God, the Light of the World is not far away from the child of God at death's door. In a very real sense, we don't *go home to be with* Jesus, because, for the believer, *we already are with* Jesus through His indwelling presence! It is at death's door when that reality is perfected. Psalms 23 came alive to me in a wonderful new way. It was there that the psalmist claimed, "Even though I walk through the darkest valley [the shadow of death], I will fear no evil, for you are with me."

When the veil between the seen and unseen world was pulled back for me, as short or as long as it lasted, His presence was overwhelming! It reminded me of the song, *I Can Only Imagine*. The song asks a number of questions, making us think about what our response will be when we see Jesus face to face. I can remember standing there in His presence, unable to speak at all.

At that moment, the destination was totally overshadowed by the glory of the resurrected Christ! Jesus, full of glory and light, was there with me all the way through the death experience. He was there at the door and there as I passed through the door. It was wonderful. It was glorious. I didn't want it to end! As sufficient as I have found Jesus to be in life, I came to find Him totally sufficient in death.

We all wonder what that day will be like. I now know, just as Pastor Randy's son and his fellow rescuer found out. It's the same thing that young teenager and the others in the van that day found out. It's the same thing that LaDonna, Zane, and I discovered.

No matter where we are, and no matter what happens to our lives, the enemy of our soul will continue to scheme against us. The good news of the gospel is sure, confirmed by what Romans 8:38–39 says: "For I am convinced that neither death nor life, neither angels nor demons, neither the present nor the future, nor any powers, neither height nor depth, nor anything else in all creation, will be able to separate us from the love of God that is in Christ Jesus our Lord."

That has always been the hope of the gospel message. It has been our joy to share it for decades, right up to the miracle at mile marker 313. It will be our joy to continue as we pick up the pieces of our traumatized bodies, and move forward, dependent on the Lord for His continued strength in this life.

We do so, as Philippians 1:6 says, "being confident of this, that he who began a good work in you will carry it on to completion until the day of Christ Jesus."

I wonder what new miracles lay beyond mile marker 313? I can't wait!